How Drive Tank

How to Drive a Tank...

... and Other Everyday Tips for the Modern Gentleman

Frank Coles

Little, Brown

LITTLE, BROWN

First published in Great Britain in 2009 by Little, Brown
Reprinted 2009

A CIP catalogue record for this book
is available from the British Library.

ISBN 978-1-4087-0182-9

Typeset in Sabon by M Rules
Printed and bound in Great Britain by
Clays Ltd, St Ives plc

Papers used by Little, Brown are natural, renewable and
recyclable products sourced from well-managed forests and certified
in accordance with the rules of the Forest Stewardship Council.

Mixed Sources
Product group from well-managed
forests and other controlled sources
www.fsc.org Cert no. SGS-COC-004081
© 1996 Forest Stewardship Council
FSC

Little, Brown
An imprint of
Little, Brown Book Group
100 Victoria Embankment
London EC4Y 0DY

An Hachette UK Company
www.hachette.co.uk

www.littlebrown.co.uk

For my friend Sam Harber, my father and my grandfathers.

Gentlemen whose lights burned brightly.

Try a thing you haven't done three times. Once, to get over the fear of doing it. Twice, to learn how to do it. And a third time, to figure out whether you like it or not.

Virgil Thomson (advice given at age ninety-three)

Contents

FROM THE GENTLEMAN'S CLUB

HAVE IT ALL

WORK AND MONEY

MAN THINGS

LUST AND LOVE

THE DIVINE COMEDY

MIND CONTROL

Introduction

Call yourself a man? You do? Do you even know what a real man is? Are you a six foot one Adonis who wears all the latest fashions, moisturises regularly, visits spas for pleasure and never does anything wrong? Or do you drink twenty pints every Friday night, batter some schmuck on the way home, spend three seconds with the misses and fart yourself to sleep? A prissy metrosexual or a monosyllabic lad? One-dimensional advertising demographics. Isn't that what being a man is?

Thankfully no. There are as many paths to manhood as there are men. A man can be buff and bucolic, a lover and a fighter, a father and a fire starter, a twist or a straight, a rock god or a tank commander and everything else in between.

Being a man means making mistakes, trying things out, knowing when to say no, knowing when to be tender and knowing when to be hard; it's neither one-dimensional nor any one thing. And let's just clear something up right now: macho is just the bluster of little boys, manly is knowledge and inner strength to find your own path – *whatever* that turns out to be.

So that's what we're here to do, to throw down a few ideas and see if there's anything you can play for a winning hand in the game of life. What you hold in your hands is the essence of a gentleman's guide but a little bit bigger, a little bolder and a damn sight more dangerous. Because it says you can do anything you want to, gives you the first steps how and then a friendly shove.

But danger doesn't mean simply putting your life on the line for extreme sports and adventurous sex although that can be a part of it – that's up to you. Danger means putting your ego on the line and challenging yourself to do and think things outside your comfort zone.

It's the kind of thing our fathers and teachers would have liked to tell us and the kind of thing we wish we could do as fathers and friends ourselves.

There are no pre-packaged life products you can buy off a shelf or order online. You won't be a passive consumer inside these pages but the manufacturer of your own experience. If you don't throw the book at the wall at least once and laugh out loud even more then I am doing my job wrong. What's more I expect abuse from you, I expect you to tell me I'm wrong and that's a good thing. Think about it.

Being a man means recapturing the idea of being a gentleman in the sense of being a truly noble man and doing the right thing, learning from your mistakes and saying what needs to be said and then just for kicks knowing how to blow shit up or jam with a guitar. It's definitely not about being a man's man; it's about being your own man. And being a man is fun. I mean really how dangerous can that idea be?

What Do You Really Really Want?

Okay before we begin there are one or two things we have to straighten out. First thing is this. I can show you any number of ways to tie a tie, scale a rock face or bodyboard a naked teen through a lake of fire but they will all mean absolutely nothing if we don't first figure out why we're here.

I won't just be making things up or copying from books on social etiquette written in the 1930s. I'll actually be doing as many things as I can so that you know I'm not just heckling you from the sidelines and to show you that whatever you put your mind to you can do too. While researching this book I burst my left retina, cracked a couple of ribs and fractured my wrist and I'd do it all again in a heartbeat. You see being a gentleman is about far more than knowing how to wear a tie pin or hold a door open. So here we go . . .

The Modern Gent

Back in the day, days of yore to be precise, a gentleman was simply a bad boy who got away with it. They gave him lands, castles and funny little coats of arms that kept him occupied and away from anything where he might cause too much trouble, say international politics. Then Henry VIII went and spoiled the party by chopping off one head too many. Suddenly the definition of what constituted a gentleman changed and became a set of rules for how to behave made up by wives intent on keeping their heads and the kind of chaps who didn't like warring and whoring in foreign parts.

They boil down to this:

Look nice, act nice, speak with authority and eloquence, have your own income, don't cause too much trouble but be prepared to step in when absolutely necessary.

There were of course the obligatory rituals stolen from chivalry: pull the chair out for the ladies, make sure they don't have to ruffle their petals unnecessarily, those delicate little flowers that need tending. Poor things.

Thank god that all changed. Women have moved on from being finishing school fops and everyday house servants. However many of us domesticated males are stuck in the roles defined by the Industrial Revolution working silly hours so that our wives can stay at home (they've stopped doing that remember?) to produce the next generation of domesticated males for the factory floor.

Times have changed but we have not. Very few of us know how to be bold, brave, self-effacing, self-critical or put our lives or egos on the line; we've become the equivalent of those delicate little flowers that need tending, only wearing a disguise of thorns. You know the look: the haircut like a foetus, the cheap mass-produced sportswear. The only calluses we have are on our game-playing thumbs and our most daring adventures are package holidays.

One Saturday night not so long ago I witnessed a painful example of the modern 'bloke'. I tried to stop another man from beating his wife to the ground and splitting her skull open. I was held back by the kind of men who would rather stand and watch hoping no one bothers them and that life passes them by. Once they'd finished with her they turned on me.

I would do it again tomorrow.

How about something worth aspiring to? The *Oxford English Dictionary* tells us that in the thirteenth century manliness meant:

1. To have the noble qualities of a man who is of mature character.
2. Having the admirable traits and virtues of being honourable, having courage and being independent.

It had little to do with class or status. The modern gentleman needs to represent the best of the old – daring, adventurous and willing to have a go – combined with the best of the new – courteous, intelligent and self-aware.

By necessity we will have to explore a few of the dark arts while we're here because rather than saying, 'Oh I couldn't possibly,' we want to say, 'I know how but I choose not to . . . for the moment.'

If you've been wanting to find a new direction now is always the time; you really can do anything you want only most people don't want to. They're scared.

So what do you most want to do?

And what are you most scared of?

Be honest with your answers: they are just for you not for anyone else. You might end up with two huge lists or not have any answers because you've never thought about this before. Whichever it is don't dwell on it; pack a sense of humour in your kitbag and let's see where we end up.

Coulda, Woulda, Shoulda . . .

. . . pursued that dream job, chased that girl, taken that trip, stayed at school, dropped out, kicked that fucker's arse, eaten the monkey brain, snorted that white powder, gone into rehab, mainlined vodka, jumped out of a plane, raised a child, driven a car so fast your ears popped, been pampered like a prince, skinned a rabbit, learned to cook, won at blackjack, cheated at poker, spoken another language, felt the warmth in a stranger's eyes, travelled to the edge of space, hit the road, taken a year out, lived on the edge, been your own boss, hired a hit man, retired young, had the sex you wanted, survived a crisis and lived to tell, said yes and meant it, taken the knocks, found meaning, woken up happy, turned off the TV, survived in the wild, learned to shoot, seduced someone truly beautiful and travelled the world.

So choose life, choose being a man. Occasionally you might even be accused of being a gentleman.

Now let's take a step in the right direction . . .

LIFE SKILLS EVERY MAN SHOULD HAVE

Don't be afraid to go out on a limb. That's where the fruit is.

H. Jackson Browne

How to Drive a Tank

The first question is why would you want to? Well let's see; you get to be that guy sticking his head out of the little hatch just like James Bond and then if the mood strikes you rebel against the herd instinct of commuter traffic by taking short cuts through thick walls and over parked cars.

Take a fully loaded Russian T55-AM2 tank for example, a more modern version of the one Pierce Brosnan drove in *Goldeneye*. It measures more than six metres long and is nearly four metres wide. Massive, unwieldy and complex it weighs in at a whopping 42 tonnes and has a 45-litre engine capable of 690bhp. It has a top speed of 50mph and in the right hands is a deadly and destructive mobile weapons system. At the very least you'll always be able to find a parking space.

My uncle Armando drove one of its older incarnations in the first Gulf War and according to him, 'You had to steer it with a hammer.'

Life often feels a little like that so perhaps as a mechanical metaphor for the intricate nuances of a modern gentleman's life it's an apt one to start with.

So is it really possible for one man to bring this unwieldy life–tank–gentleman thing under control? Possibly even with a little finesse? Could you do it? Could I? How do you drive the square tank of life into the round hole of happiness and fulfilment?

Well as tanks can drive through buildings, crush cars and take out the enemies of an easy life and abundance with one well-placed shell I'd say let's hold on to our helmets, floor the accelerator and see what happens when we actually drive one.

The easiest way to do this is to get yourself on a red letter day where you'll be taken out with a handful of other equally deranged people and allowed a few minutes on a tracked vehicle of some sort which could range from a small armoured people carrier to a Chieftain tank.

Of course the most effective and life-changing option is to join the army and attend their training school in Bovington. But remember: you are basically sitting in a target on tracks and there will be plenty of unfriendly armies and air forces out there eager to shred you into bite-sized chunks.

As a private individual to make the most of the Bovington facilities you'd also need a *Top Gear*-sized budget to play with and a lot of patience as you wait for the cogs of military bureaucracy to clank round.

Alternatively you can contact private tank owners direct. But be warned: they are an idiosyncratic breed. They tend to be men with large tracts of farmland to play with and a fair few quid in the bank. They spend their cash on tanks sourced from various armies around the world. The cost of these vehicles can be anything from tens of thousands of pounds to hundreds of thousands. Good examples are regularly serviced and in full working order, the other type end their days as unique talking points next to the water feature.

You could buy your own tank and then take your H licence, the same one you need for a tracked digger and then drive it legally on the road. But buyer beware: make sure private individuals offering H licence training in their own tanks can deliver on any promises and aren't more interested in money than in training. If you are thinking of taking this route my advice is to go through a commercial firm that trains construction contractors. After all the training vehicle doesn't matter as long as you get the licence.

But you don't need a licence to drive off-road on private land. I used the rolling farmland of the Tank School in Usk on the Welsh border. Where Alastair Scott is the proud owner of the only T55-AM2 in the country. He bought it from the Polish government and agreed to show me how to drive it. He assured me that it was nothing like the older version of the T55 that my uncle drove and definitely didn't need a hammer to operate the steering or the fully operational laser-guided targeting system.

However if it hasn't been used in a while the beastly T55 does need some warming up. Before you can take it anywhere you have to prepare the engine, the fuel and the pressurised heating and cooling system. Not by flipping a switch as you might in your compact high-spec modern family motor but by setting a fire beneath it. Literally. On a mild winter morning Alastair lit what looked like a mini flame-thrower built into the machine underneath the chassis and we waited outside for the tank to boil. Once the toxic fumes cleared he fired it up and we were ready to roll.

Lurching out of its garage we clambered on to the behemoth's back and with Alastair at the controls headed for the combination farmland and woodland training area.

I then took over Alastair's position in the front driving seat and he strapped himself above me onto the side of the tank so that he could coach as we drove. My uncle had also warned that Russian tanks were designed for small people

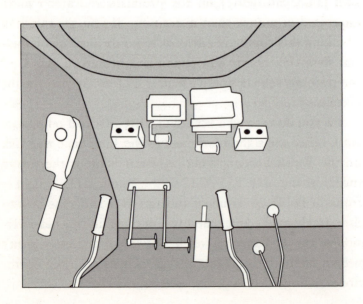

and it was a tight squeeze for a broad-shouldered lump like me to fit through the small driving hatch.

Core Combatives instructor Mick Coup (you'll meet him later on) still holds his H licence from his time in the military. When he heard that I was going to handle one of these babies for real he said, 'They're easy to drive, you'll love it.' Conflicting information. Somebody had to be right but who? With the engine idling over it was time to find out.

Surprisingly the controls of the T55 tank are almost identical to those of a manual car. There are only two differences. First the thick chrome gear stick can be slightly harder to move and has an unfamiliar five-speed shift pattern with gear one in the bottom middle rather than the top left.

Second there's a distinct absence of steering wheel. Instead on either side of you are two steering levers that extend to shoulder height and move along an arc that runs parallel to your body.

To start moving you press the clutch down with your left foot, pop it into gear, push the levers all the way forward and then take your foot off the clutch. Next to the clutch is a brake pedal and accelerator set out just like your car. A firm stamp on the accelerator and away you go. Easy.

Now how do you turn without a steering wheel?

Simple: both steering levers have a middle braking position. If you want to turn left pull the left lever to the halfway point. This stops the track on the left side while the still moving track on the right pushes you round in the direction you want to go.

It is a far from dainty procedure. With all that power under the bonnet any other machine would be shaken to pieces but with so much weight beneath you it is an unexpectedly smooth ride. And for such a big vehicle the turning circle is smaller than some 4×4s I've driven as Alastair proved by having me perform ever tighter figures of eight on my first go at the controls.

You probably wouldn't be able to take it into the nearest multi-storey car park without removing a few walls but get your head around the size of the machine and it really is that simple. There is a little less finesse rounding a corner but then you *are* in a tank; you don't have to worry if you hit anything smaller than an elephant.

And when you finally open it up on the straight, in our case a wide open field, it's like shoving a chilli up an elephant's backside: it's stupidly dangerous, surprisingly fast and something mechanically wonderful to behold. Anything in your way is like the pub doors ahead of a monk after his final day of abstinence: splinters.

To change gears you go through the whole levers forward process again. Despite Alastair having to shout his commands over the rapid fire ack-ack-ack of the engine's pistons that's all there is to it. Black smoke pours out of the rear exhaust but that doesn't affect you at the front. It's no more difficult than driving a car. Anyone could do it. Yes even you. But as in life it's where you take it and what you do with it when you get there that counts.

In fact tanks are so easy to drive that they are regularly hijacked in civilian uprisings. This happened in Paris in 1944, Budapest in 1956, Prague in 1968 and most recently in 2006 when protesters in Budapest (again) seized a museum display tank and drove it away. Unfortunately for them the museum piece ran out of fuel a hundred metres down the road slap bang in the middle of a protest and they were instantly surrounded by police.

It's actually quite surprising to find that there are a great many tanks littering the British countryside and as I found out many of them fully operational. But for anyone with lofty guerrilla ambitions in the British Isles you'd be a bit of an obvious target trundling into your nearest service station and trying to fill up with diesel.

It takes four people to make the T55 fully operational so if you and your pals do decide one drunken Saturday night to take over the neighbouring tower block or village you'll need more than Dutch courage and a foolhardy plan to make your hopes for world domination a reality.

How about this? You could try dressing in a chauffer's outfit then each take a different service station one tank at a time and tell them you're drivers from www.tanklimo.com. You never know it might just work.

You see learning to drive is the easy bit. Like being born the tricky bit is all the stuff that comes after it. As I found out during my training without effective knowledge of how to operate one of these bad boys the tank's laser-targeting system is likely to permanently blind you, the moving turret liable to rip limbs from your body or crush your skull and if the smoke alarm goes off you've only got thirty seconds to remember how to unlock the hatch before poisonous gases flood the interior and kill you outright.

Still that's life: dangerous, full of obstacles and just like a tank an outrageous amount of fun if you learn how to use it and then give it everything you've got.

Handbrake Turns . . . and Other Naughty Driving Skills

Early marketers fooled men into buying Ford Model T's because they claimed it made men more manly. This campaign strategy helped usher in the age of the car. It became a modern myth so successful that later generations of Freudians and feminists used the penis-substitute label to denigrate any man who owned a car for simply being, well a man who owned a car. And they had a point: there is nothing particularly masculine about exchanging money for a product.

On the other hand knowing how to drive a car better than the next man is. Clever chaps in white coats have demonstrated that for women risk-taking in men isn't an attractive trait but between peer groups of men it is. Risk-taking is hard-wired into us from our days as hunter-gatherers when not taking extra risks to hunt for food meant our tribe might starve.

So it doesn't matter if you drive a Fiat Punto or a Bugatti

Veyron; it's the combination of skill, quick thinking, calmness under pressure and control at speed that are ultimately desirable and distinguish you from your average boy racer or the kind of hunter that would run in waving his arms and scare the monkeys away.

For any modern gent it's not enough to only know how to parallel park and it's unlikely the skills learned for your formal driving test will help you escape the clutches of Russian spies, dodgy London geezers, boyz in the hood or even ex-wife number six. And it's not hard to learn the extra skills you need in order to achieve this. They take less than a weekend of study and are the kind of moves you see on the big screen and real-life police shows. You know the kind of audacious moves that make tyres smoke like a campfire and make you squeal like a soprano in nipple clamps.

You can even teach yourself. For this you need three things: first a car you don't mind hammering a little. It doesn't need any special modification; a standard roadworthy car is just the ticket.

Second you need space. Lots of space. Such as a large empty parking lot or industrial area.

Third you need the stones to just have a go. You'll be amazed how easy some of these moves are to execute; a little harder to master but then this is one of the key themes of the book. Fear. It's not always an easy thing to overcome but overcome it you will.

You can of course pay someone to teach you. They then provide the cars, the space and the expertise to make it all happen and logistically it saves a whole lot of headaches for you. A security professional friend of mine considers power slide days and stunt courses to be as good an option as any bodyguard's driving course and they cost about a tenth of the price. So under the tuition of a firm called Dynamic

Drivers I found myself in a disused airfield in the West Country. First out the bag . . .

The Handbrake Turn

Not just any handbrake turn but a turn into an empty space between two parked cars. Just like in the movies. To do this you need to find a suitable parking space. Approach from about 50 metres out and keep the parking spot on your right. In first gear bring the car up to around 3500 revs. When you reach the empty spot between the two cars put your left hand on the steering wheel at nine o'clock and spin it round to six o'clock. As soon as you begin to turn the wheel pull on the handbrake. Then correct any oversteer with the steering wheel.

You can also approach from the other direction. Just reverse your hands on the wheel, start at three o'clock and turn anti-clockwise. That's it. Simple and effective. However it is easy to overcook it so you may want to practise a little before trying this anywhere near real cars or pedestrians.

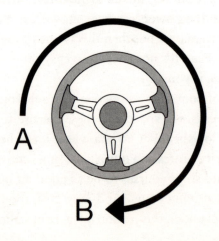

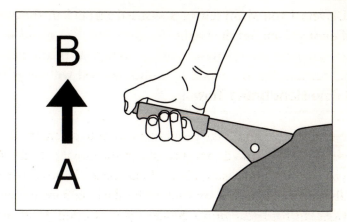

To do this you'll need four traffic cones. Lay them out just over a car length apart in your large empty area. Two on the outside edge representing the road side of the parked cars and two on the inside to mark out the area where pedestrians walk and manslaughter charges apply.

For hairpin bends we use the same principles. From whatever speed you're doing drop down to second then first gear, turn into the corner, clutch down, apply the handbrake so that the rear wheels lock and the back end comes round. Once you're pointing in the right direction it's clutch up and back on the power.

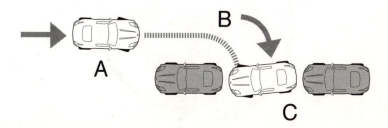

It might take you a few goes to master these techniques or like me you might get it right first time and then spend several attempts overanalysing things until you finally get it right again. But it's a skill that once learned will never be forgotten. As is the following.

The J-Turn

This is the classic move from big screen car chases from James Bond to *The Fast and the Furious*. It's also known as the Bootlegger. So if you want to feel like Steve McQueen this is the one and it's surprisingly easy to achieve whether you're using an automatic or a manual, front or rear wheel drive. Here's how.

Manual transmission

Step 1. Find your straight line through the rear window. Fix your eyes on a spot in the distance, this should keep you on course.

Step 2. Pop it into reverse and floor the throttle.

Step 3. At around 25–30mph take your foot off the accelerator. This doesn't need to be a pretty or smooth

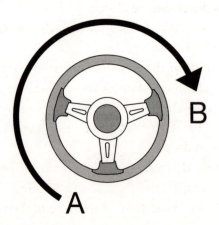

manoeuvre but it does need to be quick as the idea is to unbalance the rear suspension.

Step 4. With your hand on the steering wheel at seven to nine o'clock throw the steering wheel away to the right. This now unbalances the front end and the car will automatically fly straight round. If it's a good J-turn the rear wheels will stay virtually still as the front wheels spin around to the front.

Step 5. Look forward, clutch down and into first gear. Drive away.

How hard is that? For automatics the final step is even easier as you don't use the clutch.

Step 5. (Automatic) Look forward, change from reverse into drive and away you go.

You may find on the first few attempts that just before you change gear you instinctively hit the brakes. Don't worry about this. During my training only one person managed it first time. Our instructor said he was the first in three months to do so.

To overcome the compulsion to brake in between each set, simply visualise the manoeuvre without the braking reaction in your mind first. Repeat until it fixes in your unconscious. This usually happens somewhere between the third and sixth attempts; suddenly you'll find the front end whipping round in front of you with a satisfying screech of tyres and the stench of burning rubber before you accelerate away.

Practising J-turns beats sitting at home twiddling away on Grand Theft Auto any day of the week. But this is one exercise that will seriously beat up your car and especially your tyres, which is why it's always good to use a vehicle you're not worried about trashing or cars specifically maintained for the job.

If you want to take this move even further you could try upping the size of the vehicle; how about a double-decker bus or a single-level coach? Or my personal favourite: the golf cart – there's nothing like scaring the boys in slacks. Even better still try a fully insured hire car. It's even easier when it's not your own car you're spanking.

The Power Slide – Variations

Easily the most desirable skill to have is the power slide. It's the one move that really gets your heart pumping and turns heads whether you're a TV presenter, a Hollywood stunt man or just keen to try out your getaway skills. The idea is to keep the car moving at a constant speed through a corner. To do this you break traction by applying the brakes just before turning into the corner then reapplying acceleration so that the car appears to be travelling in a different direction from the one you're actually going in, usually sideways.

It really looks the business but there are different ways to do it depending on the type of car you're driving. In a front wheel drive you're using oversteer to get you round the corner; in rear wheel drive or four wheel drive it's the power through the back wheels. When you do this from corner to corner without regaining traction that's called drifting.

FRONT WHEEL DRIVE: The Scandinavian Flick

While you can modify the previous hairpin handbrake turn to accommodate your edge of the seat needs, at speed it is easy to get wrong. Here's a simpler technique.

Once again the aim is to unbalance the car so at speed drop down into third gear then quickly turn the wrong way into a corner to unbalance (that's right, away from the corner you're turning into) then immediately turn back the right way.

Now let the rear end slide out as far as your nerves can take and hit the throttle to power out of the slide.

It takes a bit more to master this technique but it is well worth it. The initial shimmy where you turn against the direction of the corner feels totally counter-intuitive and if you're trying it on a mountain road with a precipice ahead for your first time it'll scare the hell out of you. Again it's a perfect manoeuvre to practise in a wide-open space such as a disused airfield, industrial estate or race track.

REAR WHEEL DRIVE

Doughnuts

Classic doughnuts are for show offs and are best performed in a rear wheel drive car. They are a useful step in building up to an RWD power slide. This is where you slide the back end of the car around in a tight circle so that the front end swivels around a circular central point. It could be described as doughnut-shaped as could the smoking tyre tracks you leave behind.

Step 1. From a standing start select first gear.

Step 2. Lock the steering wheel over in the direction you want to go.

Step 3. Apply loads of revs.

Step 4. Release the clutch.

Away you go. Simple, perfect doughnuts every time. If you're attacking it from a rolling start simply squeeze on the handbrake before hitting first gear and locking the steering wheel.

Power slide in a circle

You will be going in a wider circle and this requires more skill than the simple doughnut. To begin have your car rolling in second gear then turn into the direction of steer and hammer the throttle.

Now comes the tricky bit: you have to balance the power with the steering and constantly adjust. Too much power and you'll spin out, too little and the car will straighten up and you'll lose the power and the slide.

Power slide into a corner

To put it all together, first turn into a bend at around 50–70mph to get the tail out then catch the slide and apply full throttle. Balance power with steering to hold the line round the corner and as you complete the turn ease off the power, straighten up and accelerate out.

Now take a deep breath and don't worry about grinning too much. If you've taken my advice you'll have practised all this in a big open space using a car you're not worried about hurting. Better still you'll have a professional there to teach you. You'll make a few mistakes as you learn these skills but like anything good in life to do it properly you need to be prepared to make a few mistakes first. So get out there and learn to make your tyres sing.

Pick Locks, Safes and Chastity Belts

We have all found ourselves on the outside looking in whether it's the high school dance, the head office or outside our front door with no key, no phone and the rain beating down on our heads. But fear not: the basics of lock picking are far easier to pick up than the endless nuances of social climbing and although it takes time to master it's fun and makes heroin addiction look like a very dull hobby.

So let's start with our front door and get out of this rain. You can of course use the brute force method and smash the door off its hinges but this can be a lot harder to pull off than in the movies and you're likely to damage your ankle or shoulder in the process. Cops use those battering rams for a reason you know. Our first entry method is one I learned as a teen and demonstrates the primary principle of lock picking – exploiting inherent design flaws – although without a pick in sight.

Examine your front door lock. If it's a normal cylinder type with a locking bolt that has a curved edge facing you then we're good to go. With the door shut simply insert an old credit card between the door and the frame until it touches the curve. Now give it a firm tap, *et voilà* the lock is open.

If the curve is facing away from you and you want to show off thread a shoelace around one side of the bolt. Start at the top, pull the other end back towards you and pull hard on both ends of the lace. Once again it's open sesame.

It's so easy that when you've done it once you'll ask yourself why anyone would have a standard lock fitted. However many modern door frames now have a line of beading that covers the opening between door and frame to prevent such easy access. But if you have a flat-head screwdriver to hand you can lever off the beading and use the screwdriver's tip instead of a plastic card or shoelace to get in.

Of course destroying your door frame is expensive and noisy, you may as well have called the locksmith.

Well now that your blood is up after a bit of casual breaking and entering you're probably feeling a tad frisky and unnecessary. I bet you can't wait to whisk your latest squeeze – let's call her Nicole – off to that little place in the country. But wait: her papa has heard about your reputation, gone medieval on your ass and imprisoned her nether regions in a good old-fashioned chastity belt with a great big clanking padlock on it. Well desperate times call for desperate measures. Time for your first real lock pick.

You'll need to practise a little first. Here's what you'll need:

Two paperclips.

One medium-sized padlock.

To make the pick: take paperclip one and unfold the first arm of metal once until you've made a right angle.

To make the tension wrench: take paperclip two, unfold two sides of the first arm and then fold this back on itself until the two sides of the metal are as flush to each other as you can get.

Insert the flattened end of the paperclip tension wrench at the base of the lock opening and push in as far as you can. Apply tension with a finger against the wrench in a clockwise direction, about as much as you would use to tighten a jam jar. Keep the tension constant.

Now insert the pick all the way in and rake back across the pins. You should feel the lock turn when all the pins are free. Congratulations. Give yourself a pat on the back. You've just completed your first lock pick with nothing more than some simple tools that you've fashioned yourself.

Troubleshooting: just in case it didn't happen for you first time keep at it. My first one popped open on the third attempt when I stopped jiggling and tried to feel the pins. Remember to keep constant tension on the wrench or it won't work. If your paperclips are made of very soft metal don't be afraid to replace them as they wear out.

Now that you've mastered this technique maybe you feel like liberating your significant other. She's been very patient so far.

Once you two have had your fun I'm sure you'll want to check out of the cute little hotel where you've been holed up for the weekend and leave the mess for someone else to tidy up. But how typical of the middle of nowhere: the code on your safe has stopped working and your passports and money are inside. What's more there's no one on reception. What are you going to do?

If you're a sneaky sort of chap you'll have already looked up the model of your safe using the hotel internet and tried the factory pre-set master code. Usually something like

888888 and then press E. Now depending on the hotel management they may or may not have changed this. If they have then usually they've been asked to input a 3–8-digit number. You'd be surprised how many choose 1234, 111 or some other simple to beat combination – after all the sleepy night porter has to be able to remember it. If you're a well-organised sort of fellow you may well have gone so far as to buy your own hotel safe, one that matches those of the establishment you're staying in. Why would you do this? Well as most standard hotel safes cost less than £100 and come with a basic override key that opens every model of that safe . . . oh dear have I said too much?

So passport and money in hand you reach the outside garage only to find that it is also locked and there's still no one around. Now it's time to get down to business, no more fannying around with paperclips.

You bring out your tool kit that contains the usual collection of picks and wrenches. You'll have already familiarised yourself with the whole range – picks with names like diamond, half diamond, hook, lifter, feeler, ball, double ball, half-ball and double half-ball, snake, patterned and profile, feeler and dimple as well as the wave picks, lever picks, tubular picks and cross picks. You can buy these from online locksmiths as complete sets or fashion them yourself from templates also found easily online.

For the standard five or six pin tumbler lock you'll need to get used to using a tension wrench and pick in exactly the same way you used the paperclips although with a little more finesse and savvy on the pick.

The way a lock works is that there is a shear line running from front to back inside it. There are then five or more equal-sized driver pins (top pins) sitting on top of five unequal sized key pins (bottom pins). Because the key pins are uneven in size they straddle the shear line at different heights that correspond to the indentations on the key that opens it.

When you slide the key in the indents force the driver pins to line up along the shear line to create an opening. This allows the cylinder to turn and the lock to open. When using a pick you need to apply tension in the direction of turn with the wrench and work through one pin at a time to move it into the correct position above the shear line. The pin that you start with and each subsequent pin you release is called the binding pin – i.e. it binds across the shear line. When you've tapped all five into the correct position the lock will open just as if you had a key. Easy right?

It will take time to master but it is worth the effort. Once you have the feel of it you can move on to other types of lock, use lock-pick guns and shims, blind-touch laser picks and slim jims for car entry and of course the professional cat burglar's favourite, the bump key. As you're driving away from your hotel you'll be kicking yourself for not making life easy and bringing a set along in the first place.

What a bump key is: take a normal key that fits your desired lock and cut the indentations down to their lowest setting (the lower line mark on the key), keeping the ridges intact. Insert the key part of the way into the lock (leaving one ridge or pin length sticking out) and give it a bump on the end – usually with a bump hammer – while applying tension with your thumb. The pins should jump above the shear line from front to back and allow the lock to turn.

You can make these yourself from key blanks ordered online although in some areas these can only be bought by registered locksmiths. You can also order pre-cut bump keys. However in some countries they are considered a burglary tool and you could find yourself in trouble if

found in possession with intent to use the tool for any kind
of naughtiness. But hey you are a thoroughly modern gentleman after all. The thought never even crossed your mind
did it?

How to Hotwire Cars and Motorbikes

Hotwiring a car other than one you own is a criminal offence and for newer models may not work. These days manufacturers often hide the components or wires and include cut-off switches – which means the engine won't start even with a key. It may also require a chipped key (hint: if there's an RFID (radio-frequency identification) chip in it stick it to the steering column before trying the following). But for older models you're good to go. If you find yourself stranded in a hostile environment like a desert or suburban housing estate you won't give a damn that it makes you look like a car thief.

Be warned: the following techniques could cause electric shocks or serious damage to the engine, internal components and your car. Use with caution.

Screwdriver in the Ignition

Take a flat-head screwdriver and use it in place of a key. Simply insert into the keyhole and turn. It's not the most flash way to do it but it'll save you a whole lot of trouble. If it doesn't work don't worry, you can use the screwdriver for the next solution.

The Old-Fashioned Way

Right make sure you're in neutral then get yourself under the steering column and remove the ignition cover – sometimes clipped on, sometimes screwed on. Typically you'll now see three pairs of wires. Each one corresponds to one turn on the ignition key so the first is the battery-on position, next lights, radio and electrics and the final one the starter motor.

Unfortunately there's no standard colour-coding system for these wires so you'll need to look in the manual to find out which pair is which. However if you've lost it or there's a bunch of hoodies banging on the window you could try the following.

Find the matching power wires, usually red. Disconnect them, strip the ends and reconnect by twisting them together. Bingo: the dash should light up. Do not touch them to anything metal in the car.

Now locate the starter wire or wires, often brown. WARNING: Do *not* touch the bare ends of these wires: they carry live current and you may be electrocuted. Now that you know this and have taken full responsibility for whatever happens next, strip the ends of these wires and cross the brown and red together. Just like the desperate hero in the movies. You should see a spark and the engine should start. Once the car is running, separate the live wires and cover the bare ends to protect yourself while driving.

Give the car a few revs to prevent it stalling and your

having to repeat this procedure. Now put your foot down and get the hell out of Dodge.

Motorbikes are even easier. Just take the ignition cover off and twist the battery and ignition wires together (check the manual to find out the exact specs for your machine or opt for red and green if you're in a jam). Now start the motor and drive like the devil himself was chasing you.

How to Defeat Security Systems

We have all seen the films where the hero blows some cosmetic powder into an infrared beam or uses a mirror to reflect the light back on itself without breaking the circuit. I mean who doesn't like watching Catherine Zeta Jones ooze her way through those red light beams in *Entrapment*? If your significant other is reading this over your shoulder then why pretend? Clearly the answer is *both* of you. But in the real world of high tech sometimes silent, sometimes scarily loud or police-alerting alarm systems, is there anything likely to work?

You bet. Our old friend the design flaw is here to help us. Alarm systems are just like network controllers, cameras or any other electrical device: many of them have default settings that are easy to exploit such as simple four-digit pass codes or call centre passwords that are nothing more than the owner's telephone number. As with most hacks a quick scan through the user's handbook or manual can often provide what you're looking for.

Cosmetic powder really doesn't work simply because the

dust particles are heavy enough to trip the alarm. On the other hand the noted security expert Marc Weber Tobias, author of *Locks, Safes and Security*, demonstrated a real-world example that does work using an off-the-shelf motion detector, the Lasershield by Motorola. To bypass the settings of this wireless system he simply bought a walkie-talkie from the same manufacturer and kept the broadcast key pressed down the entire time he was in the building that used the Lasershield. As they both operate on the same frequency this blocked any alarm signal sent to the base unit from the sensors. It's just like the hero's mirror trick only he uses sound rather than light. As a great many wireless sensors can be defeated by radio jamming it's also one of the best kept secrets in the industry.

Of course there are all kinds of reasons to hack an alarm system other than sneaky peeking in your neighbour's backyard. You can rig these systems to launch freaky phantoms, fog machines and spooky lights for Halloween, or MP3 players, CD systems, PowerPoint presentations and air horns that sound whenever someone walks past. Basically anything with an on/off switch.

Yes but what about technology and the constant forward march of progress I hear you cry? Biometrics (fingerprint sensors) and retinal scanners for example? Well like everything in life there's always room for improvement. Take the average fingerprint scanner on your laptop; while it might appear safe most manufacturers will tell you somewhere deep within the documentation that it isn't. Microsoft's Fingerprint Reader for Windows states, 'The biometric (fingerprint reader) feature in this device is not a security feature and is intended to be used for convenience only.'

So how do we get past this device without hacking off the owner's finger? There are several ways to do this. The advanced geek route uses a combination of a USB sniffer and custom message player along with a scanned copy of your own fingerprint; drop it in the unencrypted folder that contains the original unencrypted fingerprint scans and away you go. For a less tech-heavy approach try using fingerprint scans lifted from cups, keyboards or whatever you can find and then reprinting or moulding them on to ballistics gel, latex, Blu-Tack or even jelly babies. Lick your finger, apply, swipe. All have been shown to work by various hacker groups online.

But my favourite has to be a simple photocopy of someone's fingerprint as used on a security door lock for the Discovery Channel's *Mythbusters* show. As most fingerprint sensors use off-the-shelf components from a surprisingly small range of manufacturers, you can bet that a flaw you find in system X will often apply in manufacturer Y's version too. Failing this if there's a human interface involved (a security guard) then send in your best looking female friend with a bunch of doughnuts and feverishly fluttering eyelids for a bit of base-level social engineering, usually the most simple workround of all.

How to Get a Gun in any City in the World in the Next Few Hours

Suppose you've just run over your mother-in-law's prize alpaca; it's too far gone and you know you need to put it out of its misery and stop that all-too-human-like screaming. What are you gonna do? Call the vet? He'll spill the beans for sure. And then it's a family standoff for years to come. Clearly the only way out is to make like Tony Soprano and do what needs to be done.

Depending on where you are in the world you might have to cut a few corners to find the necessary tools for the job. If you're in legislation heavy UK then your first stop will of course be friends in the know, failing that the local gun club. Hang around for a couple of hours and 'have a word' with any likely looking characters who might be able to hook you up. Worst-case scenario head for the roughest pub you can find; you know the kind of place where you fear for your life as soon as you walk through the door. Now make like Samuel L. Jackson in a Tarantino movie: just be cool and ask around. The barman is a good place to start. Inevitably he'll point you in the direction of the scariest guy in the place. But hey family harmony is worth the trouble right?

In some countries it is ridiculously easy to get tooled up. America as you would expect gives the necessaries away free with bank accounts as Michael Moore showed in his documentary *Bowling for Columbine*. Most recently Max Motors in Butler, Missouri, offered a free ultra-lightweight Kel-Tec .380 handgun or gas card with each new car. Sales quadrupled with most new owners opting for cheap armament over cheap fuel.

Of course if you're in the so-called developing world cut-price arms are everywhere. Take Cambodia aka War Disney where at the Kambol Shooting Range you can blow up a cow with a bazooka or RPG for around £200–£300. The bulk of that price tag is the cost of the cow not the weapon. Think you might be able to do a little back-door negotiation there? It's the kind of place where you can also throw a hand grenade into a flock of chickens – for fun. I'd say that's a big yes and even though these practices remain illegal in Cambodia it's the healthy stream of bloodthirsty backpackers that makes it all possible.

If the thought of minced alpaca seems a little excessive remember that wherever you are in the world all you have to do is just be cool and ask around. There's always going to be someone who can help you with your mother in law problems. Hell if she lives in Missouri she might even lend you the freebie that came with her new SUV.

How to Disappear Without Trace

In February 1995 Richey Edwards, the guitarist and lyricist of the band the Manic Street Preachers, disappeared but not without a trace. His car had been left in a notorious suicide spot next to the Severn Bridge on the border between England and Wales. The Severn River has one of the highest tidal ranges in the world and if he had jumped in it's likely that anything left after he hit the water would have been dragged out to the Irish Sea or Atlantic Ocean and never seen again.

However in the weeks before his car was found he'd been taking the maximum daily amount of cash out of his account and it was reported that he'd read books on how to disappear. Although his family declared him legally dead in 2008 the jury's still out on this one. I researched a project on his disappearance in 1999, ever since then I always like to think that he's reinvented himself and is living a low key but happy life somewhere sexy and sub-tropical.

There are many reasons why you might want to disappear. Some of the most common are escaping abuse, debtors or an unhappy life, to business people who fear kidnapping or celebrities who can't stand the limelight any more. There are also more extreme cases such as that of Bosnian Serb leader Radovan Karadžić who changed his identity, occupation and appearance to escape prosecution for war crimes. Then there's John Darwin who famously made anyone who'd ever considered disappearing groan with disappointment when a photo of him and his wife buying a place in Panama surfaced five years after his fake death.

If you are considering your own vanishing act then there are a few basics you need to know beforehand.

You can live either off-grid or on-grid but both require you to separate everything you do in your new life from everything you did in the old. Both methods follow very similar steps; the trick is to create a firewall between you and you old life either through legal structures or new ID.

Preparation:

- Create your new life first – give yourself months rather than days.
- Tell no one of your plans.
- Use pay-as-you-go phones and international calling cards for all communications relating to your new life.
- Use internet cafés, libraries and other public computers to conduct any research.
- Use cash; don't leave a credit card, checking or Paypal trail.

Manufacture Your New Identity

A simple legal way to create new ID without a huge paper trail is to nominate a new name through a statutory declaration with a lawyer (people who have sex changes, actors and immigrants who anglicise their names do this all the time) or through what is called 'common usage'. For example my first name is Francis but I rarely use that for anything other than official government documents. I can legally use Frank for everything I do as long as I'm not planning to defraud anyone.

The darker path involves stealing ID from cot deaths, infants who died around the same time you were born (check obituaries then apply for their birth certificate and take it from there); buying passports from developing countries in return for investment money; or persuading someone who you know will never leave the country to allow you to use their passport to establish a parallel identity.

In *Other People's Money* the inventive real-life fraudster Elliot Castro successfully hijacked or created several new identities to tap their lines of credit and siphon off funds to his own Swiss bank accounts.

Whichever route you choose once you have a new ID you need to build up a layer of believability: so a home address, bank account, medical card, social security number, passport, Blockbuster card, library card, bills and so on. You might not be able to get all of them but get as many as you can.

You can then establish an International Business Corporation (IBC) in a territory with no mutual legal assistance treaty with your home country. No shareholders or directors are listed, which means you can then use your corporate ID to run your new life. This allows you to use:

- 'Black' credit cards – that list no transactions.
- Sign up for email, fax and secretarial services.
- Have a phone anywhere in the world.
- Own property.

Once you're gone:

- Always keep a low profile.
- If you must contact family or friends use calling cards or pay-as-you-go phones in an area that doesn't relate to you then throw them away.
- Don't go home ever.
- Don't use anything from your old life such as credit cards, email accounts, social networking sites or like John Darwin your old library.

Why is all this complexity necessary? Well because there are people out there paid to find you like American skip tracer Frank M. Ahearne. In his revealing article 'Learning How to Disappear' he says that for guys like him 'it's a game we get paid to play. We can make as many mistakes as we want; the one you make is the one that most likely leads us to you.' So if you fake your own death there are insurance investigators to watch out for and if you run out on significant debts the creditors can be unrelenting. Kiwi Owen Bruce Taylor found this out when the police pulled him in after he had been living for four years with a new identity when he ran out on NZ$3 million in debts. The detective agency tracking the New Zealander found him 950 miles away from home in Queenstown. By then he was the director of a local company and well established.

However take heart: there are plenty out there who do get away with it. You generally only hear about the ones that don't. Take Ivan Manson who disappeared successfully in 1975 and only reappeared twenty years later in Queensland, Australia, when a postmortem revealed his true identity after a fatal car accident.

Steve O'Keefe, co-author of *How to Disappear Completely and Never Be Found*, demonstrated how easy it is to build a new identity by making mail-order purchases in his dog's name. He always paid cash, which means his pooch now has one of the best credit ratings in Washington State and regularly receives pre-approved credit card applications.

I still have one of my own faux identities from when I first started playing with this whole idea a few years ago. With no credit history at all and nothing more than an address I managed to convince one British credit firm to offer a Mr F. Spunkmonkey a credit card. Maybe they thought this was a quaint ethnic name.

Remember: the rules change regularly so keep your research up to date. When you are set up give me a call on a disposable phone and I'll come and join you for a caipirinha somewhere sunny. Until then enjoy the beach.

How to Hide a Dead Body

So whaddya mean you've never killed anyone? What about the alpaca? You missed? Oh you hit your mother-in-law. Damn. Well look on the bright side. At least you won't have to give her the gun back.

If we are going to look seriously at how to dispose of a dead body then clearly we need to start with those two infallible sources of information, the movies and the internet.

Mafia-style

Anyone who's anyone knows that once you've whacked a guy you've got to remove the hands and face if you're of Russian extraction or fingers and teeth if you're Italian – that's if you don't want the body to be identified. You'll also need somewhere quiet and easy to clean like a tarp or bathroom and plenty of sharp tools capable of cutting through bone. Oh and a strong stomach.

The unrecognisable body can then be dumped anywhere

you like. If you're a perfectionist then you could of course dismember it into small pieces and deposit it in bins or dog bowls around town.

If you're in a rush then a heavy weight (think front axle) tied to the body and deep water should do the trick. If time is on your side you could drive around town with the body in an ice-cream van's freezer to throw off the time of death on the coroner's report – just like real-life Mafia hit man Richard 'The Iceman' Kuklinski. By the time the body defrosts you should have come up with a plausible alibi for the fake time of death.

Eat and Be Merry

If you're an out of work sociopath named Hannibal then clearly you might want to provide a silver service option for you and your girlfriend. Alternatively if you're the landowning type you could feed your victim to whatever animals you have that will then be sold on to the general public. Or if you're really enterprising you could go the way of Sweeney Todd and his girlfriend Mrs Lovett and get a production line going. They opted for meat pies. For a modern, culturally inclusive variant how about a late night kebab shop? Think anyone would notice the man-beef difference?

The Fargo Effect

You could of course put the dearly departed limb by limb in the wood chipper or garbage masher. Once you have a suitably unrecognisable mush on your tarp – you did lay one down beforehand didn't you? – either take it out into a forest, a lake or the sea and distribute as wild animal food.

Acid Bath

If these all feel a bit hands on then you can always do what deranged serial killers and Mexican drug gangs have been doing for years: simply take your cadaver and drown it in sulphuric acid. Over time the body will turn to sludge and you can dispose of it wherever you like.

Old School

If you're not a deranged killer and simply want to dispose of a family pet in a civilised way then do what gravediggers have been doing for generations. Dig six feet down – far enough to prevent the attentions of hungry animals – lay on some lime, cover and leave. Calcium oxide (CaO), commonly know as burnt lime, lime or quicklime, is used to both disguise the smell of decomposition and increase the rate of decay. You can also use salt or natron (a natural mineral used by the Egyptians for mummification) to hide the smell as both dry out the body and reduce acidity, making it a hostile place for bacteria to live. There really is no smell that lingers quite as much as that of a dead body. That reminds me: remember to wash your hands before you eat.

Make Things Go Boom

Blowing things up is one of those simple pleasures that some of us learn as children. This either kills you, gets you in trouble or you get away with it. When these same children become adults many go on to make money doing exactly the same dangerous things only with more dramatic results. Usually in the military, construction or as a creative in film or theatre. I'm going to focus on the last element here, the theatrical and the mostly harmless.

Remember: if you use any of these methods or techniques at home the onus is on you to take responsibility. Therefore if you blow yourself up using these instructions or by say adding twenty times the amount of accelerant specified here then that clearly is your own damned fault.

For all of these recipes I recommend that you conduct your tests outdoors away from the wind, flammable materials, other humans and animals, and with a fire extinguisher close at hand. If you doubt any of your recipes or ingredients simply abort your experiments. Burning or wounding yourself or others or setting fire to your house is just not worth it.

Let's start with something simple and idiot proof.
What you'll need:
Two litres of Diet Coke (not normal Coke).
A packet of Mentos (the mint ones not fruit-flavoured).

The Coke Geyser

Open the bottle, add one to four Mentos and stand back: the Coke should plume several feet up into the air provoking gasps of wonder and admiration from those standing around followed by shrieks as they get covered in sticky, frothy goo.

The Coke–Mentos Bomb

This is best performed in a wide-open space away from other humans or animals. Repeat as above but before the plume shoots up screw the Coke bottle lid back on. To avoid the cap flying off and hitting you in the head screw it on as tight as you can. Then with the bottle pointing away from you throw it hard at the ground and as far away from you as possible. It will explode with a bang and shoot up into the air.

Quick and Easy Smoke Bombs

Yes yes I know, pretty tame right? Where's the fire and brimstone? Well we're getting there. Remember we're going for the theatrical and practical and the type of thing that won't get you picked up by Homeland Security or MI5. The quickest type of smoke bomb requires the following:

One ping pong ball.
A sheet of silver foil (say 30×30cm for good measure).
Lighter or matches.

Place the ball in the middle of the foil and wrap it around the ball without tearing it. You need to leave a foil tail to act as a handle – if it looks like a giant silver spermatozoa you've got the right shape. Take it outside and light the foil near the ping pong ball (yes foil does burn). Throw the smoke bomb away from you then stand back and watch the smoke stream away. Always remember not to breathe the smoke from any smoke bomb as this could be harmful. To make it bigger cut two to three balls into little pieces and wrap in the same manner. More fuel for the fire so to speak.

Still not big enough? Okay let's try something a little more ambitious.

Big Smoke Bomb

If size and dramatic effect are what you are after then we're going to have to get a little more sophisticated. This is an entry-level smoke bomb using fuel, propellant and ignition. What you'll need:

Saltpetre, aka potassium nitrate (KNO_3).
Powdered sugar.
Tissue paper.
Something to lay it on outdoors (make sure it's not windy).

Potassium nitrate is used in any number of things from sausage-making or curing meats like ham, pastrami or Irish spiced beef to its more common use as a garden fertiliser. Since the stuff you get in garden centres is now treated to make it burn slowly you will not be able to use this. You're better off getting it unrefined from your pharmacist or on eBay. However if you begin to order this stuff in large quantities without a valid reason you should expect your door hinges to last for a shorter time than usual. Big Brother is watching after all.

Mix three parts of the nitrate to two parts sugar, say 30 grams and 20 grams to begin with. I seriously recommend you start with small quantities at first until you understand the burn rate. Remember to do this well away from any buildings, sheds, garden furniture, washing lines or anything else which could be damaged including you. Then layer your well-mixed powder on the tissue paper then set fire to the paper. See the flame? See the smoke? Good. Now let's scale it up.

Now you will need to add:

A narrow cardboard box, some sparkler powder (scratch off the outside of a sparkler) and a fuse (I'll show you how to make one of these in a moment).

Increase the quantities by a factor of ten. Mix very well; they're both white powders so once you think you've got it right do it again to make sure. Lay the mix in the narrow box. Lay a thin line of sparkler powder across the mix. Then plug a long fuse into the mix through the sparkler powder – this faster-burning material will ensure that the whole mix burns as one rather than from corner to corner.

Light the fuse and step way back. You'll see a fair bit of flame and lots of smoke. Hopefully no one will call the fire brigade. Keep a fire blanket nearby to smother the flames should you need to.

How to Make a Simple Fuse

Get some string, dip it in white spirits and let it dry. Take care. This fuse will have a rapid burn rate. Alternatively you can make a variety of more efficient fuse wires using string, glue and potassium nitrate but for a controlled burn rate and sheer ease of use I suggest you order a big coil of the stuff from your nearest theatrical supplies shop or online.

Shape a Charge for a Better Smoke Bomb

You can make another variety of smoke bomb that allows you to mould it into shape and carry it around. For this you will need:

KNO_3.

Sugar.

Baking soda.

Salt.

A solid container (e.g. a hard plastic bottle) and a fuse wire.

Mix three parts KNO_3 and two parts sugar in a pan on a low heat. When the sugar begins to caramelise add one table-spoon of baking soda and one teaspoon of salt. Keep stirring until the mixture has formed a brown gooey caramel.

Pour into the bottle. Make a hole in the cap and screw back on. Thread the fuse through the hole into the mix and leave to set for one hour. Wrap gaffer tape around the body of the bottle and you're done. Light the fuse. The bomb will burn for a minute or more. Do not put it on its side as it will probably take off like a rocket with unpredictable results. So once again do this in a secure and safe environment outside and away from living creatures and flammable objects.

WARNING: whenever you're heating up potentially flammable and combustible materials it is essential you take precautions so do wear heavy, long sleeves and protective gloves to prevent nasty burns and blisters should the mix-ture stick to you. A full face shield is also advisable – you really wouldn't want this stuck to your face. Keep a ready supply of water and an extinguisher close by and if possible cook the mixture outside on a camping stove or specially prepared area. You can always join your local rocketry club for experienced guidance on preparing these kinds of charges.

Flash Bangs and Electrical Detonation

Back in the days when I worked in TV I learned to make a theatrical explosive for war scenes. You get a flash, a bang and a cloud of smoke but by using surprisingly simple ingredients and without blowing anyone up.

Ingredients:

Gunpowder mixture from a firework such as a rocket.

A small pot such as the base of a tea light candle (preferably made of cardboard, shrapnel is no fun).

Talcum powder.

A sheet of paper.

16-volt battery.

A few metres of electrical cable (like the wires leading into a plug).

First cut out a circle using the tea light base as a template. Then fill with half the firework mixture and layer double the amount of talcum powder on top. Put the circle of paper on top of that to keep the mixture dry. You'll find it useful for transporting pre-prepared charges.

Now take your cable and cut into two equal lengths. Make a shallow hole in the ground to hold the charge. Make a hole in the paper and place an end of each cable in the mix. Run the other ends off a safe distance then touch the ends to the positive and negative terminals of your battery. Boom! Perfect war zone stage explosions. You may have to experiment with quantities here: more gunpowder equals bigger bang while more talcum powder creates a bigger cloud of smoke.

Play safe. With potential for electric shock and because you're using explosive materials it's a technique probably best left to the professionals or failing that your local amateur dramatics society or art college should be able to teach you how to perform this or the next recipe in a safe and productive way and without any real life drama.

Theatrical Napalm

This can be used for a variety of effects from creating thick black clouds of smoke to fire writing on concrete or wire sculptures. When I was younger this was primarily made with soap or eggs but the modern interpretation is effortlessly simple and therefore requires an extra degree of caution. Again take all necessary steps to ensure your safety and if possible guidance from a professional. Napalm is used in war to create devastation and psychological havoc; it can be anything from a thick syrup to a gel and once lit is extremely hard to remove from whatever it's stuck to. It's also hydrophobic – i.e. hard to put out with water. So as I say be careful. Original napalm is banned internationally for use against civilian targets although later variants such as the Mark 77 bomb used in the second Gulf War used a kerosene rather than petroleum base of the modified napalm-B variant that we'll use here (minus benzene). It burns for longer and up to temperatures of 1200°C/2200°F.

You'll need:

Petrol.

Styrofoam (the pellets you find as packing in boxes are ideal).

Metal can (it eats plastic).

Pour a little petrol into the bottom of the metal can. Add Styrofoam chunks. Make sure you do not breathe the noxious fumes as they dissolve rapidly in the petrol. When you have a sticky white residue that's it: you're done.

Whereas original napalm burns for around fifteen to thirty seconds the B variant can burn for ten minutes and lends itself well to fire writing. Take a stick and write your name with the napalm mixture on a non-flammable surface i.e. something that will not burn easily when subjected to heat for long periods of time, concrete for example.

Then strike a long fire-lighting match and apply.

Wow look at you burn baby, you're on fire!

Drill It 'Til You Can Kill It – How to Shoot Any Gun

I'm not teaching you how to shoot; I'm teaching you how to fight with guns

JC, Edelweiss Tactical

On patrol your opposite number spots trouble.

'Contact!' he yells.

The drills kick in instantly. You turn and run back down the Baghdad street. Before you've even had a chance to shout 'Moving!' you hear the first shot from your oppo's AK74 on the other side of the road, followed by a controlled three-shot burst then another. You hit ten metres, turn and yell 'Back in!' as hard as you can and lay down covering fire.

You know he has started his own run when his gun goes quiet.

At least you hope he's running.

Forget that; get the rounds down now. One-two-three-four-five-six-seven-eight-nine shots in quick succession into the targets ahead. Ammo is limited, precious, no random gangbanger squirts of automatic fire allowed here.

His shout and shot reach you at the same time. You take

off again turning outwards and scanning the street behind looking for the ambush.

'Back in!' you shout and lay down more rounds from the twenty-one left in the mag.

You hear his next 'Back in!' and then it's your turn to run again.

'Stoppage!' he shouts.

Shit. You skid to a halt, turn and scream 'Back in!' You've lost count of the rounds you have left. In the enclosed space each bullet whips through burning gas as it leaves the barrel of your AK74.

Click.

Fuck. Out of ammo.

The silence of the guns is deafening. You're exposed. Too exposed.

'Reload,' you shout.

Again the drills kick in, the same actions you've run on the pistol all week: remove the mag, stash it, grab a full one from your chest rig. Reload the fresh mag, rack the bolt . . . fire, fire, fire.

Happiness is a loud gun. Warmth has nothing to do with it. The short silence was terrifying and that, well that scenario was only a drill. Not a real street in Baghdad but a mock-up on a 50-metre shooting range somewhere deep within a mountain in the Swiss Alps. And it's a rare opportunity to train in these deadly skills.

When I asked my private military contacts to recommend firearms courses in Europe the same name came up time and time again: Edelweiss Tactical. After five days on their intensive Tactical Firearms course I'd have a selection of National Rifle Association certificates that covered pistol, rifle and law enforcement qualifications up to the company's own exacting test standards – 30 per cent higher than GSG9

Special Forces or US Air Marshal standards. That's proficient enough for any modern gentleman.

The AK74 drill above came as part of day four's individual team contact drills where my oppo Tom and I were taught how to react when we needed to fight for cover or fight through and tackle multiple targets from multiple directions.

The drill and choice of weapon were both based on real fire fights in Afghanistan where Russian Spetsnaz special forces found that the effectiveness of the AK74's 5.45×39mm round was more reliable and more accurate over distance than the AK47's 7.62×39mm round.

By the end of the day JC the lead instructor gave us credit for having worked the day's best team drills – a huge compliment.

The other men on the course (women also take part and according to JC they do very well indeed) were a mixture of ex-military, close protection and police. Participants usually come from all over the world and work in high-risk environments that you or I only read about in newspapers or watch on the six o'clock news.

Most of these guys don't have the 'normal' military mindset either; they are at the level where they are autonomous and the money they earn goes straight in the bank and doesn't get squandered. For obvious reasons I can't use real names here.

Until three days before I had never really used a gun. Not properly anyway. But the training takes you so far out of your comfort zone and up a learning curve so steep I doubted I would ever find it again.

What's more in Britain you could never take this kind of live-fire tactical course. Legally they just can't exist. Your only option would be to shoot pheasant and grouse on overpriced excursions with the aspirational tweed and City set. As one of the ex-military characters told us even your normal soldier doesn't receive anywhere near the same level of firearms training.

This is one of many things that makes this sub-Alpine training experience about as Jason Bourne as it gets. To reach the ranges you have to enter the tunnels of a research mining facility and hang a left up a long flight of stairs for the 25 and 100-metre ranges or turn right for the cavernous 50-metre range big enough to hold cars as well as build killing floors and recreate realistic scenarios. It's also deep enough under Alpine rock that you would never have to worry about waking the neighbours. Throw in a few international police forces on training assignments wandering about and you've got a place that feels more than a little special.

The system they teach was designed by JC and two other ex-military and close-protection professionals. It took years to develop and test, analysing real gunfights either from personal experience or from video material sent to them from private military companies and international law enforcement agencies. They picked apart these real world situations, took the best of the tuition already on the circuit and refined it so that it is not only scaleable – what you learn on a handgun works just as well on a rifle or machine gun – but adaptable so that you are quick and effective in any combat shooting situation whether it calls for rapid fire instinctive shooting or surgical precision.

It's so effective that their training method has already been adapted as the benchmark for a police special forces unit that once again has to remain anonymous.

It's a learning system that is uncomplicated, uncluttered

and based on higher-level principles. Too many systems fill your mind with jargon, surplus facts and shallow content. Not this one. JC filled the atmosphere with knowledge, expertise and laughter. Whenever the hard pace of training got to us – and it did – he either took the mickey out of one of us or himself, cracked a joke or told a story of sexual misadventure so outrageous I doubt my publishers would let me write up even the first sentence. Swingers at the CIA springs to mind.

The most basic of basics on the first day was familiarisation in the rec room with the range of weapons we would use that week. Cradling an unloaded SIG 552 Commando assault rifle in my arms I lined up the sight on my colleague Mario. The moment the little red dot appeared on his forehead I realised that this wasn't a game; guns loaded with live ammunition aren't toys for boys but machines that kill. And for a number of reasons from the profane to the professional we were there to learn how to use them.

Before we fired a single round the following morning we began with the draw. Simply how to grip the gun as you pull it from the holster with your finger off the trigger – no safeties, the guns are always made ready to fire – and into a closed guard. Then punch the gun out, right hand over the butt, the left covering it with the thumb pointing forward. An aiming device that helps keep your shot stable.

We dry drill it until it sticks.

The hand position is one they've developed themselves which uses the thumb as a pointing mechanism so that when you're involved in an instinctive shooting scenario your aim is more accurate. You'll still be expected to line the sights up of course but it makes the shot more stable when fear and adrenalin kick in. We're encouraged to be aggressive and unafraid of the gun. As in unarmed combat it's about learning the realities of a high-stress situation that no amount of movies, arcade games or toy guns will ever teach you.

A moment of clarity hits when you do something like this: we think we know guns because we see them so often in cop shows and play with them in computer games but we don't. We really don't. Learning how to fight with guns is the difference between pornography and real sex. There are no fluffers in the firing line and no second takes.

Then we learned to squeeze the trigger properly.

'Single tap is surgical,' JC tells us. 'Pick up, feel first pressure, press, follow through.'

More dry drills.

'Load five and five,' he says. 'Go.'

Make ready then holster.

Draw to closed guard.

Punch out and single tap, one shot in the coloured piece of A4 pinned to the target over the central area between chest and lower head.

Check gun for stoppages.

Back to closed guard.

Holster.

Repeat times five then tactical reload, an existing method of reloading quickly while retaining the empty magazine but refined with a touch of Edelweiss diesel plus.

After the first ten we review.

'Single tap is an aimed round not a lot of force. They're going to feel it. It's going to hurt. It's not really going to kill them . . . unless you hit them in the right place.'

'Load ten and ten. Go.'

We do this time after time until the technique is ingrained

but for newbies like me not necessarily comfortable. On the first live fire there was so much adrenalin pumping through my hands that I could barely keep them steady. I saw the same thing once in a young military policeman when filming outside the Edwards Air Force Base in the Mojave Desert in California. We were making a documentary and had wandered on to one of their unmarked ranges. Three military police vehicles screeched to a halt beside us. The MPs jumped out guns drawn: 'Get your hands in the air,' they screamed. It was my first project as an associate producer my baby supposedly, my director simply said, 'Frank you deal with it.' I was in my mid-twenties and the MP with his gun in my face was even younger than me. His hands were shaking. We waited for what seemed like for ever as his colleagues stripped our vehicles. I watched his trembling hands and thought it was fear.

It wasn't. Okay well a little bit – it is a lethal weapon after all – and after my first ten live shots in Switzerland I was like the young MP so adrenalised I could barely load bullets for the second set of ten and ten.

The drills changed constantly. JC would lower the lights, tell us to do it one way then another, upping the sense of pressure, shortening the time on the drills. It focuses your attention on what you really have to do and forces the skills into your unconscious without you even realising.

Then came the double tap, a method that makes the most of the natural movement of the gun after the first shot is fired: aim for the chest, tap, as the gun rises, tap again in the head. That's the theory anyway. JC was more interested in getting us to fire quickly and under control. Legally the technique is considered excessive force for armed policemen. But in reality when you're in a situation you will do what you have to do.

Instinctive or surgical? It doesn't matter. Concentrate. Use the 'big fucking boom stick' and change to snap shooting combined with double taps.

Closed guard, punch out.

'Hit the A4, two rounds in the body.'

'More holes more goals.'

And this is how it goes.

The following day we worked hard through the drills covering a range of subjects and shooting skills: taps, double taps, immediate action drills, continuous shooting, ambi lefts, ambi rights (ambidextrous = one-handed either hand), shoot them to the ground, kill shots; as well as the different types of weapons retention: closed guard, covert guard; different guns, different loading patterns. Emergency action drills, i.e. stoppages. Contact positions: Sul, contact ready, closed ready.

When shooting you're taught to always move off the line of fire. It's like boxing: guy comes in for a jab you get out of his way. As JC eloquently puts it, 'In a bun fight no matter what move. You must always move.' Step aside, drop, level change, walk, run, kneel, whatever is practical at the time. Shooting, moving. Always shooting and moving. It's a key training philosophy.

By the following afternoon I've loaded so many bullets that criss-cross slices have appeared on my thumb where the skin has caught on the mag as I push the rounds in. I keep bleeding on the shiny brass of the bullets but then I remember bullets are supposed to make you bleed.

JC lays down a situation of two British special forces operators working in a South American country. They found themselves in a room full of drug cartel members all guns pointed at them and then it kicked off. Outnumbered the two men shot their way out in a matter of seconds. They lost body parts in the process but both men lived, the others didn't.

Before I know it I'm standing on the 270° range in a room with five targets in random positions all waiting to shoot me. From the moment you draw you've got to clear the room as quickly as you can before the bad guys have a chance to fight back. Tap-tap, tap-tap, I hit the two targets ahead of me with a standard two handed grip, tap-tap, tap-tap for the two on the left and then one-handed I reach back 180° and tap the last guy on the right.

As JC rightly said I'm learning to fight. We dress our daughters in pink and give them dolls' houses to play with and our sons toy guns. For many men it's something we're programmed to do from an early age. As an adult to get your head around the images of men with guns we're fed from childhood and really own them is like a rite of passage.

'Work on your weaknesses,' JC had drilled into us. Until then my weakest skill had been the ambi rights and double taps. As I left the floor Vlad, a seriously well-muscled close-protection professional working in a high-risk desert country, complimented me on the ambi move. Until he pointed it out I hadn't even realised I'd used it. The ambi right is a one-handed firing position not dissimilar to the homeboy handhold you see in movies but more refined to provide a stable shooting platform. Unconsciously it had become one of my strongest skills.

JC brought me back down by telling me I reminded him of James Blunt. I took it as a modest compliment. Then when my ego started to show JC asked me how long I'd been a gay swinger. Cheeky blighter.

Still a bit of teasing made me laugh and took my mind off

the adrenalin shakes coursing through my hands as I loaded up for the next drill.

For teachers of tactical firearms the attitude was also refreshingly non-confrontational. We heard a story of how during training with around forty US police, special agents and military there was an exercise that didn't require lethal force. The scenario was an upset overweight female customer in a fast food diner. Hardly a life-threatening situation. However JC and his training partner were the only ones not to pull their weapons. The reason the Americans gave for pulling their guns? 'But she could have been armed.'

'Well then,' JC had responded, 'you learn to draw quickly.'

When the two firearms' specialists demonstrated how to defuse the situation with a healthy dose of sarcasm and the threat of a taser the Americans pushed them further on why they hadn't drawn their guns. Their logic was this: if your gun is out then you can be forced to shoot when you don't have to. Instead you can control a confrontation with verbalisation, pepper sprays, batons, tasers or any of the other tools you have to hand using the escalation of force model.

To emphasise the point JC told us, 'I don't need to draw this gun. The only time I'm going to draw that is when I decide you are going to die. I can no longer contain this . . . you're going down.'

Makes you wish more cops took their kind of training.

This is the reason for the different types of guards: retention and disguise of your intentions to minimise escalation.

The movement drills came into their own during the night shoots. We were given three distinct methods for lighting up a target with a torch or a clip-on tactical light, all scarily effective. The drill worked like this:

Flash the light on for the briefest moment. Locate target.
Move in the dark.

Flash on, aim, fire.

Move and reposition in the dark. Repeat.

Moving stealthily around a pitch-black room, appearing in unexpected places and nailing the target with a single tap are seductively sinister and lethal skills to have. As is firing a Remington 12-gauge pump-action shotgun from an open car window. With a 1oz rifled slugger round it's more elephant than ninja and destroys targets rather than scores neat holes in them. According to JC it's also the surest way to stop a car. Either aim for the driver or the bonnet.

By the morning of the final day I had more bloody gashes across the top of my hand from learning to rack the AK74 and then doing it overhand rather than underhand and gouging chunks of flesh out on the safety. I only noticed the blood afterwards. Ah the joys of adrenalin.

The Heckler & Koch MP5 with its Gucci looks was no harder to use than a handgun. It is the weapon of choice for law enforcement special response units and military Special Ops. It also uses 9mm rounds which are easily interchangeable with handgun ammo.

My favourite long weapon during the course was easily the AK74SU with the fatboy muzzle. The 'U' stands for '*ukorochenny*' – 'shortened' in Russian. It's a Bulgarian-manufactured version that bridges the gap between sub-machine gun and assault rifle. It is primarily designed for special forces, airborne infantry and as a defence weapon for tanks, guns, helicopters or other armoured vehicle crews. It's great for tight spaces such as the back of a small car just like the 'Scheisswagen' Tom and I found ourselves working from on the last day. It was restrictive, cramped and we were shooting out of the back window. Due to the lack of space I had to learn to fire the AK with my left hand at the last moment. Despite the nausea and headaches from the smoke and fumes when we finally rolled out of the cramped little Hyundai I found I'd loved every second of it.

There were seemingly endless supplies of Fisherman's Friends being doled out to take away the taste and smell along with the occasional line of snuff beforehand to get us in the mood. A Swiss hunting tradition apparently.

But shooting rifles is easy: you aim, you shoot, you hit. Child soldiers can work any of the AKs; the AK47 is the people's gun after all. And as JC said about rifle tests, 'You look at it, you breathe on it, you pass.'

The handgun tests were a different matter. Again the scenarios were based on extreme real-life situations, which is why halfway through the test we each scrabbled for eight bullets dug into the dirt, loaded four and four and shot all eight rounds into the targets with a tactical reload in well under forty seconds. This replicated an FBI gunfight with armed robbers; the agents died when they couldn't load quicker than the time it took the bad guys to reach them. Hence the need to load under pressure.

The rest of the test was equally challenging and true to form I was nervous as hell. Tests have always filled me with dread. I beasted myself from the inside and got on with it. My aim was poor compared to the rest of the week. I also over-racked the breech and was furious with myself. But I passed. And I'm still stoked to this day. It was far more rewarding than any A-level, driving test or Master's Degree.

In the last handgun shoot of the day, a wind-down shoot, I relaxed, added a little more aggression and got my eye back in. For my Glock 19 and me every shot was in the A4.

At the end of each day it was our job to clean up the thousands of shells that littered the floor of our cavernous dojo with shovels and rakes. On that last clean-up although tired, aching, cut and digging spent shells out of the dirt with my fingers I was sad to be leaving. The camaraderie among the guys was life-affirming, I think because they work in environments where they depend on the men around them rather than shooting each other in the back as you'd normally expect to find in everyday corporate cock-fights and proletarian pissing contests.

I can only speak for myself here, that we came such a long way in such a short time is proof of one thing. Anyone can shoot a gun: you load, you rack, you aim and then fire. But without doubt learning to fight with a gun is one of the most rewarding things I've ever done.

I realise it's only training, I've not been shot at for real and neither have I shot at anyone else. I'm neither a fictional Jason Bourne nor a real-life Chris Ryan. But if ever I have to I'll know how to respond with a weapon of last resort: with confidence, aggression, accuracy and flexibility.

If you're wondering whether I'd be scared the answer is yes. You only have to listen to some of the guys' stories of blood and see the pain of lost friends in their eyes to drop any macho veneer. However it wouldn't stop you doing what needed to be done.

At the airport the following morning one of the group, an ex-soldier just about to deploy to another high-risk hotspot for a private military company, asked me: 'How are you going to go back to your normal life after this?'

It's a question that I am still not sure how to answer. In

load

rack

fire

the same situation how would you? On the plane home as you pause for thought during note taking perhaps you too will look down and realise you're sitting in a closed guard with your pen where the gun was only the day before.

How to Fight – The Everyday Application of Extreme Force

> Fighting is like Christmas, it's all about the giving.
>
> *Mick Coup*

One of the key skills many men say they lack is the ability to adequately protect themselves or their families. Me included. The sad truth is that our home country can be a pathetically nasty place. And like many I want to learn to fight. I mean really learn to fight.

So if you are hoping for a hands-off magic-bullet technique or 'how to punch' chapter that means we won't have to talk openly about violence I apologise up front. This isn't it. However if you've ever wanted a fundamental skill set that will give you an edge over the average thug, skills that you can call on at any time or pass on to your kids then this is for you.

From my own encounters on British streets I know that the reality of violence is usually pant shreddingly scary, brutal and short. I've personally been involved in seventeen one-on-one fights and a further thirty-two 'confrontations' –

that I can remember. I only ever initiated one of these situations; trouble usually found me. Now this isn't a win/loss
chart or the brag of a professional fighter just the tally of a
normal man and someone who is far from a hard man.
Most were inconclusive results, some I won and many I
lost. Some were deeply disturbing, some even comical and
only two were reported to the police.

So let's take a quick candid look at some of the characters
from my world and probably yours too.

UK predator attack format: usually a point man opens with
a 'What are you looking at?' line then overwhelms the mark
(usually someone weaker) with punches. When the mark is
on the floor the point man's friends run in and stamp-kick
the mark's head until he doesn't get up.

Scumbag example #1: a guy I used to know his special-
ity was heads. He didn't need friends to back him up; he
enjoyed taking the head out in ever more inventive ways.
I witnessed him use a bike on one occasion, a bin on
another and on one memorable evening his feet as he
jumped from a wall to the head on the concrete below.

Scumbag example #2: a well-to-do educated guy, a friend
once upon a time, turned to me and one other while walking
home from a night out and said, 'See that guy over there on
his own? Let's fuck him up.' Needless to say he didn't stay a
friend for long. But what if we'd said yes?

Miscellaneous real-life scumbags: neighbour from the
apartment upstairs visits and lets slip (shows off) that he's
got someone tied up and has been torturing her for days.
What do you do? Two guys come into your pub regularly
and trash it, scare the customers and start fights before
extorting money from the landlord. What do you do? Point
man befriends you then a car turns up with his pals and they

force you to get in. What's the worst that you think could happen? What do you do?

Learn to Fight

It's not as easy as you think to gouge someone's eye out. According to Mick Coup, my instructor, 'It's not like the movies where the eyeball pops out and dribbles off your thumb.' He shows why with a little test gouge on my own eyes. I flinch, recoil and twist away from him. But the reaction is all he needs; he never intended to pluck my eyes out. In his world of swift, extreme violence it provides more than enough time to pummel me to the ground.

Mick teaches Core Combatives or C2 for short. It's a no-nonsense system based upon the ugly realities of actual combat rather than the acceptable ideals of the training hall. It can be studied on its own either in regular lessons or for both mine and Mick's preference in intensive blocks. Mick says he prefers to teach not train.

He certainly has the credentials: a twelve-year military service career specialising in combined infantry and intelligence-related roles and several years of extensive practical experience as a private contractor. He has operated in many of the world's conflict hotspots from Northern Ireland to Iraq. Mick currently works as a threat management consultant and specialises in personal security, surveillance and protection. He also provides expert training for military, law enforcement, civilian agencies, corporations and individuals throughout Europe and the US.

C2 applies a military approach to combat training: take skills tested in high-pressure real-world situations, strip them down to the essentials that work and train them hard and well.

At six foot two and 110kg of lean mass Mick is also an imposing physical specimen and although the teaching is initially delivered like a corporate seminar he's disarmingly honest and humorous – it's anything but a boring flip chart session.

A Solid Foundation – Combat Management

The hard skills, how to manage combat and survive a fight, are always taught first regardless of whether you're special forces, a housewife or a plumber. Build a strong foundation and the end result can be developed into anything you want.

First out of the bag:

Attitude

The driving force behind everything is to develop a survival mindset that is positive, relentless and instantly combative as and when required. By far the most important attribute of this is tenacity or the will to endure, supported but not surpassed by aggression.

To give you an idea of how raw this really is if Mick had five seconds to teach you how to have a fight in the room next door he would say, 'Don't give up – *whatever fucking happens* – don't give up.' That my friends is tenacity.

Strategy

Now you've got the right attitude your overall game plan is to achieve *constant offensive pressure* and maintain attacking momentum whatever your position or situation. Mick calls it the GLF principle or in everyday shorthand, 'go like fuck'.

'There's no point in having a load of tools and no idea what you're going to do with them,' he says. 'You need that overall aim. Our strategy is going to be constant offensive pressure. That is profound enough to me; if we are in-fight there is never a time when you are looking at that guy and waiting for stuff to happen. Competition is different. That's a possible go or a possible no; this is a definite go we're assuming it's on. Green light. Everything you do has offensive capability. You're not waiting, there's nothing passive about it, you're going the whole time.

'The guy on the street doesn't have any tools, he doesn't have any tactics, he just goes like fuck.'

To clarify the concept he asks, 'How do racing drivers win races? They destroy their cars don't they? They've got no concept of holding back. It's a new engine every race; they'll destroy it because they'll take it to the limit.

'How do guys win races at the Olympics? Because they're willing to do more than the other guy.

'That's what you have in a fight; you've got to have that constant offensive pressure. He might pick you up and ram you across the room, all the way there you're gouging him in the eyes.'

Attitude and Strategy

If Mick had ten seconds to prepare you for a fight next door he would simply say, 'Go like fuck,' and then add, 'Don't give up.'

'Most guys who you're going to be fighting that's all they've got anyway. All they have is a set of balls on them and the will to never take a step backwards. And they're the guys that beat you.'

Mix in better tactics, better tools, a few secondary tools in case things don't go as planned and a whole load of support skills to fill in the gaps and you've built yourself a better mousetrap.

Tactics

There are two straightforward tactical plans, both impact-based:

Simple repeat strikes: use the same limb into the same target. This maintains the most damaging strike position and effect and relieves your brain of any extended decision-making.

Reverse repeated strikes: use these when higher output is required, mainly counter-attack. Alternate simple strikes between sides to overwhelm and regain any lost initiative. This can reduce your power and accuracy but your increased rate of fire is used for maximum effect.

Mick's military background regularly appears in his teaching. Reverse strikes are likened to 'suppressive fire to come off an ambush. Get off the killing area, the X,' he says. 'The best way to get off it is at him. Then GLF and repeat.'

It's a deceptively simple approach, one used by boxers Mike Tyson and Nigel Benn when I was growing up and then copied by the most effective street fighters I knew.

The Goal – Put Their Lights Out

In a nutshell: hit them repeatedly until they lose consciousness using the same target, the same tool, the same path.

'It's all about stopping people. People will talk about

slashing with pens and keys and kicking them in the shins and tearing their ear . . . wounded. Stopping is generally blunt force trauma to the head.'

Let's use Mick as an example; because of his size most people wouldn't trouble him in a fight. If he was attacked by let's say an average-height woman she would never do anything that would worry him. Other than blasting him in the head with her whole body weight.

'I only teach what I fear not what I favour,' he says. 'You see it often in a pub: one guy grabs another by the shirt and then right-hands him all the way down to the floor. Someone grabs him by the hair and repeatedly kicks him in the face.

'You see exactly the same thing done in the cage or in the ring they generally use exactly the same combative model as a human fighting outside a nightclub. They'll steam in and overwhelm the guy, put him on the defensive then usually isolate him and repeatedly strike with one hand, one leg or whatever until the guy goes down.

'I want one thing that can handle multiple situations rather than multiple things that'll handle one each. I want it to be instinctive rather than deliberate in how I do it.

'It's impact-based rather than grappling-based [because] you can fight multiple people using impact techniques; you can only fight one person using grappling. Impact concentrates your force in a split second, grappling elongates that force. Time is never on your side. Ultimately I want it to be high percentage not low percentage so I want it to be probable not just possible. High percentage means it will work for most people against most people in most circumstances. Low percentage means [only] an expert could do it on that guy in that situation.'

Primary Tools

These are all simple, versatile, adaptable, recoverable and durable. Each uses a repeatable delivery strategy and you switch tools according to range and target availability only:

Highline impact tools: use either *palm*, *fist* or *elbow* in a direct line of attack to strike 'online' targets above the waist – usually the head.

Offline impact tools: for 'offline' targets outside a direct line of attack use the hammerfist or elbow.

Lowline impact tools: if no highline target or tool is available you attack below waist 'online' targets using the shin or knee from a variety of angles.

Palm

Fist

Secondary Tools

'If you have a good right hand and you *can't* use it what are you going to do?' Mick asks. 'Don't try and do what's best for you in a fight, do what's worst for him.'

Sounds good to me. So when you can't use your best primary tool secondary tools create opportunities that let you get back to using them as soon as possible. Secondary tools include: the *hook*, *headbutt*, *gouge* and *stamp*.

Support Skills

These either assist your primary and secondary tools or make them even more effective.

Elbow

Indexing: this technique is so effective that it is banned in most fighting sports. Fix your target in position with your spare hand and then attack. Direct or indirect indexing improves your first and successive strikes with devastating effect.

For example: grab a scumbag by the neck, collar or hair with one hand and pound their face with the other; every time they recoil or try to move away they can't especially with their back to a wall. Your targeting also improves dramatically. Other support skills include: *controlling*, *positioning*, *movement* and *covering* and *shielding*.

Who said kicking ass needs to be complicated? Once you've learned these Combat Management fundamentals you move on to Threat Management to improve your awareness, assessment and reaction to threats around you. Followed by Contact Management and how to handle confrontation, immediate threats and minimise risk.

Overall the fighting element is the smallest facet of the whole package but it's taught first as the default reaction if the other two fail. As Mick says, 'It's too late to put your seat belt on in a crash so you put it on whether you have a crash or not.'

Training

Remember this isn't a magic bullet so you do have to train to get your skills down but you won't have to marry the dojo or worship the gi. And once you have the foundations in place they are always there. Mick compares not having the fundamentals in place to someone joining the army and immediately entering a squad or battalion without basic training. They would be useless.

The context of training is always in-fight; and the way it's taught is more like learning to drive or tactical firearms training. You get the basic skill set drilled down into your unconscious and then you either add to it or maintain it as time progresses.

Take the fighting stance, something everyone teaches as a first principle. Mick considers it 'a snapshot from a real moving picture. People still get stance orientated, they say, "Oh you're a bit open there," and I say, "Well tell me how open I am when I'm punching you in the head repeatedly." "Yeah yeah but . . ."

'If I'm fighting him why aren't I hitting him now? My fighting stance is my hand bouncing off your head.'

That's certainly easy to grasp. There are also no belts and you're required to leave your ego at the door because it's not about looking good either. It's about being able to handle any situation that comes your way.

Mick believes that when you look at the anatomy of a real fight you'll find three big myths that are rarely addressed in training.

Myth One – Time

We usually believe we're going to have time to do all this fancy stuff, time to prepare, but in reality we never do. If anything our reactions have to be entirely spontaneous unless you're the bad guy of course because he's normally just ambushed you.

In fact you normally get beaten in a fight before you even know you're in one and rarely are they long drawn out affairs. You either don't have time to react because of what he's doing to you or even if you are controlling it his mate could walk out of the toilets in a moment, the police could turn up, or you'll be cut and bleeding out. You can't let that fight last a long time.

Myth Two – Space

'In sparring you're always trying to get closer to the other guy to hit him,' Mick says. 'In a fight you're always trying to get away from the other guy because he's trying to hit you. You're always trying to create space in a fight; in sparring you're always trying to close it.

'Try fighting with a sparring model. It doesn't work. I've proved this over and over again. I get two guys up to spar and show me then I say, "That's great." Then I take them both to one side and speak to one guy, usually the guy that's better than the other guy, and give him loads of generic stereotypical sparring advice about timing, footwork and stuff. To the other guy I say, "Forget that sparring bullshit just steamroller him next time, don't take your foot off the gas. Redline and go through him."

'Now he thinks I've just told the other guy the same thing and he's shitting himself thinking, I'd better get in there quick.

'So when they start to spar again the guy who got beat the last time steamrollers the other guy and beats him on that base tactical model.'

Real fighting is like the blitzkrieg (lightning war) tactics used in the Second World War or the 'shock and awe' tactics of today. As Mick says, 'Pound the living fuck out of them with everything you can rather than have that standoff stalemate, pointing guns at each other for years.'

Myth Three – Effect

'Last one possibly the biggest one that upsets most of the martial arts guys and the combatives guys and the other guys is that you're going to have a big effect,' says Mick.

The one-punch knockout from the movies rarely happens

in real life and as we've seen in the tactical firearms chapter if the effects of gunfire on people aren't always a definite why expect a hand or a kick to be? People take extensive damage from stabbings and bullets and still keep going.

So can everything you do work in an extremely small, scary, spontaneous time frame? Can you pull a technique out of the hat and fight back with zero preparation?

In C2 you train to minimise the effects of limited time, space and effect. You'll be put in a bad position, eyes closed, hands down and then almost knocked off your feet as the go signal. 'What I want to do,' Mick says, 'is give you some heavy physical contact, back, shoulders, whatever disturbs you physically and psychologically.'

As an example after a few minutes' work on the small pad he can see I am anticipating where it will be next, learned responses rather than reactive and adaptive. He then positions me with legs together, eyes shut and hands by my side.

I wait.

He talks to distract me, make me relax and drop my guard. Relax even though I know one of Mick's blows to the chest will be coming soon. I expect it to hurt.

It does but I react immediately, open my eyes and go for the pad. I have no idea where it will be – high, low, to the side, behind me. I have to hunt for the target just like in a real fight. Then it's my job to stay on my feet and GLF. It's clever, the strategies and tactics are pre-planned but the application isn't.

He says afterwards that if I can go adequately from that terrible position which I'm never going to be in when I am off guard in the real world and see something kick off out of the corner of my eye I'll be in a far better position to handle it. It's all about training the worst case scenario rather than easy, repeatable setups.

'You want to see guys on [normal] shooting training,' he says. 'They know the drill, they know exactly where the targets are gonna pop up. That's not a tactical drill, they're so prepared they're actually mentally modelling the exact technique they're going to employ. So you need to catch that guy unawares; how do you get that guy in a passive situation where he's unprepared?

'You've got to change the variable all the time otherwise you find a shortcut, which is only ever good for that one shortcut. We train in an abstract way; we want to cover lots of bases in an abstract fashion rather than being specific to only one.'

He sums it up like this.

'If it's perfect in training it'll be probable on the street.

'If it's probable in training it'll be possible on the street.

'If it's only possible in training it'll be impossible on the street.'

It's essential that any training you take part in emulates the real world. For example in the next pseudo surprise attack it's feet together, eyes closed then knocked off them, rammed up against a wall and then resist and retaliate.

For future sessions it could be this exercise, one of many: two guys are held down on the floor, you fight your way up, get over to the other guy and beat him down. Or it could be from a seated position or from a car or in bed.

But this all depends how far you want to take it. If you want to learn to hit hard train for a few hours. If you want to get the foundation elements down train for a solid week or more. If you want to train for security and law enforcement roles then you need a defensive programme or offensive tactics if you're aiming for the military.

Mick tells me I'll love my future training and I believe him because there's something he said that isn't on the official syllabus. But it's left a wicked grin on my face throughout our session.

He said, 'When we're training leave the nice guy outside.' This makes training reinforce how best to respond in the real world because you will be in the right mindset during practice. In a fight you can't be like I was for so many years, polite and mild mannered. Although don't get me wrong: that is a good thing. It means I am civilised and not a cowardly Saturday-night scumbag who gets his jollies whaling on others.

But when you are up against someone who has nothing but bad things planned for you turn the nice guy off. Seriously this took me a long time to learn. The first time I used it I won fight two of a very hard evening. Before then I'd honestly stood around getting hit about the head with feet, fists and foreheads and been more worried about the other guy getting hurt if I hit him even when he was intent on destroying me.

Being given permission and giving yourself permission to give that nice guy some time off is liberating both in training and on the street corner. You see if someone attacks me or the people I care about I want to be able to react instantly with explosive, unrelenting and effective aggression that I will not stop using until the other guy or guys are on the floor and I have bulldozed out the other side. If they knock me down I'll get back up or fight from the ground. And if I lose I lose. Because if I don't fight back I already have.

But hey this isn't the Mick Coup Show and I'm not advocating any one system. You've got to do what works for you first and foremost. And I always recommend training with someone who you've asked questions of and who can answer them. Ultimately they've got to be able to prove themselves.

I settled on Mick after exploring several military-derived training options in Russia, Israel, the US and all over the UK and found his the most well thought out and consistent. I was even approached by one guy with Chuck Norris style pictures on his website who couldn't explain what he taught and was asking a ridiculous £18k to learn it. So seek out the good.

After training with Mick I also ran the C2 fundamentals past a mixed martial arts cage fighter, a boxer, a ju-jitsu instructor and a′long term tai-chi and aikido practitioner. They all agreed with the first principles presented here:

- Turn the nice guy off.
- Aim to put their lights out.
- Go like fuck.
- Do not give up.

I'll let Mick finish up: 'You start talking to people and they go, "That makes sense." Why shouldn't it? You cannot plan under pressure. When the pressure is on you just do what you planned. That's why you don't work out "Where shall we assemble?" when the fire alarm goes off.'

True. That's what fire drills are for. The rest is up to you.

How to Survive the Wild . . . Because You Never Know When You Might Need To

Whenever I've been with cultures who live more traditionally they think of us as children.

Matt Upson, Woodsmoke

The world could end tomorrow, the oil could run out, the ice could descend as the earth warms or the Mayan calendar completes its cycle in 2012 and the poles reverse. The water wars could begin. Famine, blight, pestilence – all the usual suspects could charge in on their apocalyptic horses at any moment at least if you believe what you read in newspapers or see on TV.

It seems preposterous, unreal even; how could anything bad happen when we have Disneyland, *The X Factor*, Wall Street and any number of organised paths to god? Doesn't the universe know you have aspirations?

What if the worst did happen and you were thrown into the cold of a winter night or the heat of a desert day with nothing but a blanket and a knife. Could you survive?

Could you prosper? Let's face it most of us could barely provide for ourselves let alone family or friends.

But you don't have to wait for the world to end to learn to be the next Ray Mears or Bear Grylls. The outdoorsmen of Woodsmoke in the UK took me into the wet, muddy and beautiful environment of the Lake District to teach me skills that we can use today, tomorrow and any time for either wilderness living or survival. Both areas share the same skill sets; it's usually just a matter of context.

If you want to thrive in either situation then you need to be able to answer this one question.

Are you too cold, too hot or thirsty?

You are? You're not sure? Either way read on because here's what you need to know.

Cold-Weather Conditions

Hypothermia

Your core body temperature is normally around the 37°C/98.6°F mark although the range varies between 35°C and 37°C. But if your temperature drops 1°–2° below your own base level then you are hypothermic.

There are two types of hypothermia. They have the same symptoms but require different treatments.

Type	Causes	Example
Slow-onset hypothermia	Slow exhaustion of energy supplies	Climbing, trekking, long periods in a cold environment
Fast-onset hypothermia	Intense shock to the system	Plunging into icy water

Lead instructor Steven Hanton neatly summarised the early symptoms of hypothermia as the umbles: stumbles, mumbles, fumbles, tumbles and grumbles. Essentially you need to look out for any fundamental loss of fine motor skills in you or your companions. Along with two types of shivering, the first is voluntary and conscious; the second – the bad type – is involuntary.

In both cases when symptoms are left to develop vasoconstriction occurs. The body can't function at the basic metabolic rate and begins to shut down – similar to dehydration – by restricting blood flow and making the skin grey and pale.

So during the early stages focus on the five ways the body loses heat: evaporation, radiation (the air around your body), conduction (what you're touching, e.g. clothing, ground), convection (wind over the body) and respiration (you breathe cold air in, heat it and breathe cold air out). These are relatively easy to treat with warm, sugary drinks, warm, dry clothing and by getting out of the wind.

However if you find someone in a more advanced condition of the umbles, say curled up in a foetal position under a rock, then they're already on their way to coma and death. Whatever you do, don't rewarm them too quickly by moving them, rubbing them or lighting a fire nearby as the blood will rush to their extremities (hands and feet) away from the heart, brain and lungs and kill them instantly. This is called 'after drop'.

The basic rule with slow-onset hypothermia is that because they were cooled slowly they need to be warmed slowly at roughly 1°C per hour.

The traditional way to do this is the body heat method as seen in adventure movies and for once it's a movie technique that works. You both need to strip down to underwear or naked then place the other person slowly into a sleeping bag, then climb inside and hold them. This works perfectly as the natural transfer of body heat is about 1°C per hour. However do remember that you will need extra energy for yourself or – like an alien sucking the life out of its host – as your body heat is transferred your core temperature will drop and you may become hypothermic instead. A handy supply of Mars Bars should do the trick, failing that good old raisins and peanuts (GORP). Remember both bodies need to be stripped down or the air won't warm up in the sleeping bag. If you don't have a sleeping bag to hand then a black bag is preferable over a reflective silver 'survival' bag. Think polar bears – their skin is black to trap the heat in, not the other way round.

If you are outrageously shy or culturally concerned about getting naked the alternative is to wait for mountain rescue: they can then apply a rapid reheating technique that involves cracking open your chest and applying heat pads to your heart. Tough choice I know.

Recovery from fast-onset hypothermia is slightly different because carbohydrate depletion hasn't happened yet. Exercise and movement are the best remedy along with a change into dry clothes – because water transfers heat away from the body twenty-five times faster than normal – and get the victim close to a fire. Left untreated the more like slow onset hypothermia it will become.

Always remove casualties who've been in water for a long time horizontally. If you remove them upright you have the same problem of blood rushing back into the extremities and the risk of sudden heart attacks. This is why rescue helicopters use flat metal stretchers.

Cold-weather injuries include frost nip (like frostbite but not as bad). The top layer of your skin becomes pale and waxy and cold to the touch. It's not a big deal and can be warmed by putting a hand or heating pack on the affected area. But left untreated it can turn to frostbite, which is a serious cold-weather injury. It starts out white and then eventually turns black; and that's your flesh freezing. Trouble is you won't feel a thing.

So in a worst-case scenario a week away from civilisation always leave it frozen as it won't hurt. But any thaw–refreeze–thaw process will ruin the tissue and irreparably damage the cells.

Defrosting can also be very painful. I speak from my own experiences at the North Pole where my fingers began to cause me trouble and needed attention. When the blood starts to flow into them again it's excruciating. Think pins and needles replaced by a thousand miniature red-hot pokers.

Also don't use a fire: you'll simply burn and damage the skin even more. Once defrosted prevent infection and get the affected person to hospital. Even then sometimes the experience is not entirely over. Explorer Ranulph Fiennes cut off his own fingertips with a fretsaw when he grew impatient with the pain in his necrotic fingertips that his doctor recommended he retained. Clearly it's best to avoid it whenever possible.

Trench Foot

This is surprisingly common if you work outdoors but also extremely easy to treat. It happens when your feet are wet and cold for long periods of time. Essentially they begin to split and rot with an accompanying smell and prune-like texture. Nice. Immersion foot is its posh title. To avoid it make sure your feet are warm and dry for several hours a day. Preventative measures like drying and powdering your feet with talc before hitting the sack each night will allow you to spend months at a time in such adverse conditions.

Warm-Weather Conditions

Hyperthermia aka heatstroke

When your core body temperature goes over 40°C/104°F your life is in danger; at 41°C/106°F brain death begins. It's an emergency situation. If left untreated you can die within minutes.

Initially your body begins to sweat and uses radiation, convection and evaporation to draw heat safely away from your core but once the body is dehydrated this system breaks down. You can become confused, hostile or dizzy and you may faint as your blood pressure drops. Your heart rate will increase as your body works harder to push oxygen to essential organs and your skin may take on a reddish hue as blood vessels dilate and then turn a pale bluish colour. Nausea and vomiting are common even temporary blindness.

Prevention and treatment are fairly straightforward: drink plenty of water and avoid the glare of the sun through shade or covering up. You can fan someone who is too hot (convection), remove clothing or wet a bandana or hat (evaporation). Again gradual cooling is beneficial here. Dunking yourself in an ice cold bath won't do you any favours but a cool bath might. Heatstroke isn't just sunburn; remember the umbles again when looking for warning signs.

Hydration is key here. The easiest way to tell if you're dehydrated is by the colour of your urine. If it's any darker than pale straw you are. So keep drinking water. And if you're thirsty you're already dehydrated so sip a little and often.

You also lose electrolytes through sweating, which can lead to hyponatremia and sudden death through heart attacks.

Many people die because they keep chugging back water with no food. So either eat something to replace missing nutrients or use rehydration salts. You can make your own using a combination of fruit juice, salt and water. For a more robust version use three tablespoons of sugar, one tablespoon of salt and one half teaspoon of bicarbonate of soda to one litre of water. It's a whole lot cheaper and more effective than sports drinks.

But remember this: pure water is always best for normal rehydration. The stomach holds on to laced fluids as if they were food rather than sending the fluid into the lower intestine where it can be absorbed. Fizzy water helps as it increases the pressure and improves the absorption rate. It's also why bar injecting it there's no quicker way to get alcohol into the body than a white wine spritzer. Also avoid coffee, alcohol, fatty foods or smoking and reduce the amount of exercise you do to conserve energy and water.

Water – The One Essential

Most of us can survive for days without much food thanks to the excess fuel hanging around our waists but without water we won't last long at all. Here's how to find your own clean supplies when you're out in the wild.

Where to Look
Environmental sources include lakes, rivers, reservoirs and streams.

Ducks and finches always live near water. Grain feeders

like doves and pigeons need water to break down their food and feed twice daily. When they're flying quickly in one direction at dawn or dusk they're probably heading to a source of water. When sluggish and hopping from tree to tree they are probably on their way back.

Mammals like deer drink once a day and amphibians are another obvious source. Bees and wasps aren't. But it is useful to know that they are never more than a mile from a fresh water source.

Trees such as the alder in northern Europe like to get their feet wet as do willow and poplar. Reeds, sedges, ferns and rushes also like to live near water.

When you've found a stream or pool of water it's always worth checking upstream first for any dead or dying animals.

Methods of Extraction

Gypsy wells

Where there isn't an obvious source of water such as near trees or swampy ground simply dig a hole about a foot square to a foot and a half deep away from any toxic plants like hemlock.

The soil will act as a filter and water will seep in. But hold on to your thirst and bail out the first filling of water. This removes the tannins and other gunk. Then use the next, clearer batch once the sediment has settled.

As it's only been filtered the water still needs to be purified before it's safe to drink. Unfortunately the little beasties that are going to cause you problems can't be filtered.

Rain water

While safe to drink, it is only as clean as the container you collect it in and what it's been filtered through. Collecting it under a yew tree could be a terminal mistake for example. The yew is one of the most poisonous trees on the planet. It only takes a few yew needles for its toxins to be effective which is why suicides and even murders have been committed using this ethereal-looking tree.

Dew mopping
Wrap T-shirts around your legs and walk through damp grass to soak up moisture. Then squeeze out the water and drink it. As you don't know what's been cocking its leg nearby, purification is also advised.

Ice and snow
Just melt and drink. Ice is the better choice as it's fifty-fifty water and air whereas snow is only one-tenth water. Melt a little bit of snow in the bottom of your pan first to get the process started.

Finnish marshmallow
Make a snowball, poke a stick through it and rest it near a fire with a container underneath. The heat does the rest.

Puddles and pools
A handy source but always purify first.

Sap
Early in the year trees like birch provide about a gallon of low-sugar sap a day but don't drink it for more than a month. It doesn't harm the tree; it simply has to drink a little more to compensate for your vampiric ways. To tap a birch make a shallow incision low down on the lee side of the tree and insert a small wooden plug to direct it into a container.

If your interest is wilderness living rather than survival you can use a hand drill to make your hole and then boil down the sap to make it into a syrup or wine. Remember to plug the hole afterwards to keep the tree healthy.

What Really Works

The Woodsmoke instructors have tested many techniques found in popular survival books. Those listed above work better than others. They say a common but flawed technique is the solar still. Here you simply dig a pit, put in a container and cover it with plastic to collect the water condensing on the underside. The instructors reported only half a cup per day using this technique but they drank two litres of water while digging the pit.

A better solution is the transpiration bag. Take a plastic bag and wrap it round the branch of a non-poisonous tree. As the tree draws up water condensation forms and collects in the bag. Tie off the end to minimise the amount of

crud getting in. Tried and tested in Namibia, this method produced half a litre per bag per day. Tie ten and you're water wealthy.

Symptoms of Drinking Contaminated Water

Diarrhoea, vomiting, stomach cramps, gargling sounds, malaise, dehydration and fever. Most of the really nasty bugs like giardia have an incubation period of one to four weeks. So when a local guide takes you into a remote area and tells you the water is safe to drink and they have never seen their guests get ill they are telling the truth. It normally happens days or weeks later when you've flown home and suddenly become violently sick.

Filter Then Heat or Treat

This is the mantra for all water supplies in the field as you want to remove any chemical, physical or bacterial contaminants from your supply.

Filter

Clear water is the goal. Along with gypsy wells you can make another natural DIY filter using a roll of birch bark. You build up three layers of moss–charcoal–moss inside to create the filter. Use sphagnum moss: the iodine it contains is antibacterial and the charcoal bonds with the nasties. You could also try sand and gravel in place of moss and charcoal or if you've nothing else to hand a clean pair of trousers; one leg inside the other and knotted at the bottom makes an excellent improvised system.

Heat

Boiling is a bullet-proof treatment method. Nasties hide inside the dirt molecules but bring clear water to a rolling boil anywhere on the planet and it's safe to drink. To pasteurise simmer at 72°C for ten minutes.

Treat

Chlorine. Available at pharmacists and outdoors shops usually in tablet form. Good for long term use but it's not 100 per cent and doesn't kill everything. If the water's pH is too alkaline it also makes any chemical reaction ineffective.

Iodine is the preferred short term method as it has a low contact time and is more reliable. It lasts thirty days and is more effective with pH variables and dirt although it can't kill cryptospiridium, which should be removed with filtration or boiling. It's also not advised for people with thyroid problems, pregnant women or children under twelve. For either solution always remember to flood the threads of your water bottle, a contaminant reservoir that's often neglected.

The preferred off-the-shelf option is the Millbank bag (a fold-up water pouch with filtration) and iodine. Other recommendations include iodine pumps by Premac, which convert sixty litres and can make even raw sewage drinkable. Or gravity-fed systems that can convert 1,000–2,000 litres (about a year's supply). They're expensive at £120 but as Hanton put it tongue firmly in cheek, 'not bad with the apocalypse coming'.

Options to avoid include survival straws, potassium permanganate solutions, silver ions, micropurs and ceramic filters.

In a survival situation simply remember this: use a natural filter and boil your supplies.

Fire

What did we do without this handy little gift from the gods? The sweet spot where you build a fire lifts morale and is used for curing, cooking, sterilising, boiling, heating, illumination, weaponry and defence. In the modern age it's all around us in the light switches we flick on without thinking, the combustion in our engines and the heating and cooling systems in our homes.

Quick Fire

In nature friction is your friend and these are the basic materials you'll need to make a quick fire like the ones you see on wilderness shows.

One deadwood base; fire-starting material such as birch bark, honeysuckle or wood shavings; kindling such as thin twigs from birch; one thin, bowed branch; a whittled-down baton, blunt pointed at one end and rounded at the other; one piece of green wood and some natural cord (or parachute cord for practice).

1. On the deadwood base cut a circular groove with a channel and place a dry leaf or wood shaving underneath it.
2. Tie the cord from one end of the branch to the other to make a simple loose bow.
3. Twist the baton into the cord and place the rounded end in the groove.
4. Hold it in place on the blunt pointed end with the green wood greased with crushed holly leaves (or even ear wax).
5. Rotate the baton using a full draw-sawing action on the bow.
6. When enough small flakes and embers collect on the leaf move it gently through the air until the embers become a glowing coal.
7. Add dry bark to get the fire going and then place your small twigs on top.

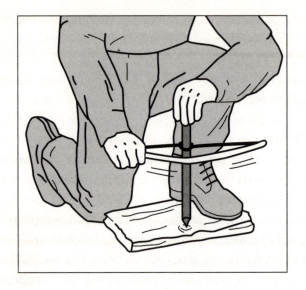

As there aren't too many people in the UK who can use these techniques effectively, master them and you're ahead of the curve.

Two other methods you might like to try are the fire steel (favoured by Ray Mears) – you strike the rough back edge of a knife blade along it to create sparks – and a one-match-only technique. Both use the same base materials as the quick fire and I'm happy to report both techniques work even in the pouring rain and ankle deep mud of a Lake District autumn – as long as you keep your tinder dry.

The entire range of ignition sources includes sparks, friction, chemical, solar, compression and electrical. Friction has given us the Victorian gent with his walking cane and embedded flint, and compression the bone firelighters of the South-East Asian sea gypsies. With the latter you plunge a bamboo piston into the hollow leg bone of a wading bird, the compressed air molecules inside then cause a rapid rise in heat and ignite the tinder on the end of the bamboo piston.

For a simple electrical fire take a 12-volt battery and some steel wool, touch the wool to the conductors and blow.

Solar fires are the stuff of Boy Scouts and cowboys. Anything you have to hand will do; it doesn't have to be a magnifying glass – eye glasses, binoculars, camera lenses, car headlamps even water in a clear bowl will do. Soft drinks cans are so effective as parabolic reflectors that manufacturers now have to frost the bottoms of cans so that when discarded as litter they don't cause bush fires. Even clear ice can be used as a solar conductor. Simply boil out any oxygen and quickly refreeze it to obtain a crystal-clear prism.

Strike anywhere matches are the ideal chemical solution. Avoid expensive 'outdoor' matches: buy the cheapest you can find and waterproof them yourself. Try using old film canisters: with the matches inside pour candle wax in to seal them. This makes them exceptionally waterproof and at the same time easier to burn.

Shelter

Shelters come in many forms from man-made tarps, tents and bivvy bags to constructions made from materials at hand. But always take your shelter to the materials not the other way round. It also needs to be situated not too far from your water supply but not so close that there is danger of flooding or insect invasion.

In warm climates you can sleep under the stars but a shelter of some sort can still be used for shade during daylight. For cold or wet climates shelter is absolutely essential. Natural shelters include thickly foliaged trees and caves. In Arctic environments a snow shelter is ideal; similar in concept to an igloo, the principle is to dig a hole with a narrow entrance that leads uphill to the main living area, which then retains the warm air. An air vent punched through the roof is essential to avoid a lethal build up of carbon dioxide from breathing and carbon monoxide from cooking. A smaller pit can also be excavated inside to channel cold air away from the inhabitants. Ideally this is built with a shovel but can be dug by hand or axe in an emergency. Once constructed the thermal properties are excellent: indoor temperatures can be 0°C even if temperatures drop to −40°C outside. It's still cold but you'll live.

We were shown how to build several types of shelter in broad-leaf and coniferous environments including an aboriginal-style shelter, a bit like a thatched tent, a tie-fighter shelter, a bender and an elaborate bush teepee, which wouldn't look out of place in a Viking enclosure. But the simplest and most satisfying structure is the Arctic lean-to, which works for any environment where you find coniferous forest. Hanton slept comfortably in one of these without a sleeping bag at −35°C.

How to make an Arctic lean-to:

1. Find two trees a body's length apart.
2. Harvest pliable roots from trees like spruce, cherry or alder to use as cord.
3. String up a cross beam at chest height.
4. Lean a double layer of poles or branches (either cut or collected) against the cross beam at a 60–65° angle (the optimum angle for rain run-off).
5. For waterproofing, add a final layer of leafy brash from the bottom upwards to a depth of a whole or half-arm.
6. For a raised bed, tie two poles off on either side of the tree trunks under the cover. Then layer body-width rungs along its length.

7. For a simple bed lay five or six body-length poles on the ground. Cover both beds with any dry leftover brash for extra comfort.

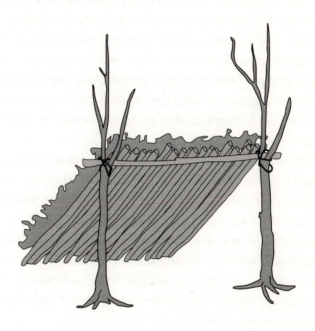

Then light a fire in front of the exposed side and you're set for the night. You can even fashion a fire 'reflector' that radiates heat back to you. Obviously choose a wind direction that compliments the angle of your living space.

Building an Arctic lean-to is extremely satisfying and an easy thing to achieve any Saturday afternoon you have spare.

Gathering

The skills needed to identify plant life and exploit its uses most often for fire, food or shelter are gathering, foraging, plant lore and collecting. Gathering is a vast subject and whole books are dedicated to trees, flora and edibles alone. But a little active study provides plenty of neat tricks to impress your friends next time you're out for a walk. For example did you know there's an easy way to pick nettles without getting stung?

Simply find the base of the stem and rub upwards a few times against the first inch or so to flatten the stinging spines. Then snap the whole stem off. Continue rubbing upwards to clear a few more inches and then grab the stem tight between forefinger and thumb and whip your hand right the way along the plant to remove the remaining spines.

Then watch as your friends sting hell out of their hands trying to master this technique. But as nettles have over a hundred practical uses there is good reason to learn this skill. They make excellent cordage and are used to treat eczema, hay fever, diarrhoea and intestinal and bladder infections. They are also an excellent source of vitamins D (rare in plants), C and A as well as being rich in iron.

Gathering definitely provides some of the most crowd-pleasing pieces of wilderness know-how. For example if you have a date with a forest nymph and need to clean your teeth beforehand snap off a twig from the alder – aka the toothbrush tree – fray the end and brush away or boil out the antibacterial tannins it contains to use as a mouthwash or disinfect wounds.

Many plants also contain saponins and when mixed with water they make a gentle and effective natural soap. Soapwort, birch and horse chestnut leaves are most common in Europe, and in North America you can use the Californian soap lily or the roots of the humble yucca.

As well as all the varieties you find in supermarkets, edible berries include elderberries, bilberries, hawthorns and rosehips. They are an excellent and natural fast food.

Knowing which ones not to eat is also invaluable. The flesh of the berries on the poisonous yew can be eaten but pay attention – *the seeds will kill you* or if you're lucky just put you in a coma. Its pollen is also considered semi-hallucinogenic and could explain the vivid dreams I had during the first couple of nights sleeping under a gnarly but beautiful specimen. Rowan berries are also edible but unpalatably tart; traditionally they were planted at the front door to keep witches away, along with everyone else presumably.

Burdock roots are still popular in Asian and Oriental cuisine and as burdock comes from the same plant family they taste a little like artichoke. They make an excellent yam or potato substitute and its jumbo leaves work well as a very dandyish sun hat.

The dark, pungent berries of the juniper bush are good to eat on their own or in a sauce. Crush them and they release the powerful and delicious aroma of gin. However in their unripened green form the berries are highly toxic. In medieval times the black form were known as 'bastard killers' as they are a uterine stimulant and can cause contractions. Even in the Victorian age prostitutes drank gin in the hope of limiting unwanted offspring. That's one of the reasons why gin houses became so notorious. Juniper is also one of the best natural tinders out there.

Tracking

'A writing that is older than mankind: the tracks in the dust, the mud or the snow. These are the inscriptions that every hunter, red or white, must learn to read or write infallibly.'

Ernest Thompson Seton

Another subject worthy of far deeper study is that of tracking wildlife. The Woodsmoke instructors opened with Seton's inspiring quote then demonstrated skills in tracking animals large and small, everything from red and roe deer to the minuscule marks of beetles, worms and a caterpillar's tiny little box-like footprints in fresh mud. They distinguished between two separate disciplines, those of track and sign, and trailing.

The first is going out and picking up individual tracks of certain species, their scat, hair or feathers along with their sleeping and feeding places.

Trailing is the art of picking up a trail and following an animal for a long time. Learning how to track and trail animals can lead you to sources of food and water in a survival situation or simply provide a rewarding hobby that really brings the forest to life.

Even a city kid like me can get to grips with it. In the past few days in the woods near where I'm writing I managed to pick up the trail of roe deer that live near by.

Hunting

I was brought up primarily on a vegetarian diet but never had any particular ethos rammed down my throat. Allowed to eat meat or fish whenever it was available, I did and still do. I don't demand it with every meal as many package-fed meat eaters do. But as a young man I decided that as a meat eater I should be prepared to kill it myself and take responsibility for the end of a life rather than simply be a passive consumer. I used to fish and shot one or two pigeons but never really knew how to process them properly. Until now.

With a little knowledge haute cuisine can be had on an

open fire regardless of whether your meat comes from the wild, the gamekeeper or the supermarket.

To prepare a wood pigeon you can use the 'rip and tear' technique to get the perfect fillet. From a basket of about sixteen pigeons my friend Carl and I both selected two. You then take the bird's wing – truly beautiful up close – locate the bone that connects to the shoulder joint and twist backwards until it comes off, removing the stringy chest tendon with it. First time I did this I took off the head and the top of the ribcage, second time I tore the little throat sac where the bird stores its grain. Messy, very messy. You then have to run your thumb flush along the inside of the ribcage separating flesh and membrane from bone. Once you reach the bottom of the ribcage – any broken bones can be sharp so watch out – you pull up with one hand and out with the other, separating the bone and breast in one hand and the bird's internal organs in the other. It's gory but if you stay focused on technique you barely notice your natural revulsion.

For a perfect game pie à la Woodsmoke with nothing more than you would carry in a basic camping kit:

1. Dice the pigeon breast into chunks.
2. Mix one handful of dried milk powder with two handfuls of flour.
3. Add ¼ cup of fat and ¼ cup of water and knead into a dough.
4. Line a camping tin with the pastry; keep some aside for the topping.
5. Fry the breast with whatever vegetables you have available. Then – a handy tip from the instructors – add instant soup powder, a camping staple, to create a gravy. In this case French onion.
6. Fill the tin with the mixture and cover with remaining pastry.

7. Put the lid back on the camping tin and place on the edge of the fire next to burning embers. Rotate 180° after twenty minutes and cook for a further twenty. For the last five minutes cover the lid with hot stones to brown the crust and then serve.

I ordered the equivalent game pie in a five star restaurant in London a few weeks later to compare. You couldn't: the pie cooked on an open fire in the rain and mud under an Arctic lean-to alongside friends was far superior.

Hunting and trapping devices generally require some form of tool to construct and these can be built from natural materials or store bought. For most devices you have to concentrate on the angles: a combination of strangles, mangles, dangles and tangles. They taught us how to construct a variety of rabbit snares that work, some of which if used on British soil would be illegal but in wilderness or survival situations would be extremely handy to know. To find out more look up *The Poacher's Handbook* by Ian Niall or *The Hunter's Handbook* by John Darling.

In this chapter I've barely touched on the range of techniques and a body of knowledge that is often overlooked in our busy modern world. It's knowledge that still exists even in developed countries and during my travels I've found groups of people living successfully off the land in surprisingly similar ways from as far apart as rural France and the jungles of Thailand.

If you want to take this rewarding area of study further then I highly recommend taking a field course to give you the working knowledge. And once you have learned a thing or two you can put your skills to the test. For example on a Woodsmoke aboriginal course you are expected to survive in the wild for three days with nothing more than a knife, pot, snare wire and your own knowledge.

In North America schools like BOSS outdoor survival in southern Utah provide even more intensive two to four week field courses that teach you how to live solely from the land. Both these types of courses are recommended as some of the best ways to learn to live independently.

The knowledge gained has a long-lasting value that you will never find through your television screen. And when you begin to explore the world beyond concrete you'll find it an immediately addictive and satisfying pursuit. Your confidence will grow along with your ability to prosper no matter what the tabloid headlines or the world throw at you.

How to Gamble – It's All in the Game

Don't bet more than you can afford to lose.
Gavin Coles

My Rules

For the first rule: reread the quote above from my father, a bookmaker (someone who lays the book on horses not a bookbinder). For thirty-odd years he watched men walk through his door with carrier bags full of cash and then occasionally when they'd lost return with swinging fists or threats and on one memorable occasion an axe. This usually happened when they'd bet the week's takings, the staff's wages or their wife's credit account. So whenever you gamble whether you're in a casino, a betting shop or at the bar with your friends you should be prepared to lose something. If you can't afford to lose then don't take the bet. It's that simple. But if you can and you're about to take that bet, well then my friend read on.

The Game

Gambling has always had an allure for the man with a bit of an edge about him. And ever since Sean Connery worked the casino as James Bond in *Dr. No* and acted like he could care less about winning, every aspiring gent has wanted in on the act. So whether you're tuxedoed to the max or just turn up in your dressing gown and slippers like a Chinese gangster I used to know you need to have your basics down. You need to know the games, how to play them, how to maximise your chances of winning and how to minimise your losses.

Blackjack

Often called 21, blackjack is a game with a simple goal: beat the dealer. It's got the best odds in the casino. The house edge is only 0.5 per cent. So that means for every £1000 you play you'll lose £5 if you're playing using exemplary basic strategy.

When you walk into the casino the blackjack tables are easy to spot: there's one dealer with up to seven players sitting facing him around a half-moon, semi-circular table. The blackjack tables are usually clustered together and on each table you'll find a placard telling you how many decks of cards are being played (hint: fewer decks = better odds) and the minimum and maximum betting table limits.

How to Play
The aim of the game is to come as close as possible to 21 without going over that number, which is also called 'busting'.

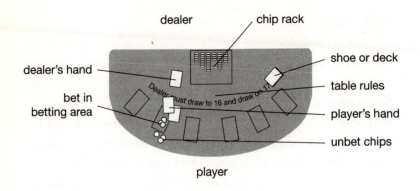

In each hand dealt the dealer will give you two face-up cards. You can win from this starting hand. Here's how.

If the cards are a 10 or any face card (jack, queen, king) and an ace that's blackjack. That's the winner.

If the dealer busts by laying down more than 21 points in his hand or your hand is higher than the dealers – you get 18 when he gets 17 for example – you also win.

Hitting

With each hand dealt you can ask for another card on top of your initial two and the dealer can also do the same. House rules say that once the dealer hits 17 points or more he'll stand i.e. not deal himself any more cards.

If you decide to take another card you can stop when you like.

Double down

In some casinos before you ask for another card you are allowed to increase the stake up to double the original bet and receive exactly one more card. If you increase to less than double this is called 'double down for less' and is not always permitted. Check that little placard for the house rules.

Split

When the cards have the same value you can double the bet and have each card be the first card in a new hand.

Surrender

If you know you're about to die on the felt you can sometimes surrender half your stake and bow out but not every casino allows this.

Basic Strategy

In 1956 four US army technicians published a paper for the American Statistical Association titled 'The Optimum Strategy in Blackjack'. They presented a system that maximised the players' average or expected gain. This was basic strategy.

Then in the early days of computing Dr Edward Thorpe published a refined version of basic blackjack strategy in his famous book *Beat the Dealer*, based on computer simulations tested by IBM programmer Julian Braun. Using his basic strategy reduced the house edge to well below 1 per cent and as a result led to a sharp decrease in casino profits. Thanks to that casinos now vary the rules of blackjack to increase their profit margins. So sometimes you won't be able to double down after a split or the dealer won't have to stand on soft 17. Most significantly the number of decks used has increased from one to four to six in some places which decreases your gains when you're using basic strategy. So always keep your eyes open; the fewer decks a casino uses the better for you.

What is a soft 17?

When an ace is dealt it can be either an 11 or a 1. The hand is considered soft when it can't be bust on the next card. So say for example you receive a 7 when you already hold an ace and a 9. If it's a soft hand the ace reverts to 1, giving you 17. If it's hard the ace stays as an 11 and you now have 27, a bust.

Whether a dealer treats his hands as soft or hard is usually clearly marked on the table with about half the casinos worldwide allowing soft 17s or to put it in plain English giving themselves a second chance.

So basic strategy looks like this for hard hands:

- Stand on 17 or more.
- When you hold 12–16 and the dealer holds 7–ace hit otherwise stand if 7 or less.
- For less than 11 always hit unless in a double down situation.

For soft hands:

- Stand on 18 or more.
- Hit on 17 or less.

For double downs:

- You hold 10, if dealer has 2–9 double, for anything else hit.
- You hold 11, if dealer has 2–10 double, for anything else hit.

For pair splits:

- Aces and 8s, always split – increases your odds of hitting 21.
- Never split 5s or 10s – both 10 and 20 are great starting hands.

For stiff hands:

Any 10 busts a hard total between 12 and 16 (a stiff

hand) so you hit or stand according to the strength of the dealer's turn of the card.

- Stand when dealer has 2-6 (weak).
- Hit when the dealer has 7–ace (strong).

For made hands:

Statistically hard hands of 17–21 (a made hand) deliver most of your winnings so when you have 17 or more stand.

Now you've got the basics down you'll probably want to rush off to the casino to try out your luck. Good for you. I recommend starting with the low minimum tables as you gain your confidence and refine your technique. Better yet before you even set foot across the casino threshold practise online. Your basic strategy should be fully established in your mind before you play chip one. As there are a great many casino variants out there you can even find out the rules of your casino in advance and play a suitable free practice table online. You can also use the 'basic strategy engine' at www.blackjackinfo.com, which will give you strategy charts that you can print out, practise on and take with you.

Card Counting – The Only Sure Way to Win

Ed Thorpe's research also brought us card counting, a statistical leverage point that sways the 1 per cent or less house edge in the other direction towards you. Meaning you can beat the casino. Hallelujah I hear you cry but wait it's not as easy as that or we'd all be doing it. To get the basics down for a simple high-low counting system will take you about twenty hours to learn. And for something that will give you everything you need, true counts, spread betting and your act. Oh yes you will need an act – those guys in the pit know all about card counting and are watching out for you.

But here's the thing: anyone with average aptitude can become a card counter if they have the will and the discipline or as Stanford Wong says, 'that blackjack devil might just decide to bite you in the butt, and believe me his teeth are sharp'.

To learn more you could try Kevin Blackwood's book *Play Blackjack Like the Pros* or Stanford Wong's *Professional Blackjack*. If you want some hair-raising inspiration on how far you can take this check out Ben Mezrich's *Breaking Vegas* for some serious number crunching madness. This book later became the film *21* where a team of MIT boffins adapted Ken Uston's team-play card counting strategies first described in his book *Million Dollar Blackjack* in an effort to win big.

Baccarat

At Le Cercle in Les Ambassadeurs club in London the sexily uptight English woman turns to the elegantly dressed but dangerous-looking gentleman and says, 'I admire your luck, Mr . . .'

'Bond,' he says and lights his cigarette as if he doesn't give a damn. 'James Bond.'

This is the opening scene that established one of the most successful franchises in movie history and one of cinema's legendary icons. But most people usually think Sean Connery was playing blackjack in that famous *Dr. No* opening scene. In fact it was baccarat, traditionally a high roller's game where

the well dressed and well moneyed congregate. But don't be put off by the opulent arrogance of many of the players or the imposing aura around the game. Baccarat is really not that much more complicated than bingo. It's a simple card game more about luck than skill and offers the best odds in the casino after blackjack. The only things likely to stand in your way are high table minimums and the size of your bankroll.

How to Play

There are only two hands and both are dealt by the croupier. One hand is the player's hand and the other the banker's. Each hand contains two cards. In traditional baccarat up to 14 players can play and each player bets on which of the two hands will come closest to a score of 9.

All bets are made before the cards are dealt and there are only three bets you can make.

Backing the player's hand to win pays even money or 1:1 so for every £20 gamble you win you receive £20 on top.

Backing the banker's hand has the best overall odds of winning. This also pays even money less 5 per cent house commission to even up the odds between the two bets. The commission is settled at the end so for your £20 win you pay £1. No commission is charged when you lose.

Backing for either way, tie or draw offers the least potential to win of all three bets but with odds of usually 8:1 or 9:1 it invariably entices the naive or the inebriated to throw away their money.

Bets are made before the cards are dealt in one of the three boxes in front of you on the table. When the caller shouts, 'No more bets,' then the deal can begin.

The Deal

Each shoe holds up to eight decks. Each player takes a turn as dealer, also known as the banker. As long as the banker's hand is winning you deal; once it loses you pass it on. If you want to bet on the player's hand before the end of your deal simply pass the shoe on. If it's your first time and you're a bit nervous you can also decline and pass on to the next player. This sharing of the shoe is one of the fun and social aspects of baccarat.

There are usually three croupiers who control the game, the money and the commissions so ultimately you don't have to worry about anything.

You deal two face-down cards, one for the player and one for the bank, then repeat.

Place the two player's cards face down in front of the player with the biggest bet (this player can peek at the cards if they like but it doesn't give them an advantage).

The caller will then turn over the player's cards and call it then ask you for the banker's cards and do the same with them.

The Score

Face cards, any 10 card or 10 score equals zero. There is no bust and there are no unknowns to contend with. The rules cover every eventuality. So if you draw a 10 and an 8 that's 8. A 9 and a 7 that's 6. Easy no?

When a hand scores 8 it's called 'le petit', if 9 it's 'le grande'. With an 8 in one hand and 9 in the other, le grande wins. When the numbers match it's a tie.

On 8 or 9 the hand stands and no more cards are dealt. But if neither 8 or 9 is drawn an additional card can be drawn on one or both hands. The basic rules about whether to draw a third card are stand on 6–9, draw on 0–5.

If a third card is drawn then the rules change and become a little more complex for the banker's hand but you don't have to worry about that as the caller controls the play and the scoring stays the same.

In essence that's all there is to it. There are variations of the game such as mini-baccarat – where the minimums are much lower – punto banco and chemin de fer, played mainly in France, where players bet among themselves and the choice of a third card is left open. There are no systems in baccarat even though you may meet a few superstitious players who will insist there are. In the long run, as in all casino games, you will lose even if you win in the short term. Keep an eye out for shills, pretty women paid by the bigger casinos to gamble at the table and flatter your ego. But really even they are all part of the fun. Simply take baccarat for what it is, a chance to dress up and mix with billionaires, wide boys and beautiful women.

Roulette

There are two flavours of roulette in the world: American and European.

The American roulette wheel has a total of 38 numbered slots with numbers running 1–36, one zero slot and one double zero slot. The European roulette wheel has numbers running 1–36 and only one zero slot.

· If you like a bit of hocus pocus at the gaming table you'll love the fact that the sum of 1 through 36 equals 666. Spooky huh? Go on: try it in your calculator if you don't believe me.

As you already know from watching movies you place your chips on the numbers, colours or side bets on the table. The wheel is then spun in an anti-clockwise direction and the ball rolled around its rim in the other. Whichever number the ball comes to rest on determines whose bet wins.

The bets are classed as inside or outside bets depending on what you're playing for.

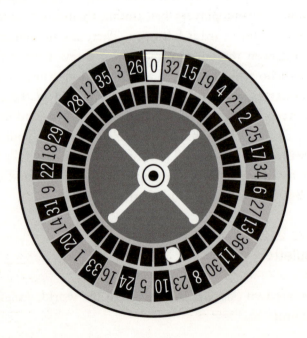

Inside Bets

These are the long-shot bets. The odds are 37:1 for any one number coming up on an American wheel or 36:1 on a European wheel. The odds don't change in between spins and over time probability evens out. What's more despite the true odds the house pays 35:1. In American that's a 5.26 per cent edge, in European a 2.56 per cent edge. Both give you the lowest chance of winning out of all the casino games so far. But typically the payouts can be huge and therein lies the bait. They are all to be found inside the square box on the roulette table.

Straight up

Gamble on any single number pays 35:1.

Split

Straddle two numbers side by side pays 17:1 for either number.

Street bet

Straddle three numbers by placing your chip on the adjacent line pays 11:1.

Corner

Place on the corner of any group of four adjacent numbers. Pays 8:1.

Square bet

Placed on the corner of 0, 1, 2 and 3 in European pays 8:1, in American it's got the extra 00 in play and is called a five-number bet and pays 5:1.

Line
Lay it on the intersecting line between two sets of three numbers, pays 5:1.

Outside Bets
These have far better odds but also as you'd expect much lower payouts. They are positioned around the edges of the central rectangle containing the number bets. 0 or 00s do not count in any of these bets.

If you want to become a casino legend just do what Ashley Revell from Kent did in 2004. He sold off his possessions for the sum of £76,840 and went for an all-or-nothing outside bet on red in Las Vegas. Red 7 came in and paid out £153,680. Not bad for a day's work. But clearly his testicles were once orbiting a small planet.

High or low
An even-money bet (1:1) and covers either 1–18 or 19–36.

Red or black/Odds or evens
Both even money bets.

Dozens
Either 1–12, 13–24 or 25–36 and labelled 1st 12, 2nd 12 and 3rd 12. Pays 2:1.

Column
Pick any column of any dozen numbers running lengthwise. House pays 2:1.

Basic Roulette Strategy
Stick to the table minimum and play outside bets only.

Or place two equal bets on the outside. One on even money and the other on a column or dozen that pays 2:1.

Neither of these plays will make you rich but they'll protect your bankroll for a short while.

Never base your plays on historical spins. The wheel really doesn't care what came last time and statistically every spin is a fresh spin. Wheel bias does occur i.e. mechanical faults over time but after some particularly big losses casinos are now scrupulous about the servicing of their tables.

Roulette systems are for suckers: none of them work. If you find one that does I'll happily let you prove me wrong. With your own money of course.

But just to show you that miracles really can happen on the longest of odds, let's meet Sean Connery again in an apocryphal tale. Reportedly he once bet on the number 17 threes times in a row at the Italian Casino de la Vallée and won $27,000. The odds of pulling that one off were 50,000:1.

Poker Staple: Texas Hold 'em

At the back of the casino you may find a couple of rooms dedicated to that other side of the game – the one of body language, giving nothing away and violent retribution for cheats and international bad guys on the make. Especially if you're the new Bond, Daniel Craig, whose character is clearly darker and moodier than all the rest, which does go some way to explaining why he'd be drawn to a game that involves a lot of pouting.

With the advent of TV poker Texas Hold 'em has become the poker game of choice. Mercifully it's easy to pick up and

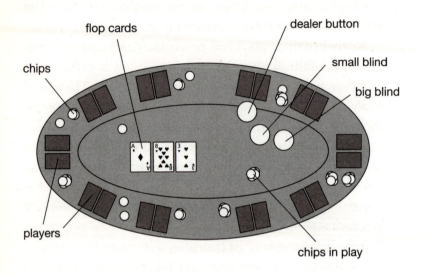

trust me there's almost nothing more fun than going 'all in' with your entire bankroll and winning.

Step 1. To begin the first two players place blinds (mandatory bets). The first player on the left places the 'little blind' and the second player the 'big blind'. The blinds are set beforehand; usually the big blind is the smallest bet possible (like a table minimum) and the little blind is either a half or third of that value.

Step 2. Two cards are then dealt face down to your left. These are the 'hole' or 'pocket' cards. Each player can look at their own cards.

At this stage the betting moves around the table. Each player can either call (match the previous bet), raise it or fold their cards and bow out.

Step 3. When the betting is over three community cards are dealt face up in the centre of the table. These are also known as 'the flop'. You use these in combination with your hole cards to make the highest hand you can.

Step 4. Now another round of betting starts with the player to the left of the dealer, who can call, raise, 'check' (place no bet) or fold. Once a bet is placed you can then only call, raise or fold. Sometimes you will get a check right round the table.

Step 5. A fourth card, the 'turn' card, is dealt face up on to the board and another round of betting begins.

Step 6. A fifth card, known as the 'river' card, is dealt. A final round of betting, pouting and bluffing ensues. At the end of the round everyone matches their hole cards with the flop to make their best possible hand. The one with the best hand wins.

If the best hand is actually the flop everyone wins and gets equal shares.

That's it. Wasn't so hard was it? When you play your first game you'll see how much parrying and thrusting can occur and how long games can last as the pot moves around the table. In 1951 legendary poker player Nick 'The Greek' Dandalos played a game in a Vegas casino that went on for five months (barring sleep and toilet breaks of course) and lost somewhere in the region of $2 million–$4 million (at least $40 million today). After fatigue set in he gave poker folklore one of its most famous lines when he said to his opponent Johnny Moss, 'Mr Moss, I have to let you go.'

It has been estimated that during his career Nick the Greek won and lost the staggering sum of $500 million. When asked by the famous physicist Richard Feynman how he regularly won so big he explained how he calculated odds at the tables and bet against other players' superstitious beliefs about the outcome. So with that in mind let's check out the strongest hands to play in order of clout.

Royal flush: the strongest hand you can play. It kills everything. Aces high such as A, K, Q, J, 10 of the same suit.

Straight flush: five consecutive same suit cards. For example 6, 7, 8, 9, 10 of hearts.

Four of a kind: four cards of the same value plus any fifth card. For example four jacks of each suit and a 2 of spades.

Full house: three of a kind and a pair. For example three kings, two 10s.

Flush: any five cards of the same suit but not in rank sequence. For example 2, 3, 6, J, K, all spades.

Straight: five consecutive cards but not of same suit. For example 6, 7, 8, 9, 10, all mixed suits.

Three of a kind: three cards of the same value, any suit, plus any other two cards. For example three 6s plus a queen and a 5.

Two pair: two pairs plus any fifth card. For example two 8s, two queens and a 6.

Pair: a pair and any other three cards. For example two 5s, plus a 6, jack and an ace.

Any card high: any five cards that do not form any higher poker hand. A queen high hand for example might run, 10, 8, 4 and 3 and be of any suit.

Introducing the Odds

Fredrik Paulsson of cardschat.com introduces pot odds like this.

'You're on the turn in hold 'em, and you're holding Q♥ 9♥ in last position.

'The board is A♥ K♥ 7♠ 4♠.

'The player before you bets. He's a tight player, and you know he's unlikely to bet without at least a pair of kings, and likely a pair of aces, here. Your only chance of winning this pot is if the last card is a third heart, giving you a flush. There are nine cards that you have not seen out of 46 in the deck (counting from the turn, not the flop) that will give you this flush so you have about a 9/46 chance to hit on the river. Another way of putting this is that there are 9 cards that will make you win, and 46 − 9 = 37 cards that will make you lose. The odds are therefore 37 to 9, or just about 4:1. If there is more than four times as much in the pot as it costs you to call you should continue since you have a profitable situation.'

Calculating your 'outs' is another effective way of improving your chances. For example in draw poker if there are thirteen hearts in the deck and four are in your hand then there are nine cards out there still to play.

If a light has now gone on and given you probable cause to find out more about implied odds, pot odds, outs and the kind of strategies that will help you win more often then I'd recommend you pick up a copy of Anthony Holden's *Holden on Hold 'Em* or his famous *Big Deal* about his year on the professional poker circuit. There is also a huge range of probability calculators for any given hand available online and plenty of practice games for you to try.

For my money poker is one of the most enjoyable nights you can have as long as you can stay in the game.

Hustles

There is a fine line between cheating, hustling and simply gaining an edge. Bluffing is part of the game when it comes to poker but marking your cards either before the game with shades and blockouts or during the game by nailing, waving or pegging is liable to make your next dental check up an emergency appointment with a kerbstone.

However there are amateurs out there who'll try it on just to see if they can get away with it and professionals with an act so smooth you'll probably encourage them without even realising.

As legendary hustler Canada Bill once said: 'It's immoral to let a sucker keep his money.' This *raison d'être* is why contemporary hustles are far from easy to spot. They range from the old-school shades in modern luminous inks visible only through adapted contact lenses to online cheats who can see your hole cards while you play – one alleged online scamster, Russ Hamilton, is reported to have nabbed $60 million between 2004 and 2008. But my favourite has to be the Roselli brothers credit scam. These professional gangsters ran an identity fraud by signing markers for creditworthy punters who never visited casinos and then losing their funds to allies in rigged games. By 2000 their take was $37 million and then they walked away never to be seen again. Best of all when the authorities caught on to the scam six months later they found that the Roselli brothers' identities they'd been passing off as their own belonged to two gangsters long since dead. An exceptional double bluff right to the end.

Back to Basics – How to Spot a Marked Deck

In his book *How to Cheat at Everything* Simon Lovell says that 'most marked cards can be detected by the very simple riffle test'. So if you're suspicious before a game starts simply hold a squared deck of cards away from you and riffle the cards by running your thumb down the shorter edge. What you're looking for is the telltale flickering just like in an animated flip book for children. Any speck or jump in the patterned back could be a sign of this. Do this twice – once up close and once further away – as some marks can be tiny. Concentrate on the top right corner of the card back as this is where most marks are and try it at both ends. Finally feel the back of the cards for any dry bumps or indents.

Marks during a game will take a more improvised form so check the edges of the cards for any marks and bends that stand out. To spot pegging – leaving a nail impression on the back of card – run your fingers over the surface. Some cheats faintly smudge the backs of cards with whatever they have to hand, cigarette ash or blusher for example (What? You really thought all cheats were men?). To avoid marked cards during play the best strategy is simply to change the deck often.

Lovell puts it bluntly: 'a professional juice player will kill you'. So if you have any doubts at all at whatever stage get out of the game.

Partner Plays

Collusion is probably the commonest form of cheating out there. Toasting is where two cheats working different ends of the tables force the players in the middle to make outrageous bets when they know they will win – it doesn't matter if the first guy loses; he'll split it all later with his partner. Between them they can even force a player out of the game by raising the stakes until the sucker in the middle runs out of cash. If you've got no cash you can't play and all they need is a simple set of signals between them – a cough, a smoothing of the hair. You'll never even see them coming.

Spooks, Drop Outs and Rail Birds

When 'spooks' leave the smaller games they often innocently ask to look at your cards as if to enjoy the thrill of play, and then signal their partner. A 'drop out' does the same while on his way to the toilet or the bar while the 'outside man' or 'rail bird' achieves the same effect by being an innocent member of the audience.

To counter these sneaks never show your cards to anyone.

Play your cards close to your chest literally or squared on the table.

Or as Lovell says, 'Never play with your back to a mirror. Don't laugh, I've seen it!'

One of the most devastating cheats is where the two hustlers signal each other before they ante up. Whoever has signalled that they have the weakest card drops out while the other plays. This is the equivalent of having two starting hands for the price of one, a bit like a soft 17 for the house in blackjack. Over time the margins will kill you.

These are just some of the hustles you're likely to find at the card table but the variations are endless from the local rules switch to pot shorting or flopping the deck. I've concentrated mainly on the card table here as the action tends to be player to player whereas whenever there's a croupier the action tends to be directed towards the house and they've got all the best moves anyway.

And finally here's rule two: the house always wins. So whether you treat the casino as entertainment or a way to make a living always remember the rules.

Learn Any Language – In a Week, in a Month, in a Year

> Go out then and 'pick' conversations in the language you're learning, like a belligerent drunk picks fights.
>
> *Barry Farber*

So just what is a verb and why the hell would you want to conjugate one? The normal reasons fed to us by advertisers and schools is that languages are best learned for business, travel, culture and literature. Expand your horizons, make yourself worthy. But is there a better reason to learn a language? Why yes to meet women of course. Or men if that's your fancy. And why not? If you have a penchant for blondes then you might want to try out a little Swedish, German, Norwegian, Finnish, Hungarian or Dutch. If on the other hand the thought of dark skin, dark hair and dark areolae drives you wild then Italian, Arabic, Spanish, Greek, Turkish, Portuguese, Serbian, Croatian or Hebrew might be a good place for you to start.

Why let old-fashioned ideas about good reasons to learn ruin your chances of opening up a world of social possibilities?

'But,' I hear you say, 'I just don't have an ear for languages.' Come on: if that was really true then explain to me how you can understand the words on this page, watch TV, surf the internet or not pay attention to your father/girlfriend/mother/teacher/boss for minutes at a time and still pick up the meaning of what they said minutes after the event.

It's understandable why most people believe they have no natural ability. We all did the same thing, studied French, Spanish or German at school until our mid to late teens and then found that in the real world we couldn't even order a cup of coffee in our target language.

For my own part I was lucky enough to stay with a French uncle for six weeks when I was eleven and managed to pick up enough French to ask someone to pass the salt or (ahem) buy a packet of cigarettes, just from listening and writing the occasional phrase down. In my first year at high school my French teacher was thrilled by my accent and abilities but by year three I'd been taught how not to speak a language and could say little more than '*Je ne comprends pas!*' (I don't understand!)

So I get it I really do. In my early twenties I had a job lined up in the south of Spain and had to take a crash course in the language. I was rubbish at it mainly because I told myself I would be. But then for one of the other pupils the idea of language learning clicked. 'It's easy,' he challenged me (we didn't get on), 'all you do is take your basic phrase such as: I would, I like etc and look up your own words to add to it.' Of course there's a little bit more to it than that but as a starting point it's one of the best. Find the basic language structure to suit your needs and then build your vocabulary. Within a few short days I was tagging the word *dance* on to the phrase *would you like* to get '*¿quieres* *bailar?*' and kissing Spanish girls. The job eventually fell through but thanks to my fellow pupil's cognitive break-through my taste for languages didn't.

Since then I've lived and worked in Spain, France, Italy, Dubai, Egypt, Thailand, Oman, Lebanon and Norway and visited many other countries. I've usually managed to find a way through the rapid fire speech of locals using the following techniques, which are based on your immediate needs and the amount of time you have for what you want to learn.

One Week – Infancy

At some point in your life you may well be taking a job or holiday to another country with little or no time for preparation. I once found myself on a plane having to bone up on a new language with only two hours to prepare first to take a group of footballers around northern Italy and then to go and take pictures of a political conspiracy. Italian football terms and political jargon are very different. But, as they say, necessity is the mother of invention so here are the tools you need. A pen and paper and a decent phrase book. I choose Berlitz or BBC for preference and then a mini dictionary if I've got the space. First read any sections you think are relevant; in my example the 'at the market section' wasn't going to be much use. Then start using what you find to build your own phrase book related to what you are about to do. I'm not talking a full-blown book with bindings, just a page or two of the bare minimum you need to get by.

Then write down all the phrases you will use whenever you meet someone, your intro script if you like: 'Hello',

'Pleased to meet you', 'Good morning', Good afternoon', 'Good evening', 'Yes', 'No', 'Please', 'Thank you', 'You're welcome', 'How are you?', 'Fine', and 'Goodbye'.

Formalise it in your head so that it becomes routine just like an actor memorising a script. This is real world communication so extend it to whatever you require. If you need to organise a coach and directions to your hotel as soon as you leave the airport then start with that. You can add as many of these little scripts as you like for whatever situation you come up against. It's easy and fun and even just doing this for the introductions will make you better than most.

Since most of your initial conversations will involve baby steps in your new language throw in the following on-the-ground language-building phrases: 'How do I say . . .?', 'What does this mean?', 'Please repeat', 'More slowly please' and some basic numbers.

One Month – Adolescence

Eventually I came across a book which used the same principles: *The Quick and Dirty Guide to Learning a Language Fast*. Not only does it have a cool title but it gives you page after page of suggested word combos and phrases to incorporate. As A.G. Hawke's book is based on a rapid language-learning system he developed as a US Green Beret it does have a tendency to suggest command words and phrases such as 'enemy' and 'target' but the learning structure is sound. After six days of one-hour, fast-track phrase and vocabulary building you move on to basic grammar but only for a day.

If like me the thought of endless grammar tables fills you with dread don't worry, all the techniques presented here use grammar to reinforce and clarify what you have already learned. Not the other way round. We're starting at the top level of language here and working down, just like children do. You learn your grammar by using it; later on when it comes to looking at tables you'll find grammar to be an old friend you're already familiar with rather than an enemy to be confronted. Remember learning doesn't have to be painful. Grammar is simply the structure of a language and how it changes with usage. Every two-year-old knows the difference between 'she go' and 'she goes'. The ending of the verb 'go' changes to the correct third person singular form 'goes'. That's it, that's how a verb is conjugated. Not so painful now is it? The high-end corporate language packages like Rosetta Stone use this method very effectively and it works.

Hawke suggests reviewing the rules for past, present and future tenses, case, gender (feminine or masculine endings), number (plural or singular), articles (i.e. a, an, the), possession (e.g. apostrophe and an 's' in English) and focusing on commonly used verbs. You'll know what they are by this point as you'll already have used them. You then incorporate the alphabet and expand on what you've learned already up to a full month by which point Hawke claims you will be functional. I've tried it. He's right. It still involves work though. This isn't *The Matrix* and you're not Neo. Unfortunately we can't just plug you in and upload a new language.

One Year – Adulthood

If your plan is to do more than order drinks and instead discuss the influences of absinthe on nineteenth-century French poetry or to repeat your wedding vows to your new bride in pitch-perfect Chinese then I recommend Barry Farber's multi-track approach from his book *How to Learn Any Language*. His system is cheap, effective and easy to use. Follow it for a year and you should be highly proficient and verging on fluent.

It's a system that's much like working out in a gym where you have a wide range of equipment to use and can mix it up every couple of weeks when your training plateaus. He recommends the following kit for your home language gym: a basic textbook (one that looks a little bit like those ones from school – but don't worry it's not going to be used like that), dictionary (make sure it's a good one that translates from your target language into your own), a newspaper or magazine, a student reader aimed at kids around age nine to twelve, a portable music player (cassette, CD, MP3, what-ever format you prefer), audio courses in your target format, flash cards and blank flash cards (that you fill out yourself) and finally a marker pen to highlight the unknown expres-sions in your *article-a-day* newspaper.

According to Farber this strategy works because saying a phrase aloud ten to twenty times is far more effective than reading it fifty to a hundred times, likewise seeing grammar in a texbook does not fix it in your memory in the way that reading it in a newspaper, hearing it on TV or radio or in conversation with another speaker does. Attempting to master a language with a grammar book alone is too boring; with phrase books alone too superficial; with audio alone too fruitless; and with dictionary and newspaper alone impossible. The multiple-track attack, he argues, makes your work pay off.

Ultimately the reason all these approaches will help you learn and then master a language in a far shorter time than you previously thought possible is because you're not forced to dwell on things that don't work, don't interest you or don't make sense before moving forward. Neither do you have to endure bad grades as punishment because where you make your mistakes is where you learn most; it simply flags up the areas you need to work on.

Punishing mistakes has been described by Dr Henry Urbanski, founder of the Language Immersion Institute, as a form of benign brainwashing. 'Why make students suffer unnecessarily?' he says. After years of pain free fun and flirtation in several languages I couldn't agree more.

Learn to Jam in a Day

First things first, give your significant other your credit card and the kids a box of matches. Tell them not to come back until they've either maxed out your line of credit or been arrested. Why? Because we're going to learn to play the guitar that's why. Every modern gentleman needs to know how to entertain a crowd and when he wants to relax and express himself.

It could get kinda noisy as we're going to learn twelve-bar blues, which works the same on just about any instrument but for now guitar will do. You only need to learn three chords and a standard progression; it forms the backbone of most contemporary, pop, rock, folk, funk and soul. You'll then have a flying start at anything else you want to try your hand at.

Once you've mastered it you'll also be one outrageously popular guy at a party, around a campfire on a cold night or on the beach.

Maybe.

But it's worth a shot right?

Now I'm no master of any instrument; however a musical friend challenged me to do this and it works. Paddy Smith is editor of *Stuff* magazine in the Middle East but at night he doubles as guitarist in a funk band. He said if he could learn to play live after basic lessons in blues chord progression anyone can. So without further ado I borrowed my grand-dad's beat-up old acoustic guitar and tried out what he recommended. First up:

How to Tune Your Guitar

This scuppers most beginners as they can get the playing technique right but because they're out of tune the guitar sounds awful. So let's make it simple: either buy yourself a digital tuner and tune your guitar in less than three minutes or if cash is tight use the free and easy-to-use tuner at http://www.howtotuneaguitar.org. As a quick reference the thick top string is the lowest open E note and runs A, D, G, B down to the second higher-pitched thin E string.

Baby Steps

Working in the key of E the twelve-bar blues uses these chords:

E (major): place your first finger behind the first fret on the third string. Then your second and third fingers on the fourth and fifth strings behind the second fret.

Strum your fingers or plectrum across all the strings over the hole. Does it sound right? If not try plucking each string

E

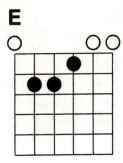

separately. If you find any strings are buzzing or notes not sounding as they should adjust your finger position until they do. Strum again.

A (major): place your first, second and third fingers behind the second fret on strings two through four. Only the top five strings are played.

A

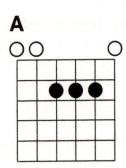

B7: finger one goes on fret one, string four. Fingers two, three and four are for strings five, three and one on fret two. Simple no?

B7

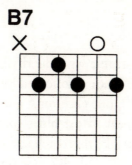

The Blues Rhythm

Find the E (major) chord and strum your guitar using down-strokes and counting out loud: 1, 2, 3, 4.

That's a 4/4 rhythm (four beats per count of four) and you're playing quarter notes. Well done. Use www.metronomeonline.com if you need help with your timing.

Still in 4/4 time let's change the rhythm a little. Count out loud: 1 and 2 and 3 and 4 and play two downstrokes per beat (great, you're now playing eighth notes).

Okay: now we're going to change the count: 1 and the 2 and the 3 and the 4. That's three downstrokes per beat. This is your basic blues rhythm and you're now playing triplets. It's amazing how quickly you're progressing. Seriously, stay with it. You're doing great.

Now for the blues shuffle count with an upstroke on: **1** and **the 2** and **the 3** and **the 4** and **the 1** (repeat).

Practise these rhythms until you've got it. It won't feel like a tune just yet; you're just learning about rhythm for the moment.

Strum It

When you're comfortable with the rhythm practice do this: play four bars on E (major) followed by two on A (major), two on E, one on B7, one each on A and E, then a final one on B7 and then repeat. Most blues songs follow this progression and it looks like this (each letter is a four-beat bar): E E E E, A A, E, E, B7, A, E, B7 then repeat.

That's all there is to it apart from practice practice practice of course. If you want to play and shout a little blues-style 'I woke up this morning' improv use that same rhythm but only play the first two beats of the bar, slap the strings for the second half of the bar or speak your mind and change chord whenever it feels right.

Solo – The Blues Scale

If you want to try a guitar solo over a band or backing track then learn this scale. To play it you simply pluck each string one after the other, first open-stringed then closed, and finish on a final open E. Then reverse back up the scale. This is excellent for building your finger skills and strength.

1. E string, the lowest note, third fret.
2. A string, fret one followed by fret two.
3. D string, fret two.
4. G string, fret two then fret three.
5. B, fret three.
6. E, fret three.

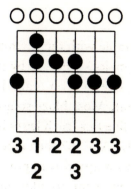

'See easy,' Paddy said when he first said to try this. 'It's not going to qualify you as a virtuoso but you'd be able to kick out a jam with a bluesman after you've nailed that.'

If you want to take either of these techniques further check out *Mojo*'s excellent www.threechordguitar.com and for a full course, www.accessrock.com. Try Mojo's two-finger plucking blues shuffle tutorial to see how much you know already. You'll quickly learn how to change key and introduce rhythm changes.

If you want to start learning Spanish, classical or rock techniques then there are loads of free resources online or you could try Richard Chapman's *The Complete Guitarist* for a good all-round foundation course.

The main thing is to have fun and enjoy it. Learn the scales and the twelve-bar progression and don't beat yourself up on the theory. Jamming with other guitarists is the best way to learn and improve as well as regular 'playing', in the true sense of the word.

FROM THE GENTLEMAN'S CLUB

Because looking good is easy

The Bare Essentials

Grooming

When raw recruits join the Royal Marine Commandos the first thing they're taught is how to take care of personal hygiene, how to wash, how to shave, how to sort their hair out.

The reason for this is that a lot of men simply don't know how usually because they aren't taught properly as children. So it doesn't matter if you're auditioning for *The Apprentice*, the Prince of Wales opening a hospital or you're going out for the night: turn up with malevolent underarms, bad breath and looking a mess and it's over before you've even begun.

Now this isn't to say that you need to spend the whole day preening yourself. Your average commando spends his days humping gear through hostile environments, muddy forests and grimy deserts getting covered in the blood and sweat of hard, dangerous work. But when they need to they know what needs to be done.

As always it pays to learn from the best. Olivier Bonnefoy is the founder and director of Gentlemen's Tonic, a select male-grooming establishment for the modern gentleman in London's exclusive Mayfair district. So if you want to hear his advice and come over like an officer and a gentleman read on.

Hair

The Cut and Style
Ensure you have your hair cut and styled every four to five weeks at a reputable establishment where time is taken to ensure you get the right advice and the right cut. A good barber will be able to advise what suits your hair type, face shape and lifestyle needs. Hair at the moment should be clean cut with texture to create movement. A sort of 'modern meets classic', this will suit most hair types and face shapes.

How to Shave

On average a man will shave approximately 20,000 times throughout his lifetime. If the average shave took ten minutes this would mean that men spend the equivalent of almost 140 days or five months shaving. But are we doing it correctly? In order to assure that you are making the most of your time and getting the best result from your razor follow Gentlemen's Tonic's step-by-step guide to the perfect shave.

Preparation
Shaving is a daily ritual for most men yet it may damage and remove up to two layers of skin in the process. It is therefore

imperative to prepare in order to protect the skin and experience a better shave.

The Basic Steps
Always shave after or during a hot shower but never before. The hot water helps to loosen up pores, cleanses the skin and softens hairs for a closer shave.

Before shaving, lightly rub in a pre-shave oil to protect the skin and to soften the beard so allowing the razor to glide easily over the face.

Once or twice a week, especially before commencing a shave, an exfoliation scrub should be used to help eliminate dead cells, excess sebum and residues from the skin surface. It will also assure a closer, safer and longer lasting shave.

Lather
It is important to use a good quality shaving cream or soap for a close and comfortable shave. Lather up a dab of your shave cream or soap with a shave brush or your fingers to soften and raise the hair away from the skin for a closer shave. If you are uninitiated with the use of shaving brushes it may be worth trying as they help generate a rich and warm lather, soften and lift the beard, open pores, bring sufficient water to the skin and help to gently exfoliate.

Shaving
The most important rule of shaving is to always shave with the grain first – in the direction of hair growth. Shaving against the grain first can cause ingrown hairs and razor burns.

Though there are many razors on the market, Gillette spent a record amount on research and development with the Mach 3 and among grooming professionals it is considered one of the best retail blades available. Ultimately however the brand name of the blade is far less important than the state it is in. Never use a blunt blade as it is distressing to the skin, causes redness and irritation and fails to shave skin evenly. The moment you feel your blade is not performing properly, replace it.

The blade is just one part of the equation. Finding a good razor to provide proper weight, balance and comfort for better control is also extremely important.

Applying excessive pressure will not change the outcome of the shave so long as the blade is clean and not overly used. Always glide the razor across the skin with gentle pressure and if you are aiming for an even closer shave re-lather and shave lightly across or against the grain using small strokes to prevent irritation or razor burns. Around the neck area where hair grows in different directions, run your finger along the skin to feel and adjust accordingly to shave with the grain. Use hot water to rinse off the blade when shaving. After you have finished rinse the face thoroughly with cold water to close the pores and pat dry.

If you have cut or nicked yourself while shaving try using an alum block to stop the bleeding. Some might find they need to use a post-shave serum that relieves razor bumps and ingrown hairs and calms irritated skin directly.

Moisturise

The last but often ignored step, which is no less important than the shave itself, is to moisturise using an alcohol-free moisturiser balm or gel to soothe, refresh and regenerate the skin and to help close the pores.

Perfect skin comes from a good skin-care routine making

sure you use the correct type of moisturiser for your skin type and paying attention to your diet and water intake. The elements are also changing: the sun is becoming stronger and we are all exposed to more air conditioning and central heating. All these factors play a big part in the overall appearance of the skin. It is important to moisturise the skin with an SPF on a daily basis whether the sun is out or not.

How to Smell Good

Shower daily using good-quality, clean-smelling products. Use deodorant and nice smelling moisturisers; also find an aftershave with a fragrance that you like and that represents your character.

For warm climates, an active life or excessive perspiration avoid deodorants altogether as the mixed smell of sweat and perfume can be more offputting than not wearing any in the first place. Instead opt for unperfumed antiperspirants with a suitably understated aftershave.

Extremities (Hands and Feet)

Finally men often neglect their hands, which is strange as they are on show every day no matter what job they do. Keeping nails trimmed (square cut for toes) and filed prevents ingrown nails. If calloused a regular hand treatment/manicure will sort that out. If you do physical work or play sports then this can be rough on your feet so if you're planning a holiday try a pedicure or moisturising foot treatment when summer comes as like your hands your feet will be on show.

So some wise words there from a grooming master. Don't get too hung up on this: remember manly Swarfega is only a hand cleaner. You simply need to know how to apply these skills and use them as effective weapons of mass seduction. Pay attention to what Olivier has said and you'll be able to make the right impression with or without your clothes on.

Urban Body Armour – What to Wear

Clothes make the man. Naked people have little or no influence on society.

Mark Twain

Twain was a wit, no doubt about it, but he understood the difference appearances can make. My take is quite the opposite: the man makes the clothes not the other way round. It's a methodology we've come across before: social engineering. Quite simply you can alpha-male the hell out of anyone who believes Twain's passive statement to be true.

The gentlemen of old were well aware of this as are the wealthy and powerful of today: tailored clothes mark them out as different from the herd who buy off-the-peg clothing. This includes designer brands. Many people who spend a good chunk of cash on a Boss or a Versace suit genuinely think they're the business but are totally unaware that they're wearing the wrong size and actually look as if they're wearing a small tent or too tight, half mast comedy trousers. Ultimately the brand or tailor isn't important. Here's what is:

Buy clothes that fit your body shape.
Buy the best that you can afford.
Keep them clean and well cared for.

Sounds obvious but for many it's not. I know from experience that if I wear even my oldest, most worn out and tattered tailored shirt I get jealous looks from men and admiring glances from women. If it's new, crisp and freshly laundered look out. Watch up and coming politicians and celebrities: they all spend on these very items as they know on an emotional level the impact good clothing has.

Now this isn't the fashion pages here, this is real-world knowledge. Most fashion houses reinvent the same old styles in delicate fabrics that have to be replaced year on year. Frankly why bother when you can spend a little bit extra and buy something from Savile Row or any number of excellent tailors worldwide that will last you a lifetime. Good clothing is an investment you'll never regret. And over time you'll build up a wardrobe with enough classic items built by craftsmen rather than designers that you'll never go out of fashion.

Suited and Booted

The Cuts
There are three essential cuts in the suit jacket that you need to know about.

Two-piece suit
This is the most popular model today. Single breasted, usually with two side vents and trousers with or without cuffs. You can also vary the pattern of this suit with three buttons and a vent down the back.

The double breasted suit
Less common these days but still fun. Think of the traditional 1920s gangster-style jacket as favoured by the hip-hop

glitterati. It usually has two side vents with no rear vent as this prevents the jacket from hanging well when you sit down or allowing you to put your hands in your pockets.

The three-piece suit

The three-piece can be either single or double breasted and come with any kind of collar, pocket or vent variation you like. The long, double breasted, three-piece as made by Mantoni is all the rage with the modern urban American gangster and royalty alike. Royalty however is far more likely to have something knocked up at Gieves & Hawkes over on Savile Row.

International Styles

As the suit is one of the most refined items of clothing a man can wear, it's essential that the type of suit you wear, the cut, the colour and the fabric match the occasion, the time of day, the season and the climate.

The English suit

The classic English suit takes its inspiration from the uniforms of the armed forces and favours an hourglass cut with side vents. The trousers are cut high to the hips and without cuffs. If you're chasing a James Bond look plain blacks, greys and midnight blues are what you should aim for while white or chalk pinstripes are desirable if you're aiming for the City or emulating royalty. One or two buttoned jackets with straight pockets and buttonholes finish off the look.

The Italian suit

If English suits are classical and uniform then Italian styling is more individual and Renaissance-inspired. The Italian suit is usually elegant and refined and opts for softer, lightweight and more colourful fabrics. Unlike in the UK there are several areas of excellence in Italy itself, from Caraceni and Belvest in the north to Kiton in the Neapolitan south. If there is a centre for traditional Italian tailoring then it's in Rome. There you'll find names like D'Avenza, Angelo, Cifonelli, Caraceni (there are four firms alone with this same name between Rome and Milan) and of course Brioni. The last have many outlets around the world, from New York and Dubai to London, that all offer hand-made suits measured onsite and made in Italy. But if you want bespoke you have to visit their Rome headquarters in person. They are favoured by American movie stars and if you want the cool, debonair styling of a Cary Grant or George Clooney, Brioni are the outfitters to seek out.

The American suit

Brooks Brothers are the benchmark for American suits and their styles usually come in two or three button versions with rounded, natural shoulders, a vent in back and usually without pleats on the trousers. They've been going since 1818 and sold their first ready-made suit in 1845. A few years later in 1864 Abraham Lincoln wore a specially designed jacket made by them for his second inauguration. He also wore it on the night he was assassinated. Prince of Wales check, grey flannel and flannel herringbone are all classic colours considered suitable for business or pleasure. The Brooks Brothers have an eclectic client base that has included tailoring the uniforms of Union officers during the American Civil War, an array of American presidents through to modern-day Hollywood costumers and celebs like Will Smith, Ben Affleck and home-grown British talent Sir Paul McCartney

The Summer suit

Something different in its own right. Normally lightweight and light coloured it's designed for hotter climates where comfort is essential. Suits made from linen or cotton are comfortable to wear but crease easily. Silk and mohair are both good materials although not commonly considered suit material by men. Cashmere or lightweight wools such as the super-100s are pleasantly cool to wear, very lightweight and almost guarantee that you'll survive a summer crease-free.

Off the Peg or Custom-Made?

Ready-made/off the peg
These suits are made in factories in just a few minutes from a basic set of standardised templates for someone of your size. They retail for around £100–£600. As they only work on an average body-type buy the larger size and have it adjusted to fit. These factory-made suits range from high-street retailers to high-end brand names. They are usually fused i.e. glued together rather than stitched.

Made to measure
These are often confused with bespoke tailoring. They are the same as off the peg except you can have a few alterations made at the factory. I've even known people who measure these suits for a living swear blind that this is bespoke. It's not. Many tailors offer made-to-measure suits as well but rightly differentiate between the two. Expect to pay £400–£1000.

Off the peg – but handmade
These are quality off the peg suits made on a production line but cut and stitched by hand. They can be turned out in an afternoon and are generally of high quality although they are still only ever made from a standardised template. But what you get is a very high standard of workmanship for a

very low price. Popular names that offer these lines include Reuben Alexander, Chester Barrie, Brioni or Oxxford Clothes. Expect to pay anything from £1000–£3000. For my money if you're paying over two you should be looking at the next option.

Bespoke

It's not a protected term unlike haute couture but probably should be. Bespoke means a suit made entirely to your specifications. You will have a unique set of measurements and therefore a unique template for your body that may change over time. The tailor will always have a wide range of fabrics for you to choose from and there will always be a high standard of personal service. You commission this type of suit rather than buy it. It usually takes four to eight weeks to make, involves more than one fitting and will last you many years of use.

Being made to feel like a king and then having a suit made that would be worn by one is one of the most enjoyable experiences a man can have. A lot of tailors say they don't like to talk money, which personally bugs the hell out of me, but on average you will be looking to pay £2000–£3000 or more on Savile Row depending on the reputation and overheads of the particular tailor.

Suits of this standard however are an investment and it's likely you'll be passing them on to your children. Think of a custom-built Aston Martin, how long they last and how good they look and you get the picture.

Knowing What to Buy

You're only limited by budget, time and imagination. If your budget is limited to less than £200 then go for a ready-made suit from the high street. Savile Row tailor Thomas

Mahon says, 'For the money, the British high street retailer Marks & Spencer makes as good a suit as anyone. I rate them highly.'

You can also pick up bargains from overstock suppliers. Whatever your source, the golden rule is to have the suit adjusted to fit your size and body shape. Don't just settle for what you're given.

If your budget stretches to the £300–£700 mark you can work with Kings & Allen who offer a low-cost bespoke tailoring option to City boys and outsiders alike. You could also look at some of the off the peg suits of tailors on the Row for their own brand of ready to wear, either hand made or otherwise.

If you're torn between a holiday or a new suit you could combine the two. Thanks to lower overheads and staff costs you can often have bespoke suits tailored in exactly the same materials as you'd find on the Row as far afield as Hong Kong and Bangkok to Turkey and Bahrain. Tailors there are generally much more open to negotiation than in the West but if you can always try and find recommendations first. All tailors are not the same. If in doubt I usually call the local Foreign Office or British Council office and pick a couple of brains there. If you're in Dubai then I can heartily recommend Royal Fashions, preferably their Karama branch (where they service diplomats and royalty). Ask for Pradeep or Daniel and the Mr Frank discount. I can usually save several hundred pounds on every suit (more, depending on the material) I commission there. *The Economist* raves about their shirts.

You can also take your favourite suit, shirt or pair of jeans for that matter to any number of tailors and have them recreated for a fraction of the price. Plus once they have your pattern they can always make more.

Shoes

Excuse me while I get a bit Sarah Jessica Parker on you here but do some women really judge a man by his shoes? Well have you ever noticed a woman check you out then check out your shoes as well? If they like them they look back and smile; if not they look forlorn and try and pretend they weren't looking in the first place. It always amuses me when it happens. Why? Because it's totally loony tunes. Just look at what I do for a living for example; unless it's a formal occasion I could be wearing boat shoes, brogues, hiking boots, trainers or clogs depending on where a story takes me. Judging you by your shoes means she's read one magazine too many and hasn't yet learned to think for herself.

But with a little social engineering when people think spoon-fed thoughts rather than their own we can always make an impression.

Again with shoes buy the best you can afford. While you can get expertly crafted custom-made shoes from John Lobb you can also pick up a perfectly good pair of formal shoes for under £100 in the shops. Again brands aren't the distinguishing feature here; opt for classic lace-ups with a defined heel and leather soles to compliment any classic suit. For a summer suit you can be a bit more informal with loafers, Italian moccasins or monkstraps in lighter shades. If you're in the media or music you can even get away with trainers by making a funky feature of them.

Shirts

If you've ever wondered why you keep your jacket on even when the temperature is rising it's because traditionally until the eighteenth century the shirt was considered to be underwear. Thankfully it's not that way any more but it explains why unconsciously you'll never take your jacket off at formal occasions unless you're specifically asked to. Or unless you're drunk and then anything goes.

Classic styling

Good gentlemen's shirts usually have several distinguishing features. If they are patterned then the patterns line up; the collars have removable collar bones, sometimes made of brass to keep the shirt collars the right shape and prevent the tips turning up; a split yoke equidistant between the shoulders to allow perfect fitting; more stitches – for durability along with reinforced gussets and several small pleats near the cuffs. Tailors often encourage you to have quite long shirts to 'avoid embarrassment' when bending over but having them cut shorter so that they can be worn out informally with jeans is rarely a problem.

The Brooks Brothers shirt

The button-down shirt has been around since 1900. It's a Brooks Brothers staple that here in the UK gained favour with yuppies and Two Tone culture in the 1980s. If you're wondering what exactly is buttoned down it's the collars. Avoid them if you want to look more Bond than juvenile Tom Cruise.

The collar

The great thing about custom shirts is that you can have the collar made to fit your neck and tie preferences exactly. The wide turndown is the most formal with varying lengths and widths between the tips. These collars always make you look more dressed up even if you're just popping out for a pint of milk.

Broad collars allow thick neckties and come in a variety

of styles. Worn wide they make a long neck appear shorter or a short neck appear longer if worn narrow.

The cutaway is the current favourite of the day: it's where the collar tips are cut away to show off the tie. Any variations on this shape look good with or without a noose.

Unusual collars out there include the detachable collar, which is almost Dickensian, a bit of a fuss to put on but does allow you to be more adaptable. The pin collar and the tab collar emphasise the tie knot and are more popular in the States than in Europe.

The fit

Whatever style you go for always make sure the shirt fits you properly. The sleeve cuffs should protrude about three to five millimetres outside the suit jacket (helps short arms look longer), cover the wrist and sit just on the base of the thumb.

The collar should only just be covered by the jacket lapel and not be concealed beneath the back lapel of the jacket.

If your shirt fits properly the tie won't lift the collar up and the tips will stay resting on your shirt. The tie should also fit snugly into the triangle formed by the collar so that your top button is not showing when your tie is on.

Bondage for Everyday Exhibitionists

How to Tie a Bow Tie

You can of course buy a ready-made elasticated bow tie that's easy to put on and you don't have to think twice about. But let's be honest: they can look a little plasticky and more what you'd expect to find on a twelve-year-old even if they are what most of us wear to a formal occasion.

A bow tie constructed by hand will always look unique and individual simply because it is never perfect. It'll make you stand out in a crowd of penguins and you will also look uber-cool at the end of the night when it's untied by the woman you're with.

Most tutorials on how to tie a bow tie miss this key point for beginners: look at your bow tie. Each side has that distinctive 'fin' shaped end and a rounded 'barrel' above it. The left hand side is the back of the bow shape and the right hand the front. Remember this point; it'll be easier later on.

Okay let's get it on.

Step 1. In front of a mirror drape the tie around your neck with the left end hanging slightly lower than the right.

Step 2. Fold the left end over the right so that both ends cross about an inch above the barrel.

Step 3. Pull the left end under and back up through the loop around your neck to form a loose knot. Place that end out of the way, on your shoulder for example.

Step 4. Now take the right end and fold it along the barrel to form the front face of the bow.

Step 5. Now find the line where the left end will hang naturally straight down over the front of the bow. Adjust the position of the tie on your neck to make it hang correctly.

Step 6. Grab the barrel and the fin of the horizontal front part of the bow and fold them gently over to one side. Where you see a small opening (locate it with a finger first if that helps) push the barrel end of the length hanging down through this gap until it's poking out the other side but stop before you push it all the way through.

Step 7. Let go. You will now see the basic shape of the final form. That's the hard part out of the way.

Step 8. With your index finger find the curved end that's poking through and while holding the fin on the other side pull on both sides to even up the shape of the back piece.

Step 9. Tweak it if you need to. Adjust the front part of the bow to make it even. I find clasping the ends of both front and back and rolling my thumbs out from behind the knot quite helpful.

Step 10. Hold all four ends of the front and back pieces and pull steadily and gently to tighten the bow.

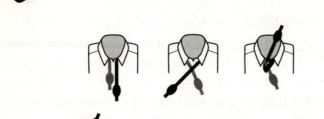

Know that everyone has their own slightly different technique and that no two ties will ever look the same tied like this, which is their charm.

Troubleshooting: if you're having problems loosen the bow tie to its widest collar setting to give you more material to play with and then retighten afterwards.

Or if you're having problems threading it through the opening or even finding the opening try placing your finger on either the front or back of the first loop of the first knot. Keep your finger there as a guide and you can then thread the barrel end through either front or back of this knot. Both work – purists might not agree – but they really do.

How to Tie . . . a Tie

Ties and tie knots go in and out of fashion but if ever you want to look like Beckham, Bond or Clooney it's essential to know how.

The Four in Hand
This is the easiest knot to tie, the one your mother taught you as a child.

Step 1. Hang the tie around your neck with the broad end hanging lower than the narrow end.

Step 2. Place the thick end over the thin end, put your forefinger on the point where they meet and wrap the broad end round once bringing it underneath and then through the loop around your neck.

Step 3. Push the broad end through the hole you've created with your forefinger.

Step 4. Hold the narrow end of the tie and tighten to fit comfortably around your neck so that the top button is covered. Give the knot a little pinch to finish.

The Prince Albert

This is my favourite quick knot as it provides a bit more body than the four in hand. Simply wrap the broad end around twice instead of once. Everything else is exactly the same.

The Windsor aka The Fat Tie

This is the godfather of tie knots named after the Duke of Windsor (the former King Edward VIII). It's always good for formal occasions and is also favoured by City boys and footballers. It's best to look in the mirror when you're first learning this one.

Step 1. From around your neck, broad end on the right, place this end over the narrow end and put your forefinger on the point where they meet. Bring the fat end underneath the neck loop and back over the thin left hand side slightly overlapping the line of the fabric beneath (not straight down over the front).

Step 2. Bring it back underneath again and then fold it over the front side of the thin side of the neck loop on the opposite side.

Step 3. Optional (for perfectionists only). Adjust both sides of the shape you have created so that they are equally spaced and it looks a little like a tongue poking out of a mouth.

Step 4. Hold this central bundle of material with one hand and wrap the fat end over the front to cover it.

Step 5. Thread it back up through the loop over the front and under the front layer then adjust as usual.

For a Half-Windsor simply leave out steps 2 and 3.

If you want to try a style that has become a slightly avant-garde cyberculture fashion statement, as was worn by the Merovingian in *The Matrix Reloaded*, do this: simply tie a full Windsor with the tie's seam facing outwards. Take it off your neck still made up and flip it over to display the elaborate origami pattern formed by the knot that is usually hidden from view. Add a subtle tie pin to finish off the look.

This movie character has spawned several variations including the Hen-Tai or 'weird' tie (also the name for Japanese animated porn), popularised by Henry Hu, a New York banker, but then found to have been previously thought up by someone called Edeity and called unsurprisingly the Edeity knot. It's basically a Windsor knot but using the narrow end to form its shape and then hidden in the back.

It is in fact a tradition to misname knots. The Duke of Windsor apparently never wore the Windsor knot; he simply commissioned ties from Hawes & Curtis with extra thick lining.

If you'd like to try out every variation seek out Thomas Fink's *85 Ways to Tie a Tie* or check out the excellent tutorials on www.lordwhimsy.com.

Everyday Wardrobe Essentials

Three black fitted T-shirts, three white.

Two black long sleeved tops, two white. These work will either on their own or as a base layer under T-shirts or shirts.

At least one short jacket, leather or fabric; both are good.

One high-quality three-quarter or full-length coat.

Two pairs of dark trousers without pleats.

Two pairs of jeans that fit you properly – don't just buy a brand name, go to a jeans shop and try on every pair you can until you find the style or brand that fits you perfectly – then always buy those if you can as many designers use their latest boyfriend as a template. He might be a skinny waif, you might not be.

One thin V-neck jumper, one crew neck and one roll neck.

Sunglasses: make sure they've got UV protection to prevent cataracts. Don't worry about brands: you will eventually lose every pair you buy.

Watches: one elegant, one rugged. But only if you like wearing them.

Stylish flattering underwear – because she will notice those and they do matter.

Now that you have the fundamentals you can apply them to every area of your wardrobe. Alternatively if you want to wear white plimsolls with your suit, some pimped out sportswear to a black tie do or think you can pull off a tight-fitting mod suit then go for it: it's your look not anyone else's. So remember whenever you need to make an impression especially if people don't think you can you now have the knowledge to own the room.

Use it wisely.

HAVE IT ALL

What would you attempt to do if you knew
you could not fail?

Dr Robert Schuller

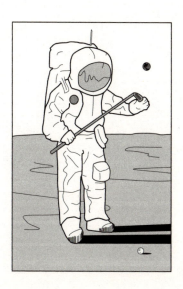

Man and Motor: Why It Doesn't Matter if the Oil Runs Out

You can always find a way to do what you want to do even if sometimes it isn't always the first thing you think of or the most obvious. Take the unhumble motorcar: it grants a sense of personal freedom unlike any other mode of transport and there are few things more enjoyable than slipping through the corners of an empty country road on a crisp sunny morning with some righteous tunes on the stereo.

But what usually happens when we talk about cars is either the very unmanly equivalent of handbag shopping – 'Have you seen James's new Aston? Ooh the rims! Ooh the torque! Can I stroke it?' – or we get stuck in a circuitous debate about oil, carbon emissions and the environment. Now like most men you can probably talk mechanical handbags all day and it's obvious why the fuel element is important – it's the obvious intangible. Will it last? Is it safe? How can we drive without it? The end of the oil age has the potential to end the dream of motoring freedom.

So if you like cars it's the most important question. But are we even looking in the right place for the answers? Oil or petrol to be more precise is not the means of transport, it's the energy source: nothing else. It's also not the only available source. There are far more ways to deliver energy than from a garage forecourt.

To prove the point we need a little historical context.

There was a time when the Cold War forced us all to sit up and behave. When I was a kid tales of naughty Russian communists and fear of nuclear attack were the norm. And thanks to public information films and BBC dramas about the impending holocaust many nights were spent staring at the ceiling worrying about when your skin would be torn from your body in a nuclear blast.

Then the Russians did an Orwellian about-turn: they began to believe in McDonald's and became our friends (although obviously that could all change if they keep dickering with our power lines).

The Chinese are still communists of course but as we are the well-behaved children of propaganda this ingenious piece of doublethink barely registers. The reds now make our beds, they don't hide under them. They manufacture our running shoes and bury our recycling for goodness' sake; stop overanalysing things, everything is just fine.

We even holiday in Cuba and marvel at their cigars and classic American cars. Communists are now cuddly.

But during those gloriously polarised Cold War years P.J. O'Rourke wrote a seminal article titled 'Why Ferrari Refutes the Decline of the West'. In it he argued that if a third-class industrial power like Italy could come up with something as marvellous as the Ferrari then the Russians had no chance of ever winning the Cold War.

So where's our bad guy?

Well first there's the grandly named 'War on Terror' and second the environment or more specifically global warming. They are intimately linked as they deal with power in the political sense and energy in the form of oil. Both determine the future of the car and potentially our species. And if global warming is to us what the Cold War was to our parents' generation is there a modern supercar that could do for carbon emissions what O'Rourke's Ferrari did for the Russians?

I thought about taking a Ferrari through the Midwest to recreate O'Rourke's trip and then an R8 along the winding mountain passes of the Delvio to Stavos road – one of the best driving roads in the world – but then from the pages of *New Scientist* the Tesla Roadster fell into my lap.

The Tesla is a proof of concept supercar that does 0–60 in 3.9 seconds in normal mode and 3.7 in performance mode with a top speed of 130mph (210kph). Impressive statistics on paper and it looks sexy as hell in photographs because its chasis is based on the Lotus Elise rather than say a square shapeless box drawn by a child – the design curse of most cars whether they are environmentally friendly or not.

Significantly it is entirely powered by electricity in the form of 6000 lithium ion batteries: exactly the same type of long-life battery that powers the laptop I'm writing this chapter on.

So I wanted to argue that if we could develop something as gorgeous and technically jaw dropping as the Ferrari (pick a model, any model), the R8 or the Tesla Roadster then environmental problems had no chance against human ingenuity. And even if the car itself became obsolete and we travelled around by jet-pack, anti-gravity skateboards or even horse and cart, ultimately the fuel source wasn't the thing to worry about.

You see the great thing about a car that uses electricity as its power-delivery system is that the fuel can come from anywhere: wind, solar, wave, nuclear and yes even oil. All that's happened is that you've changed the means of delivery from a pump to a socket. It's a method that is infinitely adaptable.

It's also something that frees the mind from fuel dependency. If one day we want to travel to the stars and that requires cold fusion or solar sails to achieve then that's what we will have to do. I'll be ashamed of our species if the best we can come up with is to circle the M25 on fossilised plant byproducts with a finite lifespan. Are we humans a thinking species with imagination and ingenuity or vegetables solely dependent on photosynthesis?

Well let's see. Are we ambitious? Yes. Aspirational? For sure. Prone to sticking our fingers in plug sockets to see what makes them work? Most definitely. So can we actually come up with something to replace the internal combustion engine, something that's sexy and that works?

I hoped so. The bods at Tesla UK delivered the car to me outside Windsor Castle, one of the many homes of the Queen and all things English. It's a car that really turns heads not simply because it looks like an Elise but because the Tesla badge on the hood marks it out as something quite different. People stood and literally gawped at it. An electric car that looks so good you'd really like to add it to your handbag collection. Who'd have thunk it?

It's so attention-grabbing you have to stand 20 feet away from it to avoid being bombarded with inane questions. I'm sure I even saw a curtain twitch in the castle. Maybe Charles, the eco prince, will be getting a green present for Christmas.

Inside you turn the key and without any noticeable start-up growl you're ready to go. Apart from a slight sci-fi hum from the heating and cooling system and a little bit of wind noise, the car is completely quiet. Silent. No grunt at all.

Some have even said that it could do with an engine soundtrack; admittedly a friendly roar might be of some help to pedestrians with their backs turned. However when I finally left the suburbs and overtook a line of cars into the face of oncoming traffic the speed and acceleration of the car were far more exhilarating than the sound of a combustion engine simmering in its own juices.

Driving further through winding country lanes it also became apparent that the many appendages we associate with combustion will also disappear one day. The gear stick for one. You really only need a switch to redirect the circuit to the drive system. Also the ignition key: a button is all that is needed there. In fact it was all that was ever needed. In the early days of motoring electric-driven cars were even more popular than combustion models. If it hadn't been for the invention of the electric starter motor in 1912 we'd probably still be cranking away like Laurel and Hardy to get our quaint and smelly combustibles going in the morning.

Apart from that simple mechanical change, which made it easy to exploit the ready availability of oil and its explosive properties, it's entirely possible that we would have been driving electric vehicles for the last century.

What prevented this was the long charge times for batteries, the lack of horsepower and the temperature-sensitive operating range of most electric motors.

Tesla gets around this by keeping the engine at a constant working temperature between 20°C and 50°C. It provides 248bhp and unlike petrol engines 100 per cent torque, 100 per cent of the time whether you're at zero or 100mph.

As for charge times on a regular 13-amp house socket

you'll be looking at a lengthy sixteen hours to charge up with a 220-mile range on completion. If you're only commuting from Windsor to London every day topping up isn't too much of a problem. Think of how you use your mobile phone; you rarely let the charge go all the way down. But for anything long distance it could be. The current workround is to install 63 amp sockets in purchasers' houses, which brings the time for a full charge down to just over three hours. Not bad. For future models they'll be looking at a fast-charge option that will bring this down to forty-five minutes. That'll leave barely enough time for lunch.

The life of the battery store is around five years with constant use or more than 100,000 miles on the clock. Performance will only drop off after that rather than stop altogether. They're not cheap to replace but as usage and delivery systems improve this overhead should also come down. Is there a future recycling or supply issue there too perhaps?

Based on figures from the US grid it then only costs two cents per kilometre to run. A Porsche GT3, which it matches in performance, costs several times that. It also produces no CO_2 emissions and even when you take into consideration the highest amounts of CO_2 released when charging it up through the electricity grid, they're still half that of anything else on the market. Of course these emissions decrease even more if the main grid also uses renewables as a fuel source.

Upkeep is minimal. Jay Leno, the American talkshow host, is a massive motorhead and after he took the Tesla for a drive he compared it to one of the many classic cars he has in his garage. In his *Times Online* article on the Tesla he said: 'I have never done any maintenance on my 1909 Baker Electric, other than maybe greasing the wheel hubs. You don't do anything. You plug it in, charge it and drive it. The motor is virtually maintenance-free. This is a car made back in 1909 I am talking about and the Tesla is the same way. There is nothing much to break or wear out in the engine department.'

Compelling stuff from a man who genuinely knows his motors. This minimal maintenance motoring also means that we men could stop pretending we know anything about modern computer driven motors when we look under the bonnet.

Theoretically there's no reason why we couldn't recharge our cars at parking meters rather than queuing at filling stations. If the mayor of even one large city was to change the fuel source of its bus and taxi fleet to electric imagine the impact that could have.

Ultimately this little energy battle between the powers of oil and electric will be fought out by lobbyists and PR campaigns designed to change political and social will, and right now it's still anyone's game. Unless of course the oil becomes unprofitable to source and refine more quickly than we anticipate. Big oil could be replaced by big battery before you know it.

I know from my own experience reporting on the energy performance ratings of buildings and the Kyoto Agreement that where there are hundreds of millions, billions and even trillions of dollars of return at stake both sides are usually willing to play dirty to win.

At the moment one side clearly has deeper pockets than the other but historically that's nothing new. According to *Internal Combustion* author Edwin Black, as far back as the 1920s Thomas Edison and his protégé Henry Ford were developing an all-electric version of the Model T that both men hoped would break the back of the powerful industrial cartels of their time.

In the world of PR hyperbole hydrogen and biofuel as viable alternative energy sources are the most obvious red herrings of our day. And once again they tie the vehicle to the fuel source. If you take them out of the official domain of high-cost hydrogen research models built for press releases and the fact that food used for fuel means less food for humans then they quickly become uninteresting.

Ultimately for me anything that can move us on from an age where we are at the mercy of oil-producing nations with apparently malicious interests is a good thing.

Happily I'm not alone; I'm writing these words a few months into a massive worldwide recession. It's a time when supercar manufacturers are lucky to have even one or two orders on their books. Tesla currently has 1200 orders. And those are for a proof of concept car not even for the production line model they plan to bring to market.

But this isn't 1909 though and it's not the Cold War. No one can say for certain what's going to happen not even O'Rourke; only hindsight gave him that almost magical ability. However what I do know is this. On the New Mile Road opposite Ascot racecourse I stamped the accelerator to test the 0–60 speed specs and couldn't stop a smug grin spreading across my face as the car took off and skipped over the bumps in the road. It hit 70mph before I could even take my foot off the pedal. The Roadster has only one forward speed and apparently that speed is quick.

It's also an extremely clever bit of kit. When you brake it uses regenerative technology to recover the energy normally lost and its engine is 92 per cent energy efficient so rather than losing all that carbon energy to heat up the bonnet, it's actually used to make you go faster.

From its heated seats and drop top to its energy gauge that tells you how many miles are left to play with or the amount of amps you use to power out of turns, by the time I had to give it back I really didn't want to. I was so tempted to just drive off . . . I did. It's now sitting in my garage as I type. At least in my imagination.

So can the Tesla refute the decline of the earth's environment and instead applaud human ingenuity? In a word yes, but only sort of. It is a car after all. I don't think any one of them will ever be totally environmentally friendly. Technically though, it is one of the most enjoyable and revelatory cars I've ever driven. And that will win it more fans than anything else. Stick one on the touring car circuit, win a few races and the rest of the world might agree.

One way or another the oil age will soon be over. Give it a few decades and it's done. And it doesn't really matter. Nobody really misses the age of steam do they? What we really need to be thinking of right now is, What next? Either that or start breeding horses by the million.

And if the choice is between humans making an Easter Island out of the entire planet as the long ears fight the short ears and use up all the resources in the process or a whole lot of high-speed fun, I know which one I'll go for.

So will the end of the oil age end the dream of motoring freedom? Clearly the answer is no. But only if we want it to be.

Being scared of change and hiding from the future is the same as if someone asked you to drive the Tesla in valet mode, which limits the speed to a piddling 20mph so that spotty teenagers can park a supercar without writing it off.

Well damn it all to hell that's just not what life is about.

High-Octane Thrills + Speed ≠ £££

Supercars are fun that's undeniable, so are all the other high-end marques that turn the heads of your peers and suck the underwear off impressionable young ladies as you drive by: you know all those Astons, Vipers, Elises, R8s, Carreras, M5s, Lambos, Veyrons, Ferraris and the like, basically cars that you and I probably can't afford.

No it's most likely you drive something with a sparky, zippy type of name like Clio, Focus, Astra, Golf, Fiesta, Passat or Punto, at a push a three-series, a five-series or an SL possibly even an Alfa. But if you're addicted to adrenalin via intravenous motoring where can you get a fix that won't upset your bank manager?

You could of course go for one of the many supercar clubs like Group20 or écurie25 that give you pre-scheduled use of an entire fleet of supercars for less than the yearly depreciation of the average Porsche.

Or if you've got just under £30k to stick in your 'future-classic research account' then you could opt for the Ariel Atom. It's the 300bhp supercharged barebones car that does

0–60mph in 3.3 seconds for a normally aspirated version or 2.7 seconds in the supercharged version. It's marketed as being somewhere between a motorbike and a car and when Jeremy Clarkson test drove it he said, 'I have never ever driven anything that accelerates so fast.' Ariel has become the bespoke end of the motor industry with many parallels to Savile Row: each car is individually commissioned, no two cars are exactly the same and you even have a master designer/engineer who builds the car from start to high speed finish for you just like a master tailor. When performance figures match or beat the Ferrari Enzo and Porsche GT3, and for a lot less money, it's hard to argue with if you've got the spare change.

Alternatively you could opt for a Caterham 7, the classic roadworthy sports car designed by Colin Chapman that also murders the competition on the track. In fact over its fifty-year history the Caterham has been so successful at boffing the competition that in the 1970s it was banned from competition to make things fairer for its rivals. It still holds its own against modern cars and still wins championships. Then there's the Caterham Academy, which teaches you how to be a race driver in double-quick time, and along with the new ultra fast, ultra light and award winning CSR models they continue to make an impression.

If your budget is £20k or less you could take a Westfield on the track, a kit built race car not dissimilar to the Caterham, slightly cheaper to buy and they don't hold their residual values quite as well but they're just as much fun. Or simply pick a racing style that suits your budget and aspirations and that won't cost you a rock star's rehab costs in rubber and brake pads to maintain.

In the Porsche Open championship you could have the lower spec 944 on the track with all safety features in place, a trailer and minimal modifications for between £4k and £6k. An entire season should cost you less than ten grand and you'll still have an excellent track day car at the end of it.

If you take to this beginner-friendly set you can then pimp your ride and move up a grade and from there win a couple of championships like the Carrera Challenge and perhaps even a Le Mans awaits you.

If you want your child to be the next Lewis Hamilton you could start him in national championships created specifically for junior drivers aged fourteen and over like the Ginetta Junior Championship or the Sax Max Championship. They can then move up to Formula Vee, the same grade where Niki Lauda started his racing. That's single-seater action with speeds up to 130mph and around six grand for a car and annual entry fees. From there it's F4 where basic Ford Zetec-powered single seaters cost around £10k, followed by F3, the place to see the next generation of F1 stars with competitions from England to India. As each car is rebuilt after every race costs are high; expect to pay £400k+ per season. Luckily sponsorship is quite common at that level too so it's not just a rich man's game.

But fear not there are so many categories of sub £10k racing that if it's thrills you're after and you've got the spare cash you're good to go. There's single-seater Locost racing, Hot Hatches, Mighty Minis, 24hr Enduro Racing with Citroen 2CVs, classic touring car championships, radicals, truck racing, vintage car club meets. The list goes on. And if you've had enough of the square edges on that sensible car you bought why not enter the Dunlop Sport Maxx Cup, part of the British Touring Car Championship. There you can enter slightly modified recent ex-production line cars and hammer the hell out of them. There's also the ultra affordable MR2 racing scene, about £1800 to get up and running with a fully modified vehicle. Peanuts.

Drifting – the Latest Craze

It was popularised in Japan in the nineties and has spread worldwide with competitions in the UK, Europe, Canada, Malaysia, the USA, Australia and New Zealand. Drivers compete in rear wheel drive cars to earn points based on correct line, angle, speed and show factor i.e. the faster you go, the more smoke you produce and the closer to the track wall the better.

In many parts of the world amateur competitions on public roads such as the Saudi Drift kids in the Middle East have become a significant problem. But as you can pick up a Nissan 200SX for less than £1500, 'the drifter's choice' according to *Redline* magazine, this will surely leave you enough money for a track day or two. There's really no need to become a menace to society or even camels.

Bangers and Mashers

For the ultimate in no-frills, virtually no-cost adrenalin-fuelled action look no further than banger racing. It costs around £200 per race sometimes even less. The concept is simple: you take a ready-for-the-scrap-heap car that's just about running and race other competitors around a track all the while trying to destroy your rivals in the process. It's the nearest you'll ever get to the types of smashes, bashes, bangs and rear ends you normally only see in *Police, Camera, Action* or *Cops*-type TV shows.

In fact if there's a type of car you're desperate to try, race or destroy then somewhere out there somebody else wants to do the same whether it's off-road in the 4×4 that you normally only use for the school run, drag racing with your eight year old at Santa Pod or rallying in a hot hatch more normally associated with a trip to the post office.

There are a huge number of racing competitions available; it really would take another book just to cover the UK variants. So if you're not sure what type of high-speed pursuit you'd like to try you could always hire a different car for every kind of race and chase available in one season, from a novice banger to a more serious Formula Ford car complete with pit crew.

Then once you've figured out which type of made-to-measure high-speed thrill fits you best just put your foot down and spank the hell out of it.

Hot Laps – Off Road in the Arctic Circle

So you've bought the supercar, been on a stunt-driving course, smashed up a banger or two and you're ready and waiting for the Russian spies to start chasing you. Unfortunately real life just doesn't work like that. Stuck in traffic again you know there's got to be more to driving than tailbacks and drive-time radio.

There is. Can you drive in a straight line? You can? Good. Can you drive in a straight line even if your car is pointing sideways? Or backwards? Or on the diagonal? It might sound impossible but you can learn.

From the air the Lapland area of northern Finland in the Arctic Circle is a wilderness connected to the commercial southern end of the country by one long tarmac road.

Zoom in a little to its northern end on to the small town of Saariselkä where you'll see the sun is coming out again and shaking off the heavy blanket of twenty-four-hour winter darkness. It's a town with a laid-back, friendly ski

resort where the beer is strong, the food hearty, the nights
long and the women lithe and healthy from all the cross
country skiing on their doorstep.

One hundred and sixty-nine kilometres of forest tracks
snake through a fantasy landscape more normally associated
with Christmas cards. Away from the town it's an unspoiled
pristine white populated only by animals and trees.

The snow is several feet deep in places, the roads are icy,
drifts common, but there are several cars and long-distance
haulage trucks on the road. How do they do it? How do
they keep moving in conditions that would bring a country
like Britain to a standstill? Unable to get to the corner shop
we'd all die of starvation. While the Finns would put their
snow boots on and pop out for a spot of ice sculpting.

Put simply they have the best driver training in the world;
they teach teenagers to power slide before they can pass
their driving test. The reason for this is that distances
between places and people can be so vast that if you don't
know how to really drive and you hit a sheet of ice in the
wilderness you're dead. That's why I've come to Lapland,
not for the huskies, skidoos and Santalands but to really
learn to drive.

So let's track a little way across town; that's right just
there towards the outskirts, over the highway and into the
forest. See the clearing up ahead? That's Saariselkä Action
Park, part of a former Test World facility designed to push
the limits of motoring in extreme conditions.

The first thing to catch your eye is the busy crosskart
track at the bottom left then the big 360° skid pan in the top
left, then over to the right there are two long tracks, one
made of snow and one made of ice.

Making its way along the snow track is a small red dot; as
you zoom in closer you catch a glimpse of forest on every

side and the rally tracks zigging and zagging through the trees. Zoom in really close now: it's a red Subaru WRX STi with full rally spec. The driver throws the back end out as it takes a sharp corner around a cone on the slalom track and pulls it back in line for the approaching u-turn.

Zoom in a final time to the interior of the car. Beneath the roll cage there's yours truly at the wheel and alongside me taking her turn as co-pilot another writer, a journalist, the uniquely named Minty Clinch. Time to put those stunt driving skills to the test.

Just before the cone I throw the car out away from the direction of turn and then quickly back in – a true Scandinavian flick. This throws the back end out and unbalances the car; as I bring the front end to face back down the track the back end flies round behind us adding power and weight to the turn. I anticipate the oversteer and start turning the wheel back out to counterbalance. It's at this point that both Minty and I look out of the right-hand window in the direction of travel. Janne 'Action Man' Ylimys, our ever-smiling Chief Instructor, has drilled into us that we must now drive the car in several directions at once not just forward so we need to be aware of what's around us and where we're travelling at all times.

To the right is the ice and snow wall that separates the two tracks. I think we're going to hit it. Then the back end settles on the new line we've turned into and we accelerate away for another run across the snow slalom.

But this is the easy part of the day; the slalom track is fairly wide and open. Janne wants to get us on the narrow forest track by night time.

On a normal road with good grip you turn the steering wheel and the car turns with it. However on the ice and snow that just doesn't happen, when you drive the car and turn the wheel it keeps going straight. That's what you have to master before you can increase the pace: driving the car in a straight line no matter which way it's actually facing.

A few slaloms and the occasional handbrake turn later Minty and I swap seats and I take a turn as co-pilot. It's a grand title at the moment; I'm little more than a passenger who occasionally tries to clarify the slippery nuances of the Scandinavian flick.

Then it's onwards to the skid pan. Janne shows us how it's done by power sliding a people carrier effortlessly round the entire circuit. Who knew you could do that? And that's what we have to master: driving the car sideways around a 360° central circle with ice walls behind us on the outside. On tarmac you can angle into the direction you want to go. On snow and ice it's a little different; you have to find that fine balance between throttle and steering, not too much, not too little, just enough to keep you moving. Oversteer and you're into the central wall of snow; understeer and you spin out into the icy wall.

In Britain we're taught to steer sensibly with hands at two and ten o'clock then feed the wheel through. But using that technique I'm doing an awful lot of tweaking to keep the car on a perfect circle. Janne says to do the opposite of what we've been taught, to use one or two hands to steer and in big arcs, hand over hand even, boy-racer style. Well okay then.

If anything it's a little like steering a boat: you turn slightly ahead of time and anticipate what's about to happen next. It works perfectly. And unlike a tarmac skid pan every time we nail it we get to spray snow at Janne as we pass him.

As you'd expect it's hard to gauge your speed when moving sideways as the speedo might read 20kph or a 100kph but depending on the momentum you've got going on the slide it could be anything in between. Janne said at one point we were moving sideways at about 80kph. But we barely noticed. He explained how counter-intuitively as the speed increases you have more time to think as everything happens in a kind of slow motion.

It's called time dilation. It's an experience common to athletes in 'the zone' or people in car accidents. It's the kind of advantage that allows professional footballers to make those spectacular runs that leave the defence standing still and F1 drivers to make death-defying overtakes on hairpin bends.

Sports psychologist Michael Sachs of Temple University in Philadelphia, Pennsylvania, has conducted an extensive 'flow state' study. He defined the experience of time dilation as 'an increased sense of well-being, an enhanced appreciation of nature and a transcendence of time and space'.

It's no wonder Janne keeps smiling. A lot of people would love his job. Anandamine, the tiny fatty acid that triggers the endorphin release associated with this psychological state, is the body's own version of THC, an opioid, as found in cannnabis. The subsequent dopamine release is one of the causes of runner's high and the feeling of time dilation. The most common cause of this particular dopamine release is risk. That explains so much, possibly even why many of us feel inexplicably happy behind the wheel of a fast car.

Yet rallying is not all about speed. Learning how to drive properly and then increasing the pace is key especially when it rains or snows. In F1 they either use a pace car or stop the race altogether but in rallying you push harder. And when your energy starts to flag the driving happens between your ears and the only contest is with yourself. For us the same rules apply and it's anything but a chore.

Back on the skid pan we're taught to slide in the same

circle but with a narrower track and half as much room to manoeuvre. Then in both directions we learn how to slide and turn back on ourselves in ever decreasing and tighter lines using the handbrake. Despite what Janne's told us about speed I keep trying to do the turn as fast as possible and hit it wide. It's only when I brake earlier and slow it right down that I turn on the spot and my speed increases, accelerating back out and into the sideways slide.

Once I have it I can't keep the smile off my face either. It's definitely addictive.

The temperature is a balmy −7°C but it does get down to −20° and occasionally −30°. At those temperatures you are driving blind, the tyres get hard and have no grip, and the bumpers become so rigid they're like glass. At −30° standing around outside can't be any fun for the instructor either.

But then the Finns are mad for it. As a country they hold more rally titles than the rest of the world. In the 1960s Stuart Turner of the British Motor Corporation (later British Leyland) decided to hire some of the bravest and best Finnish amateur drivers to push cars like the Mini and the Austin Healey to their limits and in the process the modern professional rally driver was born. The Flying Finns have dominated the rallying scene for four decades now and since it began in 1979 they've won the World Rally Championship fifteen times. Finnish rally stars have also brought fame and glory to Porsches, Saabs, Fords and Mitsubishis as well as giving us F1 several champions such as 2007's Kimi Räikkönen as well as Mika Häkkinen and Keke Rosberg. Finns are so crazy for racing of all kinds they'll charter two dozen planes just to attend F1 meets.

If you want to become an amateur rally driver the first things you need are enthusiasm, time and a local club to join. To become a professional rally driver you need skill and financial backing. The cars cost a lot to buy and maintain and should you land in a tree you'll have to buy a whole new car.

The Subaru we're driving has Monte Carlo rally tyres on its wheels, which are designed to tackle both tarmac roads and ice and snow. They're wide, slick tyres with studs and are seen on many rally-winning cars. If you ever watch the Monte Carlo Rally and see lots of drift they're probably using these tyres. They only get changed once or twice a season on the ice and snow. However Scandinavian rally tyres, which are narrow with long studs and give better grip than on tarmac, are often changed after every exercise and are liable to shred the ice to pieces.

And there is an exciting natural progression; while Minty and I are learning to drive in any direction, if you take it to the next level you learn to drive when the car is not even on the ground. 'You drive with the car and you jump with the car,' Janne says. 'Nobody is doing this normally.' But if you're a pro there is good reason to master these skills because on a professional rally circuit the road surface bucks like a roller coaster and you're driving flat out.

It's a hoot. And before long we are back on the snow track for a full length slalom with more runs, tighter turns and even closer to the snow wall. I've overwritten any sensible road habits with tyre-tearing rally skills, 'driving like he would', says Janne – the car's rear end flying out around corners as I keep the hammer down.

In driving terms I've gone from current champion Sebastian Loeb who drives direct-line races, 'quick like crazy', as Janne puts it, to the legendary Colin McRae who drove 'maximum sideways' and was a very special talent indeed. His basic speed was on an unbelievable level; he drove quicker sideways than all the other guys driving as straight as they could.

Of course those guys are sprinters by comparison and I'm the OAP on a Zimmer but I can dream.

As night falls Minty and I are given our first mock rally, going from the ice track round to the snow track. It's a different experience altogether and Janne wants to test us to see if we're good enough to hit the forest track with him as co-pilot.

Going as quick as I dare Minty calls the turns ahead of time. As I really am going as fast as I can and have to anticipate each turn I quickly discover that the co-pilot's input is invaluable. At speed if you had to assess each turn without prompting even with a rack of full-beam lights on the bonnet that illuminate the track ahead you'd be in a tree before you could say 'What's that green thing?'

The surfaces are also both very different. The car feels easier to control on ice but if you oversteer the results are harder to correct whereas on snow it feels more forgiving. This is what you learn about rallying; it's about feeling what the car is doing and knowing instinctively what to do next. Driving sideways through those turns is like throwing a motorbike through a corner but stopping short of having the back wheel smack you between the eyes.

By the time we've finished my general driving is pretty good but my 180° handbrake turns need work. Minty gets hers spot on but on the other hand finds the flicks harder to master. As always it's a case of build on your strengths and work hard on your weaknesses. As Janne says, 'It doesn't mean anything . . . you just have to be as good you can be and that's the way it goes.'

By the time Janne takes the co-pilot seat for the forest track and says, 'Give it to me,' I feel like I could drive all night. I take all the corners tight or long without destroying anything, speed uphill over humps and with great satisfaction swing the back end through a particularly tight corner. I'm hyper-focused and hyper-thrilled. 'You were doing hot laps,' Janne says at the end and of course I immediately want more. He obliges and shows me how he does it. He's far less polite than I am and hammers the Subaru round the corners at speed, grazing snow walls and pushing it as hard as he can. It's a revelation. I'm almost there but just a little too concerned about the well-being of the car.

I instantly want to come back and show that I can do the same. I want to learn to do that on a forest road without snow walls and I want to learn to drive a car when it's jumping in the air. That goes for Minty as well. We swear blind that we'll be back for the three day course next season.

But as we pull back from this snow-swept landscape and adrenalin-fuelled night you can rest assured that these skills aren't just window dressing. Little did I know that within a week I'd be using them on British roads. As I whizzed around the country in a hired van moving house and office a snowstorm hit Britain that saw babies born in trapped cars, the gritters run out of grit and the southern end of the country skip work for about half a week.

Gunning the van out of a service station on the M54, an articulated lorry hit a patch of ice and began to slide back towards me. I hit the brakes and was forced to steer across the same patch of ice covered in a thin layer of snow.

But I got to keep my rental deposit. Who knew you could drive a transit van sideways?

On the Water

Have you ever dreamed of owning a boat that's bigger than a dinghy? Of being the highest of high rollers on your super yacht, running drugs on your powerboat or escaping the rat race as you sail round the world? Well it's yours to be had.

The Super Yacht

Let's start at the top. If you're a made man with a billion or two in the bank then your 'yacht', if you can ever call a small floating town a yacht, will be anything but humble. Take Saudi prince Al-Waleed bin Talal bin Abdul Aziz Al Saud, nephew of Saudi Arabia's late King Fahd, and his mega yacht the *Kingdom K5R*. This imposing craft is usually moored off Antibes near Monaco and Cannes. If you ever see it you may recognise it as the *Flying Saucer* from the Bond film *Never Say Never Again*. It was originally built by Italian firm M&B Benetti for Adnan Khashoggi and named *Nabila* after his daughter. The original spec included 3 elevators, a 12-seat cinema, 2 saunas, a swimming pool, a disco, jacuzzi, billiard room and it had 11 guest rooms with hand-carved onyx bathroom fixtures along with gold-plated door knobs and a master suite of 4 rooms, the bathroom of which had a solid gold sink. It nearly bankrupted its builders.

When Khashoggi famously hit financial trouble Donald Trump picked it up at the bargain price of £15 million, gave it an $8 million refurb and renamed it the *Trump Princess*. When he in turn hit the financial doldrums the Saudi king's nephew snapped it for an undisclosed sum, but its initial asking price has been reported as $30 million for the boat and $55 million for all the luxury extras and equipment. Since then it's also had a couple of multimillion-dollar upgrades. But as one of the largest shareholders in News Corp, Time Warner, Motorola, Apple Computers, Canary Wharf, Disneyland Paris, Saks, Walt Disney, Four Seasons and Citigroup, he can afford it.

But if that doesn't float your boat you could always downgrade to former Iraqi dictator Saddam Hussein's 269-foot super yacht, which at the time of writing was going for the knock-down price of €23 million. However according to an

Iraqi government adviser his playboy yacht is so lavish that even the Russian mafia find it too kitsch. Even with a highly practical secret passage running the length of the ship, mini-submarine pod and full medical operating theatre for those little emergencies . . .

Still these older models are quickly being overtaken by a new breed of designs like those crafted by Ken Freivokh who prefers sleek high-performance super yacht designs that look more like alien mother-ships or stealth bombers than mere yachts. He will of course make you a traditional ketch or schooner as well; it won't be like any ketch you've ever seen but at least it'll have sails.

Still if you don't have a continent-sized current account able to handle a bespoke super yacht a modest £2 million–£5 million is all you need for an off-the-shelf, made-to-measure super boat from a desirable manufacturer like Sunseeker or Maoira.

As in the high end of the car market, fractional ownership is becoming more common. Why outlay for a boat, crew, mooring and transfers for an entire year when you can use it for the days you want at a fraction of the cost and minus the management headaches?

A Life Aboard

For many it's not about how much money you spend it's about a passion for the sea, a chance to see the world or living how you want to live.

Dream It

Every year hundreds of people sell up, buy a boat and set off either on a mission to see the world or just to take some time to enjoy life before it's gone. If you look online at the many crewing agencies you'll find plenty of skippers who've taken the plunge and now need crew. Want to spend three years sailing round every island in the Pacific from Thailand to the Polynesian Islands then Hawaii? It's yours for the asking. How about joining one man's voyage of discovery as he sets off around South America or tooling up to take a yacht through the more pirate-infested areas of the Indian Ocean?

You can volunteer for an organised race like Clipper Round the World where teams of normal, everyday people race ten clippers across five different continents and 35,000 miles. Or hop aboard an event boat like the biofueled powerboat *Earthrace*. It set a new world record for powered circumnavigation and as I write needs volunteer crew for its promotional tour.

Alternatively you can just sell up and buy something that will get you where you want to go. Unlike super yachts ocean-going yachts start at tens of thousands of pounds not millions. One way or another you can go anytime you want. Just decide to do it and seize the opportunities that arise.

Work it

Of course perhaps you don't have tens of thousands in the bank. Well never fear: there are even more ways to get on the water. If you've ever wanted that millionaire lifestyle without having the millions then one of the best ways is to take a job as a mate on a large yacht and work your way up to captain. Your earnings should start high and only get higher. Wages will be tax free of course. Uniforms and room and board are also thrown in. And as the owners of super yachts rarely spend time on them – no they're making the money to pay for them instead – you can enjoy what they can't: sunshine, foreign travel, young women in bikinis. Have I put you off yet?

According to www.superyachtuk.com a junior captain on a smaller super yacht (less than 30 metres) could expect a salary of between £3,500 and £5,500 per month. With more experience captains on medium-sized super yachts (30–50 metres) should expect between £4,500 and £7,000 per month. Very experienced senior captains on large super yachts (more than 50 metres) can expect to make between £6,000 and upwards of £10,000 per month, rising to £15,000 per month in exceptional circumstances. That's more than most investment bankers make and with a better lifestyle and perks. And all you need to wedge your foot in the door is a basic safety training course then work your way up through the qualifications.

If a life under sail sounds more appealing then a world of yacht deliveries, charters or racing awaits as long as you build up your hours either through volunteer crewing at your local club or by taking some training.

The Practical Man

Of course you can also work as a deckhand, engineer, boat-yard manager or any other role that requires trade skills. With those skills you could also turn your hand to a house-boat in the city. Think less wandering sea gypsy and more plush urban loft as popularised by Nick Cave with his Chelsea houseboat or Damien Hirst with his. Depending on mooring fees houseboats can make living in a modern metropolis like London far more affordable and fun. But do your research: if you moor next to Tower Bridge it's going to cost you a lot more than say Kew Gardens. It is definitely the romantic's option and that's no bad thing. Boat choices range from traditional narrow boats, which can be snapped up for mere thousands, to purpose-built static houseboats and spacious sea-going barges that can be refurbed and turned into floating penthouse apartments. Pick up a good mooring and the basic boat value effectively triples. Keep your boat seaworthy and you can even weigh anchor, motor across the Channel or the North Sea and find a berth in Paris or Amsterdam if you fancy a change of scene.

Powerboats

Boats can affirm your status as a financial player, liberate you from your old life and give you options far removed from the suburban humdrum. But in keeping with the modern gentleman's penchant for adrenalin let's tap a vein and ask a question. What goes faster than most supercars, costs less than an average family saloon and is one of the most accessible ways into powerboating?

Thundercats – 'Big Dicks and Psycho Chicks'

No not the animated TV series but the entry-level powerboat grade that anyone can enter. Alongside the quay at a recent Motorshow in London's Excel Centre – more usually the home of power slides, supercars and all the latest marques – there were a few super yacht manufacturers touting for business among the City bonus buyers. Next to them were Thundercat Racing UK in what appeared to be a small Bedouin tent. On the pontoon were several rigid inflatables that looked like the safety boats I used to muck about on as a teen.

But there's a big difference between these deceptively fast inflatable racing machines and a normal monohull rib. Descended from South African lifeguard boats they have lightweight catamaran tunnel type hulls and a 50hp outboard that gives them roughly the same power to weight ratio as an F1 car. They are designed to be raced in extreme surf, raging rivers and any other condition where a normal boat would flounder.

There are two classes of racing: the P750 Standard and the P750 Blueprint. The engines of the first class use standard factory-made engines with rev limiters while the Blueprint class are allowed to remove them.

When Fiona Pascoe, the event organiser behind Thundercats, asked if I wanted to have a go . . . well what do you think I said?

So imagine hitting 0–60 in around three seconds; now imagine it on water and not slowing down on a 90° corner. Using the hand holds, handles and ropes on the inside of the boat my job as co-pilot was to throw my weight around to keep us stable. If it's calm and flat then the tiller man and co-pilot both have to get their weight over the back of the boat on the straight and then for corners and waves it's forward over the front of the boat for me and hang on for dear life. There are no electrical gizmos to make life easier: it's white-knuckle action that turns heads even at car shows.

As you don't get many waves in south-east London I didn't experience the exhilaration or terror as the boat rears up and launches off a steep wave. But it's easy to see how it could quickly become addictive. Imagine riding in a motorcycle sidecar race but with faster acceleration and on a log flume with sharper turns than a roller coaster and you're getting somewhere close to how it feels.

As an entire boat package can be picked up from as little as £2500 used, brand new hulls for £3400 and a complete race-ready package for less than £8k, it's also one of the cheapest ways to get your adrenalin fix on the water and enter the world of powerboat racing.

Due to its low cost, sponsorship is also easier to obtain particularly when the events are televised on Sky Sports and broadcast throughout the world.

Over the years it has become a popular sport in the southern hemisphere with major events in Australia, New Zealand and South Africa. The UK is now set to become the fourth major player.

If offshore racing is the ultimate goal it's also the best way to learn to race using your head and skills rather than your chequebook.

Trust me; you'll be scraping the grin off the inside of your helmet by the end of your first race. You can then move up to Thunderbolt Racing, a monohull series that also has two grades: first the E900 standard class with 16-foot production hulls, 90hp engines and 50mph speeds. Then once you've left clear water behind you it's up to the E1500 High-Octane grade using 18–20-foot hulls and single 150hp outboards reaching speeds of 70mph plus.

P1 – Offshore Powerboat Racing

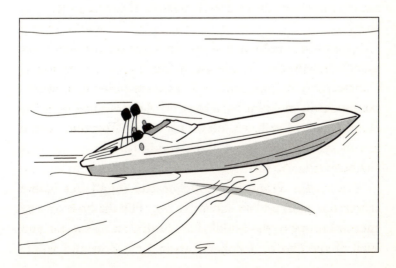

The growl of the Apache powerboat's engines is like listening to the devil gargle with sulphur. As we head out of the Portimão harbour on Portugal's Algarve for a test run in the open-topped Supersport boat the untapped aggression builds up in the two 900hp engines behind us and struggles to break free.

Once past the harbour walls the beast is unleashed. Cue the loud rock soundtrack and aerial helicopter shots as the throttle man pushes forward on the large chrome levers and the helmsman steers us towards the biggest wave he can find. We take off, there's a breathless moment and then slam down hard over the first wave and hit with a bang on the next but the boat doesn't seem to have slowed down. I know from watching the previous day's racing that from the outside it doesn't look so hard. But unlike a car there's no suspension on water: from the inside each landing is like a pleasurable punch on the nose.

Glenn Chidzoy, the throttle man, pushes the speed up even further as a wide area of sea opens up ahead. Matt Dix, the wheel man, takes that as his cue to hunt for the biggest set of waves he can find and then it's throttle up to meet them.

I just have to hold on and try not to get thrown out as the giant boat launches off another wave.

After a few heavy hits the varying pattern of waves coming at us makes it hard to control the landing of the v-shaped hull. Matt has a job on his hands. Together he and Glenn synchronise speed and steering to take us through the busy Atlantic surf.

You need a certain force of character for P1; it's both a dangerous sport and an expensive one. Flip the boat on a P1 race in Europe or the Middle East or drive it up the harbour wall at the end of a Poker Run in Key West and you're either breathing saltwater, on fire or a stain. 'We're all on the edge,' Martin Sanborn, former champion throttle man and current P1 commentator, told me, and as he normally seems calm, politely spoken and easy-going I have to take this statement seriously. 'We know it's dangerous as heck, I mean I've lost friends . . . I've been upside down at 90 . . . not something I ever want to do again.'

There are two classes of race in the P1 competition: there's the Supersport category for standard open-topped production boats between 33 foot and 42 foot in length. Usually twin engined they're powerful boats that can easily do over 100mph but in competition they're limited to 85mph to level the playing field and ensure the speeds aren't, as Sanborn put it, 'catastrophic'.

This is the same as the boat we've been bouncing around on, which eventually we have to turn around and take back in so that the racing can start.

As we head for harbour after a good soaking and less than gentle beating Glenn tells me about one of Apache Powerboat's commissions. There have been various rumours flying around the P1 campfire and he confirms that they're building a 52-foot boat with three monstrous triple 1200 engines for an unnamed client with business interests on the Black Sea. It doesn't have the usual sparkly boat name of the owner's girlfriend or their daughter's first pony. Oh no it's called *Cold War*.

And that is the thing about offshore powerboating: it's a scene that involves large amounts of cash, international travel, beautiful women and plenty of intrigue. Especially since so many of the American powerboat manufacturers and racers are based in Florida. From the late eighties on many racers and boat manufacturers were lured there by easy drug money and big adventure. In 1987 Peter Kerr wrote in a piece for the *New York Times*, 'It may be Florida's most profitable and illegal sport: a 50-mile dash past high-speed Government patrol boats, helicopters and balloons to smuggle marijuana and cocaine to the American shore.'

Then came the high-profile murder of Don Aranow, the godfather of modern powerboat racing who founded many of the early races, teams and boat builders and sold them on. His biggest success was the Cigarette, which gave him worldwide fame and is still a generic term used for any large, high powered speed vessel.

His wealthy and powerful friends in both legitimate and illegitimate business circles included mobster Meyer Lansky and former US President George H. W. Bush. He sold boats to King Hussein of Jordan, 'Baby Doc' Duvalier in Haiti and another former US President, Lyndon Johnson, who used them to race his secret service staff in theirs.

The apocryphal story surrounding Aranow's death says that he first built boats for the drug smugglers that could outrun the US Coast Guard then foolishly he built even faster boats for the Coast Guard that could catch the smugglers. As revenge they blasted him off this mortal coil.

That story is still strong on the circuit even though rival boat builder Barry Kramer was eventually arrested for his murder. Kramer's own story grabbed attention when he attempted a daring escape in which a helicopter flew into his Miami prison yard and whisked him away. Unfortunately so many other prisoners tried to climb aboard on the way out that it snagged on the barbed wire fence and crashed, putting him straight back inside.

It's easy to see why these stories still permeate the offshore racing world. Poker runs are still one of the main forms of competition in the US. Competitors race past staging posts and at each one are given a sealed envelope with a playing card in it. After five stages whoever has the best hand wins. But as Sanborn explained, 'They make a big point of telling us it's not a race. But you get two guys sat side by side in a fast boat and there's a race going on whether you want to call it a race or not.'

In Europe at least the characters are more refined. They tend to be self made men like P1 founder Asif Rangoonwala whose firm supplies half of all baked goods in the UK. But the racing hasn't changed: it's still bad to the bone, fast, furious, edge-of-the-seat action and ambitious Asif is busy trying to make the P1 competition the third pillar of motor sport after F1 and the World Rally for cars and MotoGP for bikes. As it's the fastest growing offshore series in the world he may do just that.

Next category up is the Evolution class where the speeds are faster, up to 110mph, and the boats can be any size from 36 to 43 feet in length. The modified production or proto-type boats all have a canopy over the cockpit. To keep the field even between light and nippy and heavy and powerful boats, all craft are restricted to 1hp per 3.5kg. As the differ-ence between them can be the weight of about twenty people this really makes the race.

As you'd expect modified boats don't come cheap and Evolution attracts big financial hitters from all over the world. 'Just the boat on a trailer was a million dollars,' Nigel Hook from the Lucas Oil Racing Team said. 'You get two spare engines for that.' Factor in a crew of seven or more, another seventy-five grand or so for a fully kitted truck, support vehicles and the costs certainly mount up: $4 million a year operating costs for some teams. You'd get change from your super yacht if you decided to part-ex but it's definitely a rich man's game.

So what keeps them coming back year on year to race in machines that face up to 8Gs of vertical g-force similar to those experienced by a fighter pilot but on rough seas?

'You try to master it,' Hook says, 'but it's like a never-ending journey to master these boats where you're going through the water and through the air . . . it's a continual challenge. It's not like you've raced on this track before like in Daytona. Every stretch of water is different every time you go out.'

And with international teams racing all over the world, he says, 'It's more like the Olympics; we're competing not only to win but representing our country.'

P1 is even going green. According to Hook, because Asif Rangoonwalla is buying trees by the acre to offset P1's carbon footprint it could even be considered 'a carbon-neutral sport'.

And why the hell not? A little extra thought and everyone's a winner. But whether it's green or not what's certain, Sanborn told me, is that 'it's a real aggressive sport . . . You're out there pushing in water that the average person would say "Are you insane?" And we're generally saying "Go go go" as opposed to saying "Ease up."'

So whether you crave high performance, high spend or high adventure there's a lot of life to be lived on an ocean wave. How you do it is up to you.

Live Fast, Die Old – How to Ride a Motorbike

With motorbikes you either fall into the 'What's the point?' or 'When can I get one?' category. But whichever side of the Marmite-covered toast you like to lick it's undeniable that popular culture is filled with generation-defining motorbike icons: from Marlon Brando rescuing his girl in *The Wild One* and Steve McQueen leaping fences to escape the Germans to the young Che Guevara crashing into cows or Tom Cruise's explosive motorbike battle in *Mission Impossible II*. Of course there's also the mods riding to Brighton in *Quadrophenia* and the truly legendary *Easy Rider* opening scene where Dennis Hopper and Peter Fonda head out on the highway on their badass choppers. These icons endure because those who ride bikes are always seen as out of the ordinary and willing to go out there and get it. All it takes is one twist of the accelerator.

Learning to Ride

I'm upside down, my eyes are shut and I'm flying through the air. It's only my first day on a motorbike and I've already had an accident. Luckily it's on the training grid at Silverstone race track where the British School of Motoring (BSM) are teaching me to ride at their new trackside school.

Unfortunately the unglamorous flying position is my own stupid fault. I haven't been listening to what my instructors have been saying. I dawdled over a gear change, accelerated and hit the back brake at the same time as making a turn. That's enough for the rear end to slide out, the front wheel to lock and throw me from the little Suzuki Van Van I've been riding. That and the rain on the tarmac.

There's a moment while I'm upside down where everything is black and I realise that the worst has now happened. That I've messed up. That it was inevitable. It's the big dark cloud that hangs over motorcycling that concerned mothers, wives, fathers and the media usually terrorise us with to protect us from ourselves. The fear of death.

But during that dark tumbling moment of time dilation I feel truly liberated. The book is over, no more deadlines, life is over, no more birthdays to forget and then apologise for, but then no laughter with friends either. Damn them they were all right, I was all wrong. That makes me some kind of fool.

Then I hit the ground. Then the bike hits me. I'm guessing at about – I didn't have time to check the speedo – a relatively sedate 20ish mph. There's a moment of shock. I don't know what else to do so I open my eyes and look over to Will and Andy, my two instructors. Will breaks into a run as

I get to my feet. But I'm okay, nothing is broken and the helmet protected my head. Andy strolls over.

'You all right?'

'I think so.'

'You're standing anyway. It's when you don't get up you have to worry. Do you want to go again?'

Despite the shakes I hop back on and ride a few circuits to work the adrenalin off. There are a few aches and pains but more importantly there's another fear overcome. One I'll learn many lessons from. I hope.

The naysayers were wrong after all. Falling off a suicycle didn't kill me. I came off my mountain bike a few years earlier at around the same speed and did far more damage than bouncing on concrete with protective gear and a sturdy helmet.

The one thing I've learned on this job more than anything else is that for anything vaguely dangerous whether it's skydiving, motorcycling or S&M proper training and practice minimise any risks and make everything a lot safer.

Silverstone is the home of British motor sport and on the fast-track direct access course you have a choice of Suzuki, Kawasaki, Ducati or Harley Davidson to learn on. The training really doesn't get much better. As Andy says, where else can you walk into your office and find Damon Hill flipping through your brochures?

And apart from my embarrassing little bounce the first day's off road training brought me up to speed on setting off, changing gear, u-turns, turns out of a junction, slow clutch control through a series of cones and figures of eight, although with its low power the slow clutch is unsatisfying on the small bike. The reason for these drills will become apparent as soon as you hit the bigger bikes but for the moment it is back to riding round the paddock. I know it's

essential – walk before you can run – but it's like being a
small child kept in on a beautiful day. Let me out already!

By the following morning it's a proper cold start to the
British winter and I'm a little anxious. Back on the bike I feel
vulnerable and exposed but lesson well and truly learned.

There is also a new instructor, Mark. With back-up from
Will they take me out for an evaluation and apart from my
u-turns everything looks good. However since the bounce
the aches and pains on my right side make it agonising to
hold the bike steady in the turn.

But after a solid morning's riding my fears are gone. I've
paid attention to my instructors' cues over the helmet mics
and navigated roundabouts, junctions and country lanes. If
I could have made the little 125 go fast enough we would
even have hit the speed limit.

It's immediately addictive: bikes are far more primal than
cars even the little ones, and I can't wait to change up.
Despite what most people who don't ride believe, smaller
bikes just aren't as safe on the road. The bigger the bike is
the more stable, more controllable and easier to ride it
becomes. Even though I've grown fond of the little Van Van
with its fat back tyre and California Highway Patrol styling
I can barely get it up to 60mph, clinging to it on a busy road
as it wobbles between my knees is unsettling.

So if an instructor ever tells you he's happy for you to
have a compulsory basic training certificate (CBT) and
happy for you to trade up to a bigger bike, you'll have that
Christmas-has-come sensation too.

The six-speed, four-stroke, liquid-cooled Suzuki Bandit
650 has way more grunt; it cruises between 3000–4000 rpm
and redlines at 12,500 rpm. With the bigger engine, 240kg
weight and easy power delivery you also have to use the
clutch a lot more. There's a satisfying 'Aha!' moment when

all the slow control drills on the smaller bike suddenly make sense – if you're not in control of the clutch you're on your back or into the wall – and my understanding falls quickly into place.

The Bandit easily hits the speed limit. On my first 70mph on the dual carriageway it feels totally secure except for my visor, which I'd left up. The side wind from two articulated lorries whipped the open helmet around, shaking my head like a rag doll's. It didn't worry the bike though and we cruised easily past.

To reach up and pull the visor down on my first overtake seemed one move too far but when you ignore the jangling nerves and take that first tentative hand off the handlebar, you realise how stable the machine really is.

Unfortunately the weight that provides the stability was still too much in the u-turns. To my utter humiliation I drop the Bandit once on the training grid and once on a quiet country road, both times at full lock. The bike lands heavily on my foot due to a combination of not enough power, too little clutch control and lack of confidence that my injured right side could hold the weight.

And when the heavier bike goes down there's no stopping it. The front brake handle snapped and my foot hurt like hell from the impact. With the injuries from the previous day and the ones I'd already picked up on the job (see intro) I was beginning to feel more than a little beaten.

Mainly because if I messed up the u-turn during the test it was an instant fail. At a certain age you expect to learn things quickly and effectively. You learn to shut off the argumentative, whiny little boy inside and listen to what your instructors are telling you. Despite myself I was frustrated. You see once you get a taste of the simple freedom a motorbike grants you really don't want to fail.

There's a moment when you're travelling along at speed where your relationship with the road and the landscape around you changes. For me it was at the speed limit on a country lane as I took the right line for a series of corners. The manoeuvres had nearly all become unconscious by that stage. The engine noise faded into the background as I opened the throttle and my centre of gravity became one with the bike. As we glided effortlessly through the curves the machine disappeared beneath me.

It's all focus, all the time. Totally in the zone, no worries about the outside world, nothing but seeing into the future as you anticipate the next corner and lean into it then the next and the next. With the sun on your cheek and the crisp winter air keeping you alert that is living properly. My injuries seem like the temporary annoyances they are. After all bones heal, bruises fade.

By the second day of riding on the big bikes I've got my road-riding technique down and in the afternoon we work on my weak points one by one and familiarise ourselves with the roads around Kettering where I'll have my test in two days' time.

As long as I get those u-turns nailed it shouldn't be a problem. My general road riding is pretty good but it's about to get a whole lot better. By the end of the afternoon both Mark and I are frozen despite thermals, neck warmers and big thick winter gloves. To the point where I'm growling inside my helmet to ward off the cold settling into my fingers.

We decide to head back to Silverstone but on the way back through Northampton we enter a twilight zone in Middle England: every time we take the turn for the A43, which will take us back to Silverstone, the roads take us north, south, west, anywhere but where we're supposed to be. After several frustrating attempts to escape the Northampton vortex we pull over and call base to find out what the hell is going on.

We soon find out the signs on the roundabouts are down – it's the reason we keep missing the junction. It's been getting noticeably colder on the side of the road and then the cold turns to a hard, sleeting snow. By the time we're back on our bikes it's coming down thick and fast and so is the rush-hour traffic. There's not even enough space to weave our way through. I'm also learning very fast that if I want to see I've got to wipe my visor down with the soft leather back of the glove. Cars are a doddle they really are.

Then as we reach the outskirts and roads that we recognise the snow settles so quickly on my visor that it's turning to ice and the heat from my body is causing the inside to steam up.

If I push the visor all the way up at speed the icy flakes hit me straight in the eye making it impossible to see. I settle for somewhere in between.

As we hit the A road I have to constantly wipe both inside the visor and the outside at the same time. I'm effectively riding one-handed and although it's an A road, because of the diminishing visibility and the heavy build-up of snow my speed never makes the limit. It drops quickly to 45mph then 35mph and then Mark says to pull on to a B road. A single file of traffic is safer than three lanes of trucks and cars in low twilight visibility. Our speed drops to 25, the cold is gnawing into my bones and I'm shouting at it to keep myself moving. I feel like I'm going too slow but then the cars around us are moving just as slowly trying not to slide.

On the first day I'd asked Will, does anyone ride in snow? He'd said, 'I tried it once and with all that ice hiding underneath I can't recommend it. My advice would be: just don't do it.'

I keep cursing the world around me. Then as we enter the village of Roade Mark tells me calmly to pull into the next service station. When we climb off the bikes we are both shocked to see that the snow has settled on us and the bikes even though we've been moving the whole time.

We won't be going anywhere. We wait inside to be picked up by a heated Land Rover. The bikes stay there.

The roads are so bad the following day I can't even escape the village where I'm staying so I miss a day's training and it's straight into the test the following day. My u-turns still suck and I put my foot down during the test u-turn to compensate for an adverse camber on the road. Instant fail. Although the rest of the test is absolutely fine. The examiner says he would have let the bike drop. Personally I think that's over the top and completely unsafe when a tap of the foot will suffice but hey sour grapes right?

A few weeks later I'm back for one last day of training with Ray, a new and hairier instructor, who maxes me out on the u-turn drills as my right side still hasn't healed properly. It's all about clutch control and thank god we did practise because the road the examiner takes me on this time is even tighter. I just make it round without putting my foot down and it's a pass even though my general riding was worse that time. Go figure.

Over celebratory tea and biscuits I ask laid back Ray why he started riding. Evel Knievel, stuntman extraordinaire of course. I'd forgotten about him. An icon to our age group thanks to a wind up plastic toy with a smiling face that when you let rip would fly across the living room, over park benches and water features and usually into trouble.

In real life Knievel, a 'crazy son of a bitch from Butte, Montana', jumped his motorcycle 151 feet over the fountains at Caesars Palace in Las Vegas, crashed into the asphalt on the other side and destroyed his body in front of 15,000 spectators and millions on TV. Everyone talked about it. After twenty-nine days spent close to death in hospital he told the world that not only was he going to walk again he was going to jump the Grand Canyon as well. When he found out it was too wide he jumped the mile-wide Snake River Canyon in Idaho on a rocket-powered bike instead. He never made it to the other side but he did survive.

And in a funny way when you pass your test you feel a little like that smiling Evel Knievel figurine: wound up and raring to go. I mean now you really get to play. Ask what's next? Which bike do you choose? And which bike-riding friends you call and say, 'So where are we going then?' The canyons can wait.

What Next?
It used to be that if you were a biker you were either one of those hairy Harley-riding gentleman of the road – a Hell's Angel – or a scooter boy on a Vespa. But thankfully these days not everyone needs such brand specific tribes to be into bikes. The range of bikes and owners is now extremely diverse. You've got weekend track racers and road warriors, environmentally friendly Piaggio and Vectrix scooter owners, for suburban semi-dwellers Goldwing tourers, classic bike builders, speedway stars and, thanks to the likes of Ted Simon, Charley Boorman and Ewan McGregor, the latest and greatest development for my money at least, adventure biking.

How Far Can You Go?

If like me you have permanently itchy feet, get bored by airports and holiday resorts and have just got your licence you might be keen to turn your wheels to something a little more life changing than the daily commute.

Why not work out which trip of a lifetime to take? Maybe it'll be north to south of the Americas or a shorter hop to North Africa to start with; perhaps one day the more troublesome Marco Polo route. The world is an open road and where it isn't that won't necessarily stop you either. But there are a few things to consider before you go.

Be Prepared

Just like a Boy Scout you need to think ahead: what type of bike will you ride, what type of ride will you face? Will you travel alone or with companions? In his excellent book *Adventure Motorcycling*, Robert Wicks says, 'Preparing well in advance for any overland adventure is where half the battle is won – get it right here and the chances of something going wrong on the trip can be reduced significantly.' So along with the right attitude for long rides, hardship and flexible living, will you need sponsorship, be self-financed or part of an organised group?

The type of trip you'll take also determines whether you'll need further training. Passing your test may be essential to ride on British roads but it's not the only thing you'll need. If you're travelling to remote areas you'll need language skills even bushcraft and survival skills for truly remote places. A bike maintenance course would be handy as well as basic all round physical fitness so you can pick that heavily laden bike up again when you inevitably drop it.

Type of Bike

Unlike your average road bike you have to be a lot more picky about your choice for your trip as there is no one machine that suits all conditions perfectly although most manufacturers do offer some kind of adventure, off-road or touring option these days. The market leaders are BMW with the R1150GS and 1200 models made famous and proven by the *Long Way Round* and *Long Way Down* trips. KTM would be the next most successful adventure manufacturer but all offer something, from the Kawasaki world traveller, the KLR 650, to the Suzuki V-Strom DL 1000 for more road based trips. Bikes like the Benelli Tre-K Amazonas are good for extended off-road trips and rally-tested models for long-distance dune bashing. If you want machines that you can maintain yourself then opt for slightly older or less technical models. Whichever style of machine you opt for, before you set out, Wicks says, 'You will need as much time with your new best friend as possible.' So get riding.

You'll also need to factor in budgeting, navigation and route planning, transportation costs, customs documents (carnets), insurance, emergency preparation, visas, money and communication.

If that all sounds a lot then that's because it is but when the view from your office could be the jungles of the Darien Gap or the breathtaking scenery of the Himalayas, your next networking event a yak's milk with Mongolian tribesmen or a samba with a Carnival dancer in Rio, you might think a two-week, two-month or two-year trip well worth all the planning.

How Fast Can You Go?

Let's not pretend: most people who like bikes also like to twist their right hand, open up the throttle as wide as they can and test the manufacturer's claims. So what else is available to you that is fast, fun and won't leave you as a stain on the tarmac?

Racing

If you want to be the next Valentino Rossi or Barry Sheene then you've got to start somewhere. First it's worth seeing if you like racing by sampling a track day at Silverstone or Brand's Hatch. If you do the next step is to join a local club, buy a race bike, set up a race bank account and start racing. It is by all accounts extremely addictive and if you're any good at it then hopefully someone will spot you and sponsor your passion. Brian Moore, the ex-England rugby international, recently described in the *Daily Telegraph* how he was hooked the moment he got his knee down on the tarmac. 'That sounds like nothing,' he said, 'but it was genuinely as thrilling as running out at Twickenham.'

There are more types of racing out there than you can wiggle a victory wheelie at. You can go for off-road thrills with trial bikes, motocross and rallying. Or on-track high-performance thrills with superbike championships, Supermoto, Hypermoto, Motosix or even MotoGP, where heroes like Rossi, Agostini and Sheene are made on purpose built racing prototypes from the world's leading manufacturers.

Let's not forget drag racing, legal road racing and the legendary Isle of Man TT races. Or for that matter quad bikes and skidoos, which have their own championships in Quad Motorcross and Snowcross. Just having a licence in your pocket opens up all kinds of possibilities. In Finland recently local guides were willing to take another biker and myself off road through that country's beautiful Arctic back country on a skidoo. Steering one of those beasts at 100kph through forest and several feet of snow at night is something altogether different.

Speedway

This is a unique form of two-wheeled racing with worldwide barnstorming appeal. At any given race two teams compete against each other on bikes that have no brakes and standardised single-cylinder 500cc engines with fixed gears that do 0–60 faster than F1 cars. The only way to control the speed is to power-slide round the corners. And those engines run on pure alcohol (methanol fuel) not petrol. Build or buy a bike, join a club and start racing.

The number of championships and categories is truly bewildering so if high-speed thrills are your thing get a bike. You'll be spoiled for choice.

How to Outrun Anybody . . . the Good Guys or the Bad Guys

There's a T-shirt doing the rounds that shows how motorcycling man has evolved. In the first frame he's hunched over a sports bike like Neanderthal man; he needs the speed. In the middle frame he's sitting a little more upright on a street bike. By the time we get to the final frame he's sitting upright on a long-range cruiser like a Goldwing. But even though that's usually how it happens (would you say no to heated grips in winter?) there is always going to be a need for speed whether you're trying to outrun the cops, the ex (again) or an angry Hell's Angel. Now track days are clearly the most sensible ways to experience speed and if you want to race that's where you need to go. But if you want to win a chase that's a different matter. This is what you need to know.

What Are You Riding?

If you are a hairy Angel then unless you're riding a sportster (which I know you all think are girly), something suitably modified or have some nitrous oxide strapped on, you're screwed. Most chopped-up bikes don't have the manoeuvrability to outrun anything other than a mod on a scooter. Don't believe it? Try taking a sharp turn with extended forks at high speed. No if you're going to ride and win then you need something fast and manoeuvrable. Any of the higher-end sports bikes should do the trick.

Is There a Helicopter Near By?

Hard to tell until the chase is on. But most often there won't be despite what you see on TV, first they have to get it up in the air and over to where you're running. So if you get away from your pursuers pull over, stash your bike and blend in with the crowd.

What Are the Local Laws?

It's a question you might not have thought of. But depending on where you are in the world you might not get chased at all. Many police departments now have a 'no chase' policy. What this means is that unless you are an escaping felon or a 'crime in progress' they'll let you go whatever speed you're doing. Why? Well simply because a chase often causes more problems than just leaving a speeding rider be. In the US this varies from state to state. In some states they are liable to jump on their bikes and chase after you at high speed. In the land of health and safety that could be a whole 80mph but here in Britain twenty-two-year-old Michael James Collins from Beckenham in Kent hit 140mph when a police rider chased him. Which begs the next question.

How Good are Your Skills?

The law won't always favour you. When asked if he'd implement a no-chase policy one American police chief said he'd rather stick with his current policy of 'Chase 'em to the ends of hell.'

Police riders also have well-maintained, high-spec bikes and the skills to match. The chase with Collins lasted more than fifteen minutes despite his repeated attempts to shake off his pursuer. You can watch the full video on www.motorcyclenews.com and if you don't think you could win a race at your local track what makes you think you could on the road?

Basic Stunt Skills

How to Get Your Knee Down

Scraping your knee on the tarmac as you turn into a bend is supposed to help you take a tighter, more accurate line on a corner in a race. Even if that's a modern motorcycling myth it does make you feel more confident and looks super cool. So here's how.

- First get some knee sliders then take your time and do this over several attempts. Don't worry about keeping up with your mate's progress; learn at your own speed.
- Find a corner that you can take in second to third gear, preferably on a race track otherwise a medium-sized roundabout on, ahem, a 'private' road . . .
- Warm up your tyres with a few laps.
- Have your weight over both pegs and a relaxed body position.

- As you lean into the corner favour your body weight slightly more over the top peg as this will help you pull out of the turn.
- Always keep the balls of your feet on both pegs.
- Slide one butt cheek off the seat into the corner and let your knee hang out a little way. Not too much or you'll mess up your balance.
- Start your runs slowly and gradually increase your speed with each run; as your speed increases you'll lean over further until eventually your knee touches down.
- That's it. If your foot pegs grind tarmac then you're already at the right angle and you need to adjust your body or knee position. Don't rush it, take your time, have fun.

How to Pull a Wheelie

Okay these are easy just as long as you're patient, take your time and don't overcook it. Clearly this is also the celebratory dance after you've lost your pursuers.

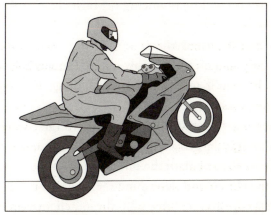

Simple wheelie

In first gear gently open the throttle until the wheel leaves the ground. Roll off the throttle and let it come back down. If you don't you'll flip – you have been warned.

Make it last longer

As soon as the wheel comes up ease off the throttle a fraction – just a fraction not all the way. Keep practising that until you can keep the wheel in the air for longer and longer periods each time. Master this first before tackling the next section or you will be bouncing off tarmac.

Clutch-control wheelie

As you slip the clutch out apply a quick squeeze of revs, not too much. You'll feel the front end lunge up. Try this a couple of times to get a feel for it.

Got it? Okay then: for the next step you need to keep the revs on as the slipped clutch brings the front end up. You will then have to control the bike with both the revs and the clutch; the clutch will determine the height. Try it.

Once you're comfortable with the clutch movement add a few consistent, steady revs to keep the bike in the air. How's that?

As you become more comfortable with this you'll find you balance the revs and the clutch first time every time and won't need to rev first.

How to Ride the Wall of Death

Okay that's just a primer and it sure beats my test-failing u-turns. But if you wanted to push your skills further you could go the Evel Knievel route and aim for some big air. Or you could try something a little more traditional. The Wall of Death. If you've never seen one it's a circular wall usually made of wood. You usually find them at funfairs. Motorbike riders either alone or in teams accelerate fast enough to get up on the wall and ride at right angles to the floor. They then ride around in circles and try not to fall off; they also have races, ride around with animals and sidecars and try to avoid the popcorn thrown at them by the audience standing at the top of the wall.

If you want to ride one for yourself the traditional method is to persuade the owner to show you how to do it in between shows. There's no riding around outside first: you get straight to it.

Step 1. Familiarisation. First you simply ride your bike round and round on the floor.

Step 2. Banking. You then hit the banking – the angled section that joins the floor to the wall – and get used to riding around this. The main problem here is motion sickness as you're operating on a different spatial plane. You have to give yourself time to get used to it, a bit like finding your sea legs. According to Allan Ford, author of *Riding the Wall of Death*, the sensation is so strong that 'after a few laps the trainer will call the new rider to a stop and rush to grab them'. It's at this stage that your legs inevitably desert you.

Step 3. Acclimatisation. You then go round the banking many times with lots of breaks in between as well as learn how to come on and off the banking. Experienced riders usually report that this is harder than going round the wall as you're neither on one plane nor the other.

Step 4. The Wall. After you've mastered riding along the crack between banking and wall you flick the wheel on to the flat and away you go. This usually takes two to three days. However Ford says, 'What happens nine times out of ten is the rider tries to flatten themselves against the wall, it being a natural instinct to straighten up. This inevitably results in a spill and the rider's first hard lesson.'

Step 5. Riding the Wall. Next time keep your head down as if you're taking a corner and try to find an equilibrium between throttle and balance. It's a bit like a frontal power slide using the imaginary 'centrifugal' force to keep you in place.

If you're impatient or can't find someone to help you learn you can always do what British YouTube hero Colin Furze did and build your own. He and some pals used 850 wooden pallets and some bits of scrap wood and built something that because of the ludicrous amount of nails, split wood, cracks and splinters was even more dangerous than your usual Wall of Death. To watch him spin out and then ride successfully check out youtube.com/colinfurze. If only he'd read this handy little how-to first.

You can take your motorbike to the corner shop or around the world. Whatever you do the better training you receive and the more experience you have the more you'll enjoy it. And trust me enjoy it you will.

Wings and Whirlybirds – Millionaire Playthings: or Are They?

So what are your options for getting in the air? At the high end there's your own private, personal jet. Let's turn to the outrageously rich Prince Al Waleed again. According to Bob Shepherd in his book on private military contracting, *The Circuit*, Al-Waleed doesn't just have one jet (complete with bedrooms, showers and every conceivable luxury), he also has a chase jet just in case his first one breaks down. No wonder Shepherd felt that both the prince's and the Saudi royal family's conspicuous consumption was 'breeding a tremendous amount of contempt among the region's less privileged inhabitants'.

At a certain level however the cost of a private jet is perfectly justifiable; if for example it costs less than paying for executive class for your upper-level minions then buying one outright could be cheaper. Or better still join a fractional jet ownership scheme and lose the management headaches of ownership.

The traditional routes to learn to fly yourself rather than be chauffeured are still either through the military or commercial airline training schemes.

There also aren't as many competitions to show off your skills in the aviation arena. The most high-profile event is the Red Bull Air Race where the world's best pilots compete using the fastest, most agile and lightweight racing planes. The pilots navigate a low-level aerial race track made up of air-filled pylons, reaching speeds of 370kph while withstanding forces of up to 12Gs. It's exciting stuff. I watched it from my bedroom window looking along the Thames last year. There were moments when both the helicopters and planes were turning, diving and defying death that would make you shout out loud, 'No please don't you'll die,' followed by, 'Now how did they do that?'

If you're paying for it yourself either to make money or for pleasure then you need to start with your private pilot's licence (PPL) where you have a minimum flying time of forty-five hours, twenty-five of them under instruction, and at least ten solo hours. You have a qualifying solo cross-country flight of 150 miles during which you have to land at two airfields different from your home field. As you'd expect there's plenty of theory, which will teach you everything you need to know about air law, human performance limitations, meteorology, navigation, flight performance and planning, principles of flight and radio telephony. There are seven exams in total but they're multiple choice and not too difficult. If you budget for forty-five to fifty-five hours of flight training this should cost you in the region of £6000–£7000 with another £500–£700 for your ground courses and exam fees.

For your commercial pilot's license (CPL) you can either choose a modular conversion route, generally the cheapest option especially if you train abroad in the USA, Canada or Australia. There are also integrated courses where you train from complete novice to commercial pilot, usually over a period of six to thirty-six months. These are good but far from cheap. They usually cost between £50,000 and £60,000 but again shop around for better prices.

Before forking out large amounts of cash it's worth taking your class one medical to see if you pass muster. When I looked at taking my commercial helicopter licence I did just that. My eyesight was out by 0.025 of a dioptre in one eye. If I'd taken the training and then taken the medical just before the exams the costs would have hurt.

Helicopters are noisy and exciting and a bit more like playing the drums with an all-limbs-moving-at-once style of flying. For your commercial licence you'll be looking at £50k+ unless you just want a licence that allows you simply to play. The PPL (H) is similar to the aeroplane licence with a minimum of forty-five hours flying time and classroom tuition. Expect to pay in excess of £10k before you pass as you pay hourly and prices start at around £225 + VAT per hour. For CPL (H) you need 185 hours flying time and must have passed the nine ground school exams.

You can also take the same course for around the same price in several places around the world from Hawaii to India. I'd use an excuse like more sunny guaranteed flying days to do just that.

So how much does it all cost?

You could pick yourself up a microlight in good condition for around £3000; you'll still need your PPL of course as you will for all the following. A single-prop Cessna in the same condition can be had for £10k–£20k, rising to £40,000–£200,000 for a twin-prop. Helicopters start with basic but fun ultra-light kit copters for under £5k like the tubular

A/W 95, rising to as little as £30k for a used two-seater Enstrom-28 to £100k+ for good examples of other smaller pleasure models. For turbine helicopters you'll be looking at upwards of £200k and for executive models that look like Airwolf you'll need a much bigger chequebook. For private jets like Gulfstream, Hawkers and Bombardiers expect to pay £10 million plus for smaller models and up to the tens of millions for bigger head-of-state-sized aircraft.

You could of course start from scratch like Yves Rossy aka FusionMan. The former fighter pilot, inventor and adventurer who built a himself a jet-propelled fixed-wing, strapped it to his back and then launched himself from a plane at 2500 metres. As he reached speeds of 200kph he had to stay relaxed and composed as steering was controlled by his body movement not by levers. So far he has crossed the English Channel between Calais and Dover in thirteen minutes as well as the Swiss Alps and Lake Geneva.

Flying can be as expensive or as cheap as you want to make it. If you want to opt for lean and green flying try hang gliding, ballooning, paragliding or gliding. The British Hang Gliding and Paragliding Association says this about their members: 'To be aloft on the breeze seems to them a rare privilege made more precious by the fact that so few of the teeming millions seem to know about it.' Nuff said. And no worries about rising fuel costs either.

Space Travel

In the late nineties few people took the idea of space tourism seriously. The idea that in a few short years everyday people like you and me could be flying into space and experiencing the profound wonder of leaving our mother planet seemed absurd.

Initially space travel was simply a Cold War dick-swinging contest that the West won with the Apollo moon landings then space became the domain of commercial and military satellites. Even though we already had the technical capability to get humans off-planet even as far as Mars, for governments it was costly and hard to justify especially if they wanted re-election.

Happily there were a few voices in the wilderness that asked why can't we do it for ourselves? In California Dr Peter Diamandis set up the X Prize, a competition that would award $10 million to the first person to fly a spacecraft into low-Earth orbit and then repeat the process with the same craft within two weeks. In Britain only a handful of people knew what the hell he was talking about. Richard Branson was one of them.

The passion and insight of those early astronauts had inspired a dream. The entrepreneurs, designers and teams who were prototyping the privately funded spacecraft, space stations and space hotels of the future were about to make history.

In 2004 Burt Rutan and his company Scaled Composites won the X Prize with his Paul Allen-backed SpaceShipOne. Branson immediately stepped in to create Virgin Galactic and offer proven commercial flights to low-earth orbit. The future had arrived and the universe was waiting for us to explore it. Here's how it begins.

Current Opportunities

Edge of Space – with Vodka-Drinking Jet Pilots
Terrestrial tourism options through a company like Space Adventures include watching a rocket launch; taking a zero-G

parabolic flight where a plane creates the effects of weightless zero gravity through a series of diving manoeuvres; or full cosmonaut training in Russia's Star City where you take part in underwater spacewalk training and learn to fly the Soyuz craft in the simulator and on the 10G centrifuge. You can also take a jet ride to what is traditionally known as the 'edge of space', 68,000+ feet in Russia or 60,000 feet in South Africa depending on your vehicle either a MIG or Lightning fighter jet, where you will see the full curvature of Earth beneath you and the universe above.

Low-Earth Orbit – with Branson and the Laid-Back Californians

Branson's Virgin Galactic already has hundreds of paid-up customers for the first sub-orbital flights in the Burt Rutan-designed craft. As one of the first space tourists your small spaceship will be mounted beneath the VMS EVE mother-ship aircraft; then at 50,000 feet, the maximum altitude for Concorde, your spacecraft will detach and the rockets will fire. Space is officially 330,000 feet above Earth and you will fly to around 360,000 feet. When the engines cut out you will be able to see 1000 miles in all directions over the earth and you will be travelling at 2500mph. That's over three times the speed of sound. You will be weightless and in space with a total flight time of two and a half hours.

Rutan has designed a clever feathering system to allow for 'care free re-entry'. The feathered wings act as airbrakes until your craft reaches a height where they can be retracted and you glide back to the spaceport. Tickets currently cost $200,000 (around £107,000) through Virgin Galactic but many other companies are offering or proposing sub-orbital flights too, among them the secretive aerospace company Blue Origin, owned by Amazon founder Jeff Bezos, and long-term pioneers Space Adventures who are offering flights for $102,000. However it's likely that Virgin Galactic will be up and running first with flights scheduled to start as soon as the rigorous testing phase is complete, with either one or two scheduled flights daily after that.

International Space Station – with a Pile of Cash

Space Adventures have already flown six private citizens into Earth orbit, starting with Dennis Tito back in 2001 and most recently with Richard Garriot, the influential video games designer. By the time this book is published they should already have flown Charles Simonyi up for a return trip; he enjoyed it so much the first time he just had to go again. For $35 million–$45 million you can spend seven to ten days aboard the International Space Station (ISS) using Soyuz as your taxi vehicle. If you want to spend a little longer and take a space-walk as well this will set you back $45 million–$55 million or you can opt for a tailor made mission of your choice.

If you're mind is boggling at the price then private space explorer Mark Shuttleworth's answer might explain why he felt it a price worth paying: 'An experience like that changes your perspective on life and on the world . . .'

Future Opportunities

Living in Space

A decade ago designs for space hotels and habitats were nothing more than exercises in blue-sky thinking to distract the board from getting any real work done. Things have changed. All the future sub-orbital carriers are interested in developing longer-term habitats; after all, more destinations means more business. Las Vegas hotel tycoon Robert Bigelow has bought NASA's Transhab programme of expandable habitats from NASA and is developing it privately, with two successful test deployments into orbit already. The Excalibur Almaz company has plans to modernise and launch it's Soviet-era Almaz space stations similar to the ISS. Several hotel chains like Hilton International have plans for space hotels and Branson is demonstrably keen but as with the sub-orbital market he is waiting to see who shines most brightly first before committing.

To the Moon and Back

Constellation Services International have had a circumlunar trip on the drawing board for a few years now but Space Adventures are already offering a round trip into lunar orbit using the proven Soyuz craft. The mission builds on space technology originally developed for manned lunar missions and has been flown over decades as part of the world's most successful human spaceflight programme.

Seats costs $100 million – hardly cheap – but if I was a billionaire I'd already be signed on and urging them to hurry up and light the fuse.

Future Prizes

The X Prize Foundation was clearly on to something with their 'revolution through competition' thinking. They've now created the $30 million Google Lunar X Prize for the first privately funded robotic mission to the moon along with a range of other prizes from progressive automotives to fast, affordable genome technology and lunar lander competitions.

Bigelow has also established a Space Prize, a $50 million purse with the goal of developing a spacecraft that can carry a minimum of five people, conduct orbital flights and ultimately dock with his own privately funded space stations.

On the back of this new privately funded space race, NASA has also proposed its own competitions with prizes potentially reaching the $30 million mark for soft lunar landings, bringing back pieces of asteroids and ultimately the hope of putting humans on Mars.

Just ten years ago space tourism was a pipe dream; now it's becoming a visible reality with commercial spaceports being built from New Mexico and California to the United Arab Emirates and Singapore. Who knows where we'll be in another ten years?

On Earth sailing, flying, driving or riding all offer enjoyable and rewarding challenges and adventure but so often at the higher end they are just ways of displaying peacock feathers to attract a mate or look good in front of our playground primate pals. A ride in a spaceship though is something altogether more astounding. Spectacular and evolutionary are the words that spring to mind. Think about it: the athletes who broke the four-minute mile made it possible for everyone else to do the same. Maybe one day we'll forget that we were once limited to the confines of our planet in the same way we thought we couldn't run faster.

When I met Peter Diamandis in 1999 he said that one of his main reasons for setting up the X Prize was because he'd never get into space as a government astronaut. Just look what a simple idea and the will to try can achieve.

People Power

Have all these six-figure combinations got to you yet? Yeah me too. Not everything in a modern gentleman's life needs to be concerned with price tag or status; in fact as a rule it probably shouldn't be. So it's just as well we've been given these amazing bodies to work and play with. Look after them and enjoy them and you'll get more satisfaction out of them than any super yacht.

Walk

If you want the royal road to health and well-being this is probably it. Every able-bodied man can do it naturally. You can walk for health (make it regular), fitness (add inclines, uneven surfaces and up the pace or distance), meditation (breathe deeply and still your inner monologue), explore (take a different route to work every day and occasionally get lost – on purpose) or simply take in the scenery around you, wherever you find yourself.

Your feet could even take you from the southernmost point of South America all the way round the world and back to Britain. In 1998 Karl Bushby decided to do just that; he's currently completed 17,000 miles and has 19,000 more to go. After walking through the Americas he crossed the Bering Strait into Russia and as I write is waiting for visas that allow him to carry on. The last stage will be to walk through the Channel Tunnel in 2012 just in time for the Olympics when he will have realised his dream as the first person to complete an unbroken walk round the world.

Run

Remember all those Ethiopian track stars who honed their skills without fancy modern training kit? Like walking running is one of those skills that we all naturally have. We all used to run around like maniacs as kids, in the park or on the football pitch. But as adults all we seem to remember are those 'cross country' days where we were forced to run around a track endlessly in the rain. The thought of running filled me with dread as a younger man. I lived on a beautiful park and one day I thought I'd give it a go. I did what we were taught to do at school – just go at it. About a hundred yards later I had to pull over, hold on to a tree and wheeze like a coal miner. I gave up. I was an extremely heavy smoker at the time, which didn't help. Then I found Hal Higdon's book *How to Train*. In it he detailed a running plan originally designed by the ex-military coach Chuck Cornett for the over-fifties. It's called the 30/30 plan and it teaches you how to run properly unlike school.

Every day for thirty days do the following:

- Go away from the house for fifteen minutes then turn around and come back to it for a further fifteen, total time: thirty minutes.
- Walk for the first five minutes – this is your warm up.
- Walk for the last five minutes – this is your cool down.
- For the middle twenty minutes jog or walk as long as you do so easily and do not push yourself. To begin with in your twenty minutes try jogging thirty seconds, walk thirty seconds and slowly build up your time.

Always listen to what your body tells you. If you want to go faster do it, if you want to go slower or walk do that too. I guarantee that after a week or so you'll be wanting to go out every day because if you don't you'll miss it.

After thirty days you'll be running a mile or three every time you go out and it won't have been painful in the slightest. After that if you begin to run a little further you'll find out that lovely little secret of runners everywhere: after twenty minutes the endorphins kick in. You won't even want to stop.

Cycle

Bikes would be my second love. It was BMXs and mountain bikes for me but for you it might be a racing bike, a fold-up or a street bike. They're about as green as it gets and while you can spend thousands for a top-of-the-line model you really don't have to: you can pick up a good second hand bike or a modest but fully functional bit of kit for £100 or so or even build your own. If there is one thing I could teach about cycling that suits all types of riding it's this: cadence.

Put simply it's the number of times you turn the crank in a minute. For example if you want to go uphill rather than stand up on the pedals and stamp away in a big gear, a muscular action that increases lactic acid and takes longer to recover from, simply drop down a couple of gears so that the amount of push needed to turn the pedals is lower. Then try to maintain the same cadence.

I first came across this concept in my early twenties when I was overtaken on my flash new mountain bike by an old codger on a rickety old road bike with a Woodbine in his mouth.

When you're on the flat, finding the rpm that is best for your gear and most comfortable for you will increase your performance no end. Mine doubled. I've been looking for a race with that old geezer ever since.

Lance Armstrong famously came back after testicular cancer that had spread to his lungs, abdomen and brain to win a record-breaking seven Tour de France competitions. One of the key contributors to his increased performance was high-rpm cadence training (around 100–120rpms for him), which resulted in his having a remarkable ability to remove muscle-stiffening lactate from his body. Hardly surprising he won so many races.

It's just like lifting a lower weight more quickly for more reps; you still lift the same amount of weight in the same time as you did before but with less lactic burn and quicker recovery times. It's excellent for toning and muscular endurance and puts less stress on bones and joints and therefore causes less injury.

Ski

Tragically, in Britain at least, skiing is often seen as either an extreme sport or something that is part of the social scene of the aspiring classes. 'It's all about the après ski darling, wah wah wah!' But in countries where snow falls year in year out, skiing is as normal as riding a bike or walking to work. And for those who come from countries where it isn't, exploring the wilderness on cross-country skis or rocketing downhill through powdery off-piste snow is far from poncey or posey. It's liberating, awe inspiring and addictive.

Again cadence comes into its own when you are going cross country; it's hard, gruelling work if you don't achieve a good rhythm. Good cadence is the thing that will allow you to travel for miles in some of the most beautiful and remote landscapes in the world.

For downhill there are plenty of options and as you'd expect by now I'd always recommend getting the best training you can afford. The Ski Club of Great Britain offer some fantastic options to get you skiing no matter whether your end goal is just to be able to enjoy a holiday with the kids or to go to places not normally accessible to man. Your experiences should always be exhilarating and fun and if you learn good technique from the outset the motor skills will stay with you for life.

So if adventure is your thing hire a leader to take you on all the best runs and avoid the queues. If getting away from it all is your thing take a touring holiday where you mix hill climbs with wide open landscapes and deserted descents; if unique experiences are your thing then aim for off-piste powder skiing and if you want to take it as far as you can try it by helicopter. Heli-skiing means you can always make first tracks in the fresh snow of pristine wilderness or make uncharted first descents in the Himalayas or Alaska. It's a big world out there and there's more than one way to see it. Try everything.

Living for Adventure

Extreme Sports – Not Just for the Little Rubber People Who Don't Shave Yet

So what exactly is an extreme sport? One man's off-piste extravaganza is another man's same old same old. For me an extreme sport is one that when somebody asks, 'Why would you want to do that?', you don't necessarily have the answer. It is something that challenges you and pushes you out of your comfort zone so that you find out something about yourself or the world around you. It's definitely not the day-glo colours and high fives of soft drinks commercials although that's not to say that never happens. That's just not what it's about.

No, extreme sports are all about the challenge. Either you against the environment, you against yourself or both. Unlike normal sports when environmental conditions change it's even more reason to do it. When the storms come that's when you surf, when the ice freezes over that's when you dive, but not always, because even though high risk is a primary factor stupidity isn't. At least not for very long.

And again unlike in the adverts the pioneers of each sport tend not to be the little rich kids doing it as a lifestyle statement to attract attention or a need to join a tribe. The Lance Armstrongs, Laird Hamiltons or Colin McRaes come from a variety of backgrounds and usually the key thing that makes them pioneers is simply a relentless passion bordering on obsession.

Case Study:	Alain Robert (aka Spiderman)
Occupation:	Solo urban climber
DOB:	7 August 1962
Nationality:	French
Married:	Yes, two children
Height:	5′ 5″
Weight:	105lbs

The first things you should know about Alain is that he is considered 66 per cent disabled due to sustained injuries and amazingly he also suffers from vertigo. But despite this at the time of writing he has climbed eighty-five giant structures around the world on his 'solo urban climbing world tour', all without ropes or harnesses. He has scuttled up the sides of some of the world's tallest structures such as the 313-metre Eiffel Tower, the 443-metre Sears Tower in Chicago, the 244-metre Canary Wharf building in London, the 354-metre Vostok Tower in Moscow and many other landmark buildings around the world from the relatively modest 64-metre Sydney Opera House to the terrifying heights of the 420-metre Jin Mao Tower in Shanghai and the 508-metre Taipei 101. Phew it's exhausting just typing that. There doesn't seem to be any stopping him add further buildings to this ever expanding list of conquered land-marks.

As most authorities couldn't be seen to condone this sort of behaviour, Alain often climbs without permission, arriving early in the morning to begin his ascent. He's usually arrested and then released without charge after a few hours or days and asked politely never to return.

And like all men who do things that look crazy to the rest of us, he first honed his skills as a young boy, climbing regularly in the French Alps. He began to mistake buildings for mountains when he forgot his keys to his parents' eighth-floor apartment one day. Guess how he got in.

He's also had seven accidents during his career, has been in a coma several times and has suffered multiple fractures. Expertise comes at a price but don't expect that to stop him.

In fact expect to see more of him over the coming years as he has a penchant for climbing the world's tallest towers even when he sometimes gets arrested before reaching the top, as he did on the Petronas Towers in Kuala Lumpur, or hits extreme weather conditions, as he did on the Sears Tower. There he met a thick fog near the top of the 110-storey building that covered the glass and metal walls of the last twenty floors with moisture making it a potentially lethal climb.

Tall buildings are clearly his thing and as he has yet to master the 553.3-metre CN Tower in Toronto or the new tallest building in the world, the mega structure that is the 818-metre Burj Dubai, it's unlikely we've seen the last of him or his Spiderman suit.

Alain says, 'Being a top athlete requires total concentration. And some sacrifices. I have suffered a great deal but here's the result. Never give up, make your dreams come true.'

Well okay Alain I will. This isn't to say that every modern gent needs to be able to wrestle bears or dive with sharks but it is all about mindset and Alain's 'Never give up, make your dreams come true' is exactly what this is all about. Whether that's parenting, making a cappuccino or what happens next . . .

Proving It – How to Jump Out of a Plane and Live

I want you to get over your fears. I know it's a lot to ask. It's not something I ask lightly either. You see once you face your fears, large or small, the world literally becomes a different place. So here's one of my biggest.

From an early age I liked to jump from things. I started out small, the back of my granddad's sofa then the high steps on the way to school. Then climbing on to the beams in the rain shelters. I remember going for a walk with my mum along the top tier of the Transporter Bridge in Newport. Apparently despite the gaping cracks in between the boards I ran on ahead, fearless. (It's now closed off to the public. Health and safety wasn't such an issue back then.)

These jumps progressed when Tony, one of the neighbourhood kids, and I figured out that if we landed on a mattress from the second storey of my house it didn't hurt too much. Of course my mum disagreed when she found out.

I also remember one of the kids up the street copied us and jumped from the third storey on to the pavement out front. He broke both legs.

One day we found the rusted framework of an old factory outbuilding near a sand dredging plant on the River Usk. We climbed the skeletal frame until we reached what would have been the third storey. My friend dared me to tightrope walk across a rusted joist about 20 feet across. Of course I did. Then I looked down. I can still see quite clearly in my mind's eye the green scrub pushing up through the sandy dirt three floors below. Gravity pulled at my outstretched hands and my stomach churned at its touch. My pulse quickened and my vision blurred.

When I looked scared my friend started to jeer. I overbalanced and fell to my knees, gripping the powdery metal beneath, then scrambled backwards on to a safer support. Unable to stop shaking I somehow found my way back down to the ground.

I didn't think about heights again until a summer camp at about the age of ten. Waiting for my turn I had no fear of the abseil wall. None at all, not until I leaned backwards out over the sucking void and found my heart bouncing off the walls of my chest. I resisted the urge to shout and run back up the wall. I made it to the bottom. It was torture. But despite the fear I wanted to go again.

Somewhere on every skydiving website there's a line from *Point Break*, one of the seminal films of my teenage years, that goes, 'How do you feel about jumping out of a perfectly good airplane?'

Well in all honesty I think it sounds ridiculous but then strangely I'm drawn to the experience. I'm also more scared by the thought of it than a grown man is usually prepared to admit. Think leg-trembling pant-wetting horror and you're halfway there.

As you can probably see from my childhood I've always had an attraction to high places and especially jumping from them. This compulsion to jump has carried over into adulthood. It's not a suicidal thing. I'd really rather not die so sensibly I've taught myself not to jump. Yet the urge is still so strong that if my cousin opens the window in his twentieth-floor apartment I have to lie on the floor. The pull of gravity towards the window and what lies beyond it is truly overwhelming.

A lengthy Google says that it's not vertigo, which is an inner-ear disorder, it's also not a fear of heights: it is an overwhelming urge to jump – which is really not the same thing at all.

It appears that I'm not the only one. Plenty of people online seem to have the same problem. It doesn't have an official diagnosis. Maybe it doesn't even need one? Not everything that scares us is an illness.

So my thinking was this. It's all very well wanting to fly like Superman but landing safely on the ground would be even better. Therefore if I jumped out of a plane from one of the highest drop zones in Europe that would appease this strange, fear-full desire and release me from its clutches. Obvious right? It had to work.

I threw myself at the mercy of Target Skysports, hosts of the British National Championships and some of the highest drop zones in Europe and unarguably one of the best skydiving companies out there. As the British climate tends to be unpredictable they offered to take me out to their sister company, Skydive Spain and their Seville drop zone to avoid the British winter.

I also chose the Accelerated Free Fall course rather than a

tandem or static line jump. The other options seemed too passive. In the first someone else is in control and for the other it's simply mechanical: you jump and a static line attached to the plane pulls your chute out for you.

No what I wanted was something that would really scare the crap out of me. The AFF has you free-falling from jump one and quickly cycles you through the eight levels you need to get jumping on your own. It was time to get on and do it.

The Arabian-influenced Andalusian countryside is a gloriously sunny and perfect place for free-fall. It has blue skies, low winds and a wide-open, friendly drop zone. However on my arrival at the Aeródromo La Juliana there was one small snag: the plane wasn't working. The company were flying the engineers in from Czechoslovakia and twiddling their thumbs waiting for them to arrive. This was a good introduction to the first part of the sport that you have to get used to. Waiting. Usually for the weather to clear.

Other pupils arrived. Skydiving is a sport that many want to try but AFF learners it seems are nearly always solo travellers. There was Richard, my partner for the AFF, and Mark, there to work the next level called 'free fly' – where you get to fly upside down, on your back, and at pretty much any angle your imagination and body can take. As well as the guys there are nineteen-year-old Karri and twenty-year-old Sophie, both fearful and courageous and both already a couple of levels ahead on the AFF.

To pass the time the others took on the labours of a packing course while our instructor Duarte put Richard and me through ground school.

Ground school can seem a little fluffy when you're doing mock free fall on a little wheeled sled with mock backpacks and jumping out of a mock door frame but it's an essential part of the training. Through repetition it begins to embed the actions that when you're falling are essential to survival and progressing through the AFF system.

For the first level there is one fundamental action – arch your body. If you get a good arch when you exit the plane or when you lose control – belly first, arms and legs in the air and relaxed – then you'll flatten out and control your fall. Without this you'll spin all over the place.

I can't imagine that is ever a good feeling when your chute opens.

As we went over the emergency procedures it became clear that there are four main areas where you might die.

If there is a malfunction with your main canopy you have to 'cut away' and get rid of it. To do this you tear away a red handle with your right hand and push down; this disposes of the main chute then with your left hand you immediately pull the metal handle which releases your reserve. If the reserve fails to open or you're too low it's game over. That's option one.

If you open and get tangled in your lines you're warned not to cut away. Just stay as you are and hope for a good landing. If you cut away with a leg under tension between your parachute's lines you can imagine what would happen. Think cheese wires. Now imagine a line round your neck. Yeah sweet. That's option two.

Option three is other jumpers crashing into you. Not much you can do about them.

Option four is the major cause of accidents: sharp turns on your canopy as you're coming into land.

Here's the surprising thing though. Overall skydiving feels quite safe. Of course it does have its dangers: you are leaping from a plane after all. However the United States Parachuting Association reports that in 2007 out of 2.2 million jumps there were only 18 fatalities and 827 injuries.

In the UK the figures are also positive. According to the British Parachute Association over a five year period the average injury rate was 0.8 injuries per one thousand jumps for all types of jumpers and a fatality rate of roughly 1 in 100,000 for the period 1990–2007. Statistically though, one thing is clear on both sides of the Atlantic: the more training you have the safer a sport it becomes. Another good reason to opt for the AFF.

There are eight levels and in theory at least from the first jump you are in control. You start with two instructors and work up to a point where you can jump on your own, deploy on your own, track through the sky, turn and land safely. Your eighth jump is at low altitude (5000 feet), followed by ten solo consolidation jumps. At that point you get your 'A' licence which allows you to jump any drop zone in the world.

By jump twenty the fear is supposed to wear off but it's different for everyone. When I spoke to Barbie, one of the onsite packers at Skydive Spain, he said he didn't truly enjoy it until around jump one hundred.

Right then and there that felt like a hell of a long way to go.

Beneath the edge of the plane's open doorway there's 15,000 feet of nothing. The wind whips at your feet. Tugging, teasing and taunting. You're not allowed to hold on to anything up there. You'd never let go.

Eight people just leaped out before me as if to their deaths. Every part of me screams that that was wrong, so wrong. I've fought the compulsion to jump for such a long time. I like life. I don't want to die.

I ignore the fear and let the training take over. I check that Alf, the jump instructor, is standing next to me on the inside and ready to go. Then I check in with Andy, the crazy man standing on the outside of the plane holding on to my sleeve. He's grinning from ear to ear.

Look at the wingtip. Focus. Ready . . . set . . . go . . . go. C'mon. Go. But I can't, my mind says go but my body says no . . . and then . . . and then I lean forward and whether I want to or not I'm falling into the backdraught of the plane.

Oh god. A hot white flash of fear. What the hell am I doing?

I arch instinctively and catch sight of the earth curving away on the horizon, taking my breath with it. Through the faraway clouds below I can see the ground. Gravity takes over and pulls me towards it.

My rate of descent rushes towards 120mph, way over the speed limit. With arms stretched and hips forward my low centre of gravity brings me to a level and stable position.

I try to tear my eyes away from the horizon.

A tap on my helmet, get on with manoeuvres.

Check altitude: '14,000,' I shout under one arm then the other. The instructors communicate using hand signals:

Two extended fingers: straighten legs, point toes.

Thumb down: arch my body more.

A shaking hand: remember to breathe; relax. How exactly?

Then arch, reach behind with my right arm to find the pull toggle then recover. Repeat three times. Try not to fight against the instructor's hand as he guides mine to the right spot.

My body is rigid with terror. Thank goodness for the drills. They keep you moving.

Clouds that seemed so far away only seconds ago now rush to meet us, swallow us and surround us. Scared but fully alive I grasp at the precious seconds of wonder and terror. The ground is getting closer fast, too fast. And I can't see it or the numbers on my altimeter; condensation from the cloud obscures its face.

Andy's hand enters my line of sight. The altimeter's face is still too blurred. Then he rams his hand full in my face and his urgent signal finally registers.

A straight index finger: pull now.

Breaking through the cloud the ground is even closer than I thought.

Wave off the instructors, reach, pull . . . 1000, 2000 . . . the start of the count sequence that stops you looking at the canopy too soon and mistaking the strange configurations of a chute opening for a malfunction. There is a reserve of course but do you really want to test its reliability before you have to? . . . 3000, 4000, check canopy.

Breathe, breathe, breathe. Check canopy again. It's big, it's rectangular and it's free of damage. Thank fuck. Thank fuck. Thank fuck. Try not to laugh too much. Thank fuck. Oh hell laugh as much as you like.

Ten minutes later and back on the ground the adrenalin crash knocked my legs out from under me. According to Pete, one of the instructors, the more scared you are the bigger the buzz and the harder you eventually fall. 'It's like the comedown after a handful of pills,' he said. He was right.

All I wanted to do was go again.

The jump instructors Alf and Andy ribbed me mercilessly during the video debrief. They said I was so tense I was like an ironing board and called me 'The Claw'. I trusted them implicitly though so despite the knowledge of what I had to put myself through I was ready to get high once more.

The fear was just as bad. The anticipation, dread and the urge to run to the toilet increased sharply as the plane rose steeply to a cruising height of almost three miles. I still couldn't quite get my head around the smiles and bravado of the other skydivers. Their lack of fear. But because of this I knew that everything was going to be okay, which made jumping out of the plane easier second time round. Still when the chute opened it really was like the coming of the Lord. Hallelujah.

After the rush of free fall the time you spend hanging underneath the open chute is relaxing, peaceful and wonderfully serene. It opens up a totally different perspective of the earth. Normally looking out of a plane window or over the edge of a cliff it's just a very long, scary way down. From under a canopy it's a landscape you interact with rather than are scared of.

It's time to fly.

Pull both toggles in, the square canopy above flares and you slow right down. At height it's a heart-stopping moment as the canopy stalls, almost as if it's about to collapse and fall from the sky.

When you let the toggles all the way back up the chute speeds up. Then fly over the other side of the runway and into a zigzag holding pattern ahead of the giant wind direction arrow in the landing area. It could be hours or seconds tracing patterns in the sky. With the adrenalin still pulsing through you it's difficult to tell.

At 1000 feet turn downwind at full speed, at 500 hang a left, at 300 take a final left into the wind and forget about any fancy manoeuvres. At 15 feet flare all the way so the chute slows, in theory enough to walk or run away and look super cool.

In my case bounce about 50 per cent of the time.

Back on the ground it felt like I had whiplash from the force of the wind hitting my body. Then the comedown kicked in again. But there's something nobody tells you about skydiving that makes it all a lot easier to bear: the people are fantastic. The camaraderie exceptional. I've rarely met a friendlier group. I talked and debriefed with instant new friends because even the most experienced there had been where I had: terrified, falling and desperately wanting to do it all over again. It's an immediate bond that crosses language barriers, social types, gender and race.

Back on the video monitor my jumps looked less than glamorous. No one was pointing fingers though; style comes with experience. By the time I'd completed my fourth jump of the day I was turning on my own during free fall and landing without radio assistance. The jump out of the plane became if anything the least scary part and I then had to deal with a different set of fears under the canopy. What if the straps came loose? What if there was a malfunction?

By mid-afternoon my body was aching so much and coursing with so many endorphins and adrenalin surges that I had to stop at jump four. I needed time to recover. But with a flight to Heathrow booked the following morning there was no time to complete all eight jumps on that visit.

On the flight home the view out of the window was not the same. It was a different world and my relationship with it had changed. I scanned the ground for places to land as we rose up through clouds that I would have preferred to be falling through.

Back in London I was curious to know whether that sickening, overwhelming compulsion to jump from high places was still part of me. So I paid a visit to St Paul's Cathedral and climbed the long stairway to heaven and the Whispering Gallery that runs around the inside edge of its landmark dome.

I remembered visiting with my father when I was a very

young child and leaning through the railing out over the congregation below and seeing nothing. My head was so full of fear. Back then all I wanted to do was leave.

But this time I leaned over the security rail and found I could make out the paintings of saints on the walls and pick out the eyes and voices of the tourists far below. I looked up and took in that magnificent dome. Every golden detail was crisp and clear. There was no panic. No anxiety. No fear. That terrifying compulsion had gone. Finally. After all those years.

Then I caught myself thinking thoughts I'd not had since I was a slightly older child. What would happen if I climbed over the safety rail and leaned backwards out over the hard tiles of the cathedral floor hundreds of feet below?

These days if I tried that they'd probably think I was a terrorist.

But now I had an answer to that *Point Break* question. I felt absolutely fine about jumping out of a perfectly good airplane.

Challenging your fears really does change your life.

Living on the Edge

Now at this point I should emphasise that nothing you see here is prescriptive. You don't have to buy a super yacht or an electric supercar or learn to live in the wilderness. There is no 'should do' for the modern gent only 'What do I intend to do?' But if you've realised that maybe working in the tax office isn't for you from reading about an everyday guy like me doing exactly the opposite then you'll be pleased to know you do have options. So if you decide to jump out of that tax office window take a parachute with you and you might just have a new way to make a living. Here are some other ideas.

Modern Explorers

Explorers are just normal people like you and me who get it into their heads that they can do extraordinary things. They have a long history from Marco Polo and Ibn Battuta to the Victorian explorers of the industrial age. And although we think of the world as being so well mapped that we no longer need to explore it, if anything as our environment changes, microcultures disappear and the same old politics and religions clash we need to more than ever.

What differentiates explorers from mere tourists is that they bring something back that changes our perceptions and that reminds us of who we are and our place in the world. It doesn't always have to be dangerous but it helps. And the stories that they bring back are true rather than the tall tales you hear in the pub or read in celebrity magazines.

The explorer who first inspired me was the Norwegian Thor Heyerdahl. He'd spent a year on the remote Pacific island of Fatu Hiva before the outbreak of the Second World War. After a long war and inspired by native legends, old reports and drawings he'd seen made by Spanish Conquistadors of Inca rafts, Heyerdahl and five friends travelled to Peru to rebuild one of these rafts made of balsa logs and sail it across the Pacific. They wanted to try and prove that migration across the Pacific had come from South America to Polynesia and not the other way round.

They sailed for 101 days, for an amazing 4300-mile (8000 kilometre) journey across the Pacific Ocean, their voyage came to an end when the soon-to-be famous *Kon-Tiki* raft smashed into the reef at Raroia in the Tuamotu Islands on 7 August 1947.

With a strong will, a small amount of cash and some good friends, Heyerdahl managed to challenge historical orthodoxy and have an adventure that if you've ever read his book *The Kon-Tiki Expedition* you'll know reads like a novel. Except that his experiences were real. He went on to recreate similar voyages from Egypt to the Americas and Mesopotamia to modern day Pakistan as well as exploring several pyramid structures in the Canaries and South America.

Another favourite is the eminent Victorian explorer Sir

Richard Burton who not only learned Arabic but had himself circumcised and then passed himself off as a devout Muslim to join a Hajj pilgrimage to Mecca. As well as translating *The Arabian Nights* and what was then considered a pornographic, sexual text, *The Kama Sutra,* he helped track down an inland African sea which turned out be the massive Lake Tanganyika, which in turn led to the discovery of Lake Victoria.

How about finding out that the real life inspiration for Indiana Jones lost one of his discoveries and then rediscovering it? In the 1980s filmmaker and writer Hugh Thomson was working cash in hand in a London pub, the kind of place that attracted gangsters trying to climb the social ladder and Sloanies roughing it. The landlord was renowned for hitting his staff and doing the morning stocktake in a giant pair of purple underpants.

Thomson happened to tell one of the regulars about an Inca fortress that the American explorer Hiram Bingham had found around the same time he discovered Machu Picchu and then lost again when the jungle reclaimed it.

Thomson jokingly told the drunk he was thinking of trying to find it. The drunk told him, 'That's one of the first ideas I've heard from you with any sense to it. Given a choice between wasting your time serving old farts like me and getting lost in the South American jungle, I'd have thought the jungle was a far more constructive alternative.'

As Thomson said in the book he eventually wrote about his two trips to Peru, 'Chance conversations are dangerous things'. With the drunk's words ringing in his ears he approached the Royal Geographical Society and raised a small amount of cash for his first trip. This ultimately set him on the road to becoming an explorer, writer and filmmaker. Sure beats working in a dodgy London pub.

But explorers aren't just interested in ancient history. Boorman and McGregor are undoubtedly explorers. So are the many unsung heroes who work for small NGOs or charities, or the anthropologists and journalists who throw themselves in harm's way to find out more about their subjects. As Benedict Allen wrote in an article on the subject for the *Guardian*, 'Travel is about shedding our preconceptions and trying to see the world from new perspectives. In other words the business of exploration today is about two things: science, but also about our own mental landscape – charting our ideas, our hopes and fears.' And he should know. By the age of twenty-two he was fleeing through the Amazon forest to escape violent gold miners and was forced to eat his own dog to survive. Since then he's travelled deserts, rainforests and crossed a frozen Bering Strait all on his own. He said, 'Exploration to me is about that – not making your mark on a place, but allowing that place to make its mark on you.'

Dangerous Places

Does the buzz of nerve shredding danger make you feel alive? Maybe it's the dusty streets of civil war in Somalia; the threat of terrorism or kidnap in Afghanistan or Sri Lanka; negotiating with Chechen gangsters; the run-up to an election in Zimbabwe; the favellas of Brazil where mugging and 'quicknappings' (forced to an ATM to pay your own ransom) are not a matter of if but when; and let's not forget Chad, Sudan, Colombia, South Africa, Haiti and a dozen other countries around the world where someone else's whim may end your life just moments from now.

Often the danger doesn't come from other humans; the

Arctic and Antarctic are both hostile, unforgiving environments where temperatures drop below –60°C, and when you call for help no one answers. The dangerous heat and animals of the world's deserts like the Sahara and the Gobi claim lives each and every year.

But for every dangerous place we would never dare visit there is someone who loves it dearly. And as Robert Young Pelton of www.comebackalive.com and Fielding's DangerFinder found after cataloguing the world's most dangerous places sometimes it's the places closest to home that you really have to worry about. Unexpectedly his home country, the USA, was one of the most dangerous countries he charted. But then it is a place where as many as 31,000 convenience store clerks are shot at every year.

After my own experiences of a murderous day on the backstreets of Moharrem Bey in northern Egypt and the mafia-run backwaters of Thailand where I felt safer than in many areas of London, my current hometown, I'm inclined to agree. It doesn't matter whether you're in Iraq, Afghanistan, Burma or Bolton, you always need to challenge your perceptions of what is dangerous. After all, danger is where you find it.

Dangerous Jobs

For most of us danger involves getting caught looking at websites we shouldn't be looking at by an overzealous supervisor. Of course just having a dangerous job doesn't mean you'll get any adventure to go with it. In the UK for example, according to the Health & Safety Executive more than six thousand people die due to work-related cancers every year. If you work in China's coal mines then life is truly abysmal. They account for more than 80 per cent of coal-mining deaths worldwide but as the statistics from a communist state are notoriously unreliable it's hard to be certain of the true count. The most reliable figures say that at least 31,000 people died in mines between 2000 and 2006, and even though they can manipulate the figures the government are still reporting increases each year. So if you're looking for a little adventure with your danger you might consider these jobs.

Outdoors Instructor/Supervisor/Sports Professional

Skydiving to Everest, tour guide to the North Pole, ice diving in Siberia (sports, salvage or research scientist), stunt-driving instructor, P1 crew, they all have their dangers and certainly plenty of stress but the personal, social and financial rewards if you find your niche will make you feel alive and are definitely going to be worth it.

Commercial Drivers

Statistically both here and in the US, road accidents are the number one killer with more than 54,000 crashes a year in the UK. Still you could be driving in a country where the driving test is of the 'drive forward, now stop, give me the money, you've passed' variety. They don't even have statistics. For more adventurous routes try an evasive driving course and then apply your skills to the military or celebrity sector, train as a test engineer/driver for motor firms or take up racing for a living.

Fisherman/Merchant Seaman/Loggers/Roughnecks

Each of these roles can attract handsome tax free salaries and serious danger. The mortality rate is high for deep sea fishermen who brave the elements in all weathers to make their daily catch: 103 deaths per 100,000 in the UK. For merchant seamen it's 53 in 100,000. For loggers in the US the risks are flying timber, falling trees and lethal machinery. There it's around 81 deaths per 100,000. Roughnecks face dangers from oil fires and heavy industrial machines that will rip off a limb as well as kidnapping and shooting in certain parts of the world. There are no reliable worldwide stats for roughnecks but on American oilfields it's around 29 bodies per 100,000 workers. Still any one of these jobs beats slipping on the soap in the bath or getting knocked over by a school bus.

Deep-Sea Divers

Commercial and military divers face drowning and risk of serious or fatal injuries from working with industrial equipment in very unfriendly environments. They are also susceptible to a series of mental and physical problems as a consequence of prolonged periods (weeks at a time) beneath the surface and high consumption of compressed gas, six times more than on land, as well as decompression and nitrogen narcosis. All that and if the air mix they breathe contains helium they'll talk in a squeaky voice too. Shark attacks are rare for commercial divers but they do happen. Industrial accidents like setting yourself in concrete, shoddy equipment or operator error are far more likely. Understandably compensation is generous.

Bomb Disposal

In the British Army a bomb disposal expert is known as a 'Felix', a cat with nine lives. But it's not a macho job; they take multiple exams to weed out the gung-ho hero types. Chris Hunter spent four months in Iraq doing what he considered 'the most dangerous job in the world'. He told the

Telegraph that people go into bomb disposal for three reasons: atonement, duty and the buzz. He says for him it was all three as well as what journalist Cassandra Jardine reported as atonement for the minor-sounding sin of 'having too many girlfriends'.

Private Military and Security Contractors

If you're a bodyguard for a celebrity then the biggest danger is going to be screaming fans or the histrionic fits of your boss. If however your work takes you further afield then be sure to go in with your eyes wide open. The market for PMSCs took off after 9/11 and the subsequent invasion of Iraq. When the occupying governments then disbanded the country's military they left a gaping hole in the national infrastructure. In *The Circuit* Bob Shepherd estimates that the US government would have needed 50,000 extra troops just to secure its portion of Iraq. However both the American and British governments promised a quick war with few casualties and couldn't commit more troops without losing face and possibly elections.

Cue boom time for PMSCs and outsourced military contractors. For British PMSCs in 2003 collective revenues were £320 million, by 2004 they'd shot up to £1.8 billion (War on Want figures) and it's estimated that out of a total $21 billion for Iraqi reconstruction 34 per cent of that went on commercial security. In 2008 there were 126,000 men and women on outsourced private security contracts and there are no official statistics for the casualty rate among these contractors. Iraq isn't the only conflict zone out there and if you're seriously considering a private military career be diligent, do your research. Rates are going down as more regular guys are trained up to join the circuit as what can only be described as cannon fodder. There are good and bad PMSCs out there; avoid designer military showoffs and companies that don't value your safety.

All these jobs are physically dangerous as are more every-day jobs like policemen, construction worker, firefighter, aid worker, cycle courier, bouncer, bus driver, journalist or pilot. And although there are lots more mortality figures available I wouldn't ever put you off doing any one of these jobs. Just go in knowing that you're doing a real job rather than counting time.

You could of course opt for something emotionally or socially dangerous instead. Drag queen on a naval vessel would do it. Or you could be a stay-at-home father, a social worker, a carer or a performer. Personally I find the idea of getting up on stage as a stand-up comedian and trying to make a room laugh out loud far scarier than most of the jobs listed above. Apart from ice diving that is: for some reason I have a recurring nightmare about that one. But hey one day maybe I'll do both. If you have the will everything is possible.

WORK AND MONEY

The more you need the money, the more people will tell you what to do. The less control you will have. The more bullshit you will have to swallow. The less joy it will bring. Know this and plan accordingly.

Hugh Macleod

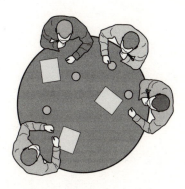

Money – The Fundamentals

'Let the market decide!' Set an alarm bell to go off whenever you hear this trite little phrase. The kinds of people who trot this nonsense out are usually lobbyists dressed up as experts or one of their gullible peers. The phrase itself has two implied meanings. The first is that you through your purchasing choices determine what is right. So if there is a market for it whatever it is should be permitted to be sold. Clearly this is so much balderdash and poppycock; there's obviously a market out there for paedophile pornography for example but I can't see anyone proposing adding that to the top shelf can you? The second unspoken meaning is 'buy what we tell you to buy'. As every good marketer knows this is what we really want so buy buy buy when the market is booming and prices are inflated. We'll happily buy it back from you at a savagely reduced rate when the market nosedives.

Remember James Bond had an expense account. He didn't actually have to pay for anything. So before we all get carried away with ideas of private helicopters and powerboats we need to get our finances in order. Foppish Victorian gentle-man were primarily trust fund babies. We on the other hand are the combination of the trailblazing OGs (original gentle-men) and the modern. We determine our own finances so whether you have an income of £60 or £60,000 per week here are the basics.

Have a Strategy

Being in control of your finances means you won't be a victim whether it's boom time or bust. So whether you want to capitalise on cheap house prices in a downturn or chase equity in a boom you need a strategy that will keep money in your accounts rather than other people's. J. D. Roth of *Get Rich Slowly* recommends the following:

- Andrew Tobias suggests a simple three-step budget: Destroy all of your credit cards. Invest 20% of all that you earn (and never touch it). Live on the remaining 80% no matter what.
- Elizabeth Warren's balanced money formula is outstand-ing. It's the budget I use. Allocate 20% of your after-tax income for savings (or debt reduction), 50% for needs and the remaining 30% for wants.
- If you crave a little more complexity try the 60% solution from Richard Jenkins at MSN Money. He says spend 20% of your pre-tax income on savings (half for retirement, half for long-term savings or debt), 60% to committed expenses, 10% to irregular expenses and 10% for fun.

Monitor Your Spending with a Simple Budget

Ever hear people say, 'I spend as much as I earn' even when they get a pay rise? These people simply don't know what they're spending their money on and if your outgoings are regularly more than your income you're heading for trouble.

You may not be a mad fan of complicated budgets but consider using a spreadsheet, Microsoft Money or a simple diary to suit your style. Track your income and outgoings as well your expenditure. Keep it simple. I used to do this even when living in a tax-free environment and didn't need to file accounts. Knowing where you stand financially keeps you sane and usually takes no more than half an hour.

These days you don't even have to pay for the software: www.wesabe.com and www.mint.com both offer similar functionality to Money. You can monitor all your bank accounts, track spending habits and set specific targets and goals all online and for free. You can also download versions for your mobile device or iPhone as well. For a downloadable Excel budget planner go to Martin Lewis's excellent www.moneysavingexpert.com.

Give Yourself a Pay Rise

Once you've got an idea of your regular spending patterns see where you can save money. Shopping around for better deals on hire purchase, utilities, TV and phone, water, gas and council tax can save you thousands according to Lewis. That's effectively an instant pay rise as well as being tax free.

Optimise Your Bank Accounts

Make your money work harder by seeking out higher interest rates and better banking products. There are several money comparison websites out there such as www.money-supermarket.com that will help you find who is offering the highest interest rates for your savings and current account in seconds.

Clean Up Your Credit

If you need credit then check your credit report by getting a copy from either Equifax or Experian, the two main agencies used by banks to assess your creditworthiness. The main things to look out for are incorrect entries that can be removed or unfavourable ones as well as making sure that all your details are correct. For example if you live in an apartment but the apartment number is wrong you could be judged on your neighbour's creditworthiness rather than your own. Add yourself to the electoral roll immediately and put one or two utilities in your name. Pay everyone off without fail. No excuses. However despite what most people believe credit records aren't everything; many banks have their own internal credit scoring system that they use. Try the credit checker on Martin Lewis's website to get an idea of what they are looking at before you apply.

Build Your Creditworthiness

If your credit rating truly sucks and this can happen simply because you're a private individual who doesn't borrow or vote, or perhaps you've worked abroad for a number of years, then you need to build a successful lending track record. The way to do this is to show that you are borrowing and paying back regularly. The easiest method is to get a credit card with 0 per cent on purchases and then use it for all purchases. Then pay this off at the end of each month or put the cash you would have used into a high-interest savings account and then pay off the credit card before the end of the 0 per cent offer (this is a basic form of what is known as 'stoozing' or gaining interest on cash borrowed at 0 per cent). This will create a track record but if you want to raise the amount of money you can borrow try this: put £500 in a limited access savings account. Borrow £500 against it as say a car loan. You will be charged high interest on this but you will pay the full amount back before the first payment is due. Repeat the process and then place the next £500 borrowed in an easy access savings account. Then borrow against the combined £1000 and pay both £500s back before term. Keep doing this and increasing the amount you borrow. You can up this to tens of thousands in just a few months using this technique.

A Warning on Credit

Golden rule: don't spend credit. A good debt is one that covers its own cost like a rental property where the value of the rent covers the mortgage; or saves you money like a mortgage that is lower than your rent. A bad debt is one that doesn't do either. If you use credit as 'real' money instead of a tool or a temporary substitute that you immediately pay back you will come unstuck. No questions. So if you raise credit, spend it and the debt can't cover its own costs look out. You have been warned. Also always pay off credit cards first before investing or saving as the interest rates charged are always more than you make through saving. It's a false economy to do otherwise.

Educate Yourself

Pick a subject area such as credit, investment, loans, day trading, share investing, property, online retail. Then buy or borrow one book at a time. Read it, understand the key subject areas, make shorthand notes of the main points that you can refer back to and research any supplemental material online until you've mastered the whole area. Once you understand it and can potentially invest, trade or do whatever you need to do, move on to the next subject and increase your knowledge.

Open an Investment Account

ISAs, mini ISAs, trackers, funds – there are all kinds of investment opportunities available to you out there. I'm not an investment expert so I'm not going to recommend which one you go for but what is certain is that thanks to the wonders of compound interest the earlier you invest or save, the better off you'll be. If you only remember one thing from this section remember this. Albert Einstein called compound interest 'the greatest mathematical discovery of all time'. So sit up and pay attention.

Here's what www.motleyfool.co.uk, one of the best sources of money advice out there, has to say about it. 'The concept is this. When you invest money you earn interest on your capital. The next year you earn interest on both your original capital and the interest from the first year. In the third year you earn interest on your capital and the first two years' interest. You get the picture. The concept of earning interest on your interest is the miracle of compounding.

'It's very much like a snowball effect. As your capital rolls down the hill it becomes bigger and bigger. Even if you start with a small snowball, given enough time you can end up with an extremely large snowball indeed.'

So if you save £100 a month for forty years and your investments compound at 12 per cent a year how much will you have? The answer according to The Fool is an astonishing £980,000. That's a staggering sum and far more than your intial stake of £48,000.

Set Financial Goals

While this is all heady, exciting stuff let's not forget what we're here for. Do you need money for a mortgage deposit,

your child's education, investment, retirement or all of these?
Set yourself small, easily achievable goals for the next year.

- Establish an emergency fund to give you a buffer against
  redundancy or illness. Save and invest the bare minimum
  you require for two months this year, enough to cover
  your housing, food and bills. Each year or sooner add
  another two months until you have a year-long buffer.
- Pay off your credit card debt. You've learned what compound interest is; if 12 per cent will give you those kinds
  of returns how much will the bank's 20–30 per cent+
  interest rates lose you?
- Fully fund a cash ISA this year.
- Save for major expenses such as cars, weddings and children. Don't borrow.

Create a Money File

If you don't already have one set one up. It could be a shoe-
box that you throw everything into or better still a proper
file for each year with sections for each bill, payment and
account. Keep it simple. Use this to give yourself an account-
ing day once a month to make sure everything is in order.
Putting aside one day a month or every week if you prefer,
will instantly make you feel more in control of your finances
and when you start to see the numbers creep up you'll be
very glad you did.

Ultimately you decide how your finances work best not
the market, your friends, your parents, spouse or the man on
the TV. Take control and educate yourself. Do it now.

Never Get Ripped Off Again –
Negotiating Skills from the Boardroom,
the Street and the Souk

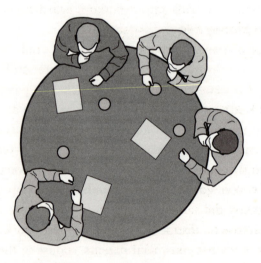

Okay in thirty seconds you are going into the next room to negotiate a deal. What can I teach you now that will mean you walk away with a smile on your face and a potentially better deal than you've ever had? Simply this: 'Don't forget your LIMs.'

To get the best deal you can there are three key negotiating points you simply must establish *before* you enter the room.

Like – what is your dream scenario? If you could have everything you ever wanted from this deal what would that be? That's what you're aiming for.

Intend – what will you settle for? You're probably not going to get everything you want no matter how much you negotiate but it would be foolish to walk away from a profitable deal. What would you be happy with?

Must – what is your walk away point? It would also be foolish to accept an unprofitable deal or where you think the deal might be more hassle than it's worth. At what point do you politely thank them for meeting with you and exit stage right?

If you know the above then you are more prepared than most people who walk into negotiate regardless of whether it's the boardroom or the car showroom.

If I had an extra minute I'd also add.

The Elk and the Wolf

Imagine you're in a sled being chased by a wolf. If you throw elk steaks to distract the wolf will it just keep coming to see if you've got more to give?

It's exactly the same in negotiation. Don't give anything away for free to distract or appease; they will only push harder to see what else they can get.

X and Y

It's essential that you present any discount or offer *after* theirs: 'If you give me X I'll give you Y.'

If you present it the other way round, 'I'll give you Y if you . . .,' a sharp negotiator will cut you off immediately after your offer of Y and say, 'Thank you very much.' Any attempt to assert yourself after this will be played off as a snub and they will act the mild-mannered wolf. You can of course work it the other way too.

If I had an extra two minutes I'd also tell you about cultural baggage. In our global market different cultural factors come into play in any negotiation.

The Power of Silence

As Britons we've been brought up to feel uncomfortable with silences of more than a few seconds. Most non-Western negotiators know this and use it to their advantage. Take this following high-level meeting between a leading European chemical company and a Japanese partner. When the time came to seal the deal and it was down to one remaining point the Japanese negotiators stayed silent, making the potential new partners feel deeply unsettled. However the European team had also been briefed on the power of silence. Forty-five minutes later when nobody on either side had spoken the European team leader stood up and said, 'I can see you need more time to make your mind up. I'll be back in a few minutes.' He left his own team sitting in silence and when he returned their new partners signed and on his terms.

Everything is Negotiable

In a Middle Eastern souk or bazaar, or a South-East Asian marketplace, you must negotiate. Culturally anything from a 10–80 per cent discount is factored into the initial asking price. So always push for a lower price. Once you have agreed a lower price it is considered rude not to buy. If however you have not agreed to the price don't be bullied into accepting it. A walk away at this point may even get you a bigger reduction.

Emotions Lose Money

This is cross-cultural. Two very good friends of mine are property millionaires, lovely people but tough in negotiation. Usually in every negotiation if one is more emotionally attached to the deal than the other they hand over to the more level-headed partner. However when it came to purchasing their new dream home emotions were a significant factor and even these two canny negotiators didn't negotiate as hard as they could have. They now have their dream home and are very happy with it so it's no big deal. But if you are going into a negotiation that is make or break for you or your company you cannot afford to be overly emotional so either check your emotions at the door or have someone else close the deal for you.

On the other hand if you know someone desperately wants what you are selling then you have a very strong hand to play.

Swinging Dicks – Office Politics and How to Win Every Time

For many of us where we work is often a barbaric place and if you want to tackle the politics head on you first need to evaluate the environment. Is it a Prada-wearing, female-focused media office, a pin-striped penile-pecking order, a meritocracy or a mini dictatorship with a boho veneer?

Understanding and not taking it personally is key to your success. Once you've established which dungeon of hell you're working in, bide your time. Observe without getting involved until you understand your organisation's political style. If you notice inconsistency or that there's more than one game being played continue watching until you understand what the patterns and motivations really are. There is more than one way to skin a corporate cat.

The Direct Approach

Rob Yeung, author of *The Rules of Office Politics*, is even more cynical than I am. For him it's a dog-eat-dog world where if you're not willing to be the alpha mutt you're going to get eaten. In a recent *Times* article he said for those who do not recognise the harsh world he describes, 'Wake up and smell the coffee.' His advice:

- Accept the reality and power of office politics.
- Get to know the bigwigs and rising stars.
- Don't waste time on no-hopers and has-beens.
- Cultivating influential people matters more than working hard.
- Think strategically and understand the office undercurrents by becoming a confidant. Even when you are bored by colleagues' stories, fake attentiveness.

It's advice all right but I'm not sure it'll make you anything more than a low-level game player. The trouble with office politicking is that for most people by the time they realise they're in the game it's already too late. The best way to do that is to not play the game at all. How do we do that?

The Real Game – Forewarned is Forearmed

Is someone doing a Frank Spencer on you, are they Kissing Like Judas or are they more than their Jobs Worth? Mike Phipps and Colin Gautrey run workshops and training seminars teaching the unwritten rules of the game through their Politics at Work™ brand. They have seventy-five workshop exercises and games that teach some of the dirtiest political tricks played on you when you're least aware. If you want the straight dope on how to survive and prosper this is how you do it. I've got twenty-two of them for you to review. See if you recognise whether someone is planning on making your life truly uncomfortable.

Photocopier Game

Deliberately leaving disinformation lying around for others to discover e.g. a document 'accidentally' left on the photocopier.

Development Opportunity

Management spin to motivate someone to take on a task, project or assignment they might reasonably refuse by pretending that it will be good for their development.

Kiss Like Judas

Declaring public support for an embattled project or individual while privately plotting for change behind the scenes.

Double Agent

Joining a group or team in the guise of help but really to secretly gather information or undermine their efforts.

Email to the Gods

Using email to shame or coerce another. Usually an email arriving from a colleague (which includes either true or false information) levelling accusations of blame, which is copied on to important others.

Tell Me More

Duplicitously resisting a valid suggestion by continually demanding more information in the hope that the other person will eventually drop it.

No Invitation
The tactic of leaving people off distribution lists so they miss important meetings or information and therefore appear disorganised, badly prepared or ignorant.

Respect
'With all due respect . . .' which is code for 'I disagree (and my respect for you is at best tacit').

Plausible Deniability
The tactic of 'skilful ignorance', remaining deliberately uninformed so as to be blameless if a plan goes wrong later.

Re-Structure
The tactic of reorganising a team or department specifically to get an unwanted person out rather than to drive improvements or serve customers better.

Talent Handcuffs/Ball and Chain
Ensuring that a talented team member is denied a rightful and deserved promotion opportunity so they stay and protect the manager's self-interest.

While the Cat's Away
Waiting until the important decision maker is away to use the delegated authority to push through decisions that they would otherwise challenge or block.

Jobs Worth
Selectively enforcing the rules against someone when for a different person the rules would be relaxed.

Frank Spencer
The tactic of being 'skilfully incompetent' so that others might feel obliged to take over unwanted tasks.

Creative Magpie
Exaggerating involvement in the ideas and good work of others or blatantly stealing their good work and passing it off as their own.

Free Lunch
The tactic of bestowing all manner of gifts and favours on another to invite them to feel indebted so as to be able to coerce them at a later date.

Rock and a Hard Place
Manipulating people by offering limited or fixed choices, expecting the victim to choose the lesser of two evils.

Tender Bender
Manipulating or using the tendering process disingenuously usually to gain ideas or solutions which are then appropriated and applied internally.

We're Right Behind You
The tactic of setting someone up as spokesperson and falsely suggesting back up or support, which vanishes at the first sign of conflict.

Absent Friends/ Re-Write
The tactic of re-writing history or facts to gain an advantage or to make people feel differently about past events – or wrongly blaming failure on people who are no longer around.

Training Day
The game of getting the trainer to do the manager's dirty work. Perhaps providing a team member with difficult feedback which the line manager avoids giving.

Divide and Rule
The game of mischievously setting up opponents to fight each other in order to distract them.

These look deceptively straightforward but to give you an idea of how powerful these tactics really are the last entry, Divide and Rule, is a political strategy that has been used successfully by every imperial power from Roman times to the British Empire to rule the lands they conquered. It's called politics for a reason and if you don't understand the political landscape around you then you are at a serious disadvantage.

Study the above and once you recognise when someone is trying to run a game on you, you can interrupt the pattern and undermine their efforts.

If you want to study this in more depth I recommend visiting www.politicsatwork.com or pick up a copy of Phipps and Gautrey's excellent book, *21 Dirty Tricks at Work*, where they've gone into detail about the main strategies used. Alternatively you could persuade your boss to get them in for a reverse Training Day scenario and watch the squirming embarrassment as your colleagues get to play some of the games that they already play.

Funny how we spend half our waking lives on the job and most of us still have little idea how it really works. I know this will help.

How to Hire a Hit Man

If the office politics have really got out of hand you may need to up the ante. Passive aggression is just aggression after all. So if the only way out or up is to off the competition you could go back to that 'hardest pub in town' we visited back in the How to Get a Gun section and have a chat with the guy who thinks he's a little tasty.

He will of course listen attentively to what you have to say then one of three things will happen:

- He will agree to do the job and ask you to pay him an 'advance' to recce the mark. When you follow up to find out when it's about to happen he will simply say, 'What advance?'
- You will be arrested as he is actually a cop.
- If the pub is in Glasgow you will hand over your £20 and wait in the pub, your alibi. He will return when the job is done and probably bum a cigarette off you.

If you are determined to shoot your way to the top you could hire a professional of course. To do this you would need to have connections either in organised crime or with government departments with the preface 'Secret'. They usually call their hit men assassins; it's the same job only with more foreign travel and a pension.

If you look online you could try www.hitman.us, an American firm that specialises in 'reliable contract killing'. For a mere $50,000 per head (excuse the pun) your basic contract includes: 'a simple killing that is traditionally accomplished by administering two rounds of ammunition, at close range, into the back of the head, through a silenced .32 calibre pistol. Typically the mark doesn't even feel a thing. We use Glaser Safety Slugs that ensure a guaranteed kill, by exploding and fragmenting inside the brain. Thanks to the small calibre pistol the entry wound is extremely small; sometimes the external damage is so minimal that the entry wound can be completely covered by the hair and is often not immediately apparent to a medical examiner [. . .]. Typically, there is no exit wound. Furthermore, we use untraceable, first-time-use weapons.'

Very professional, I'm sure you'll agree. Quality control is important whatever line of work you're in. However if you're foolish enough to send them a cheque or even ask to join their organisation then expect a sarcastic email and at best a company T-shirt with 'STAFF' emblazoned on it.

There are many reasons to hire a hit man; the usual ones are to improve your job prospects or solve a business dispute, to secure your inheritance, get rid of a spouse because you're not man enough to ask for a divorce or simply to put that noisy dog next door out of your misery.

A real hit goes something like this recent one on notorious Colombian cocaine lord Leonidas Vargas as reported by www.topnews.in.

Madrid January 2009
A man with his face partly covered by a cap and scarf entered room 537 at a hospital in the Spanish capital. 'Are you Leonidas Vargas?' he asked one of the two patients in the room with a South American accent. The patient pointed to the man sleeping in the other bed.

'Turn your back and keep quiet,' the visitor instructed, turned towards the other patient, and shot him four times with a gun equipped with a silencer.

By the time doctors and nurses had rushed into the room, the killer and his suspected accomplice, who had kept guard behind the door, were gone.

Still now you know that if a potential hit man ever asks you if you're you, say no.

One wannabe hit man, a Mr Essam Eid, an Egyptian-born poker dealer living in Las Vegas, apparently couldn't wait to get his hands dirty and set up a website called hitmanforhire.us under the alias Tony Luciano.

A woman with the contact name Lying Eyes hired him to kill Irishman P. J. Howard and his two sons for €90,000.

Lying Eyes turned out to be Howard's partner Sharon Collins. According to the *Irish Times* Howard said at the closing of her trial, 'Sharon has a very positive outlook on life and she was very loving and giving of her time to our extended families.' A bit too attentive and giving of her time perhaps. Eid double-crossed Collins and demanded €100,000 from Howard to call it off. Maybe she should have asked the guy down the pub.

Still there's definitely a market for it. A quick Google will find you a few more virtual hit men touting for business.

Alternatively she could have done it herself by getting hold of a copy of the controversial book *Hit Man: A Technical Manual for Independent Contractors* originally published by Paladin Press in 1983.

In 1993 a triple murder was committed in Montgomery County, Maryland, by James Perry who may have used the book as his guide. He was hired by Lawrence T. Horn to retrieve the proceeds of a trust fund that resulted from his ex-wife suing a hospital. The families of Mildred Horn, her son Trevor and her nurse Janice Saunders then sued Paladin Press and won. Since then although the book is not in the public domain it has been published on the internet. I'll be sure to post a link to it on my website.

You could also ask your trader friends about Assassination Markets. These are theoretical prediction markets where anyone can make a trade (place a bet) using anonymous electronic money and pseudonymous remailers on the future date of death of a given individual and collect a large payoff if they 'guess' the date accurately.

Any would-be assassin is then incentivised to make the kill on the correct date and collect their winnings. Because payment is simply the payout from a bet, or shorted stock, it is significantly more difficult to assign criminal liability for the hit.

The theoretical set-up was initially proposed in 1994 and then according to www.answers.com, 'These issues arguably left the realm of the theoretical when U.S. stock markets based in Manhattan took a trillion-dollar hit in September 2001. A serious investigation was launched in Autumn 2001 by the U.S. Securities and Exchange Commission to determine whether large blocks of short-sold airline stock could be traced back to Al Qaeda, the group responsible for the terrorist acts carried out on the 11th of September; the investigation eventually announced that the short-selling was part of a legitimate hedging strategy unconnected to Al Qaeda or other extremist groups, but did not disclose the identities of the beneficiaries.'

The extensive cooperation of fundamentalist terrorist groups and suggestions that they were in fact trading targets and objectives in different nations, gave rise to the idea that a covert assassination swap market may well already be in global operation. A group could perform an action in one place and a seemingly unrelated group in another place would profit from the act.

There's clearly a market for assassination at many different levels of society. Unfortunately the reality is nothing like the romantic image portrayed in movies. Russia currently holds the title for most hit men per capita with their penchant for poisonings, gold chains and tacky sports gear while the cowardly religious men of Iraq are paying $100 per head for 'honour' killings. According to the *Guardian* in 2008 eighty-one women or girls were executed in Basra alone.

There is also another kind of wannabe hit man out there and one you need to be on the look out for. In 2006 emails started to appear from senders claiming to be hit men hired to kill the recipient. They would then demand money to not take the job, just like Mr Eid. In 2007 the emails grew a little more sophisticated with claims that they were the FBI in London. By 2007, 115 complaints had been lodged with the FBI.

In one case a recipient responded that he wanted to be left alone and threatened to call the authorities. The scammer, who was demanding an advance payment of $20,000, emailed back and reiterated the threat this time with some personal details about the recipient – his work address, marital status and daughter's full name. Then an ultimatum: 'TELL ME NOW ARE YOU READY TO DO WHAT I SAID OR DO YOU WANT ME TO PROCEED WITH MY JOB? ANSWER YES/NO AND DON'T ASK ANY QUESTIONS!!!'

Bill Shore, a special agent who supervises the computer crime squad in the FBI's Pittsburgh field office, said recipients should not be overly spooked when scammers incorporate their intended victims' personal details in their schemes.

'Personal information is widely available,' he said. 'Even if a person does not use the Internet or own a computer they could still be the victim of a computer crime such as identity theft.'

The basic rule is if ever you are approached like this don't respond. You have been warned.

Cruising Without the Bruising – The Four-Hour Work Week

Is there another way to live and work? One where you don't have to turn up on time and be grossly overworked whether it's for yourself or someone else? Where you can be the independent modern gentleman you've always wanted to be? Timothy Ferris, author of *The 4-Hour Work Week*, believes there is. He writes, 'Life doesn't have to be so damned hard. It really doesn't. Most people, my past self included, have spent too much time convincing themselves that life has to be hard, a resignation to 9-to-5 drudgery in exchange for (sometimes) relaxing weekends and the occasional keep-it-short-or-get-fired vacation.'

Sounds great but what about the rent, the bills, your expensive car and the holidays you already booked? Well quite. So how does he propose doing this? Through a combination of skills he's learned from what he terms the New Rich, those who understand that 'gold is getting old' and are using currencies he says have far more leverage: time and mobility.

One way he proposes to do this is to apply the 80/20 principle to your life – that you currently receive 80 per cent of your results from 20 per cent of your input.

Step 1. Interrupt the interruptions. Take emails for example. They speed up communication, facilitate information sharing and increase productivity. Or do they?

How many times do you invent things to do to avoid doing what is really important? How easy is it with email? Organising folders, sorting spam, taking ages to write the perfect response when a simple yes/no will do. Instead check emails twice a day only. Then only respond to the emails that need responses. Ignore everything else. Then add an automated response that advises them either to call your office phone at predetermined times if it's not urgent or your mobile if it is urgent. And then keep it brief. This trains you and yours to get to the point. Why? 'Emergencies are seldom that,' Ferris says. 'People are poor judges of importance and inflate minutiae to fill time and feel important.' So far from decreasing your effectiveness this strategy forces you and others to evaluate your actions and decrease meaningless and time-consuming contact. Try it today; I'd have barely had time to shoot things if I hadn't done this one thing.

If you like this then Ferris has a whole lifestyle design plan mapped out to turn you into someone who can work from a beach somewhere exotic or run your own business with minimal input i.e. four hours a week.

His own model is based on online retail but it could be anything that works with the kinds of people you know and the kind of markets that are open to you already without you even realising. Property management through an agent is one alternative that we Brits know very well but what about revenue from copyrighted works, reselling other people's products on eBay, automated information services. What else can you think of?

Step 2. Outsource your life. Delegate time consuming tasks to a personal assistant, usually based in a foreign country where the interest rate favours your currency, who is usually more qualified than you are. I've yet to try this but really it is one I should have used to collate the research for this book.

A. J. Jacobs, editor-at-large for *Esquire* magazine, had this to say when he tried it for himself: 'I've been assigned to write a profile of this woman [*Esquire*'s Sexiest Woman Alive], and I really don't want to have to slog through all the heavy-breathing fan websites about her. When I open Honey's [his remote PA's] file, I have this reaction: America is f*cked. There are charts. There are section headers. There is a well-organized breakdown of her pets, measurements, and favourite foods (e.g. swordfish). If all Bangalorians are like Honey, I pity Americans about to graduate college. They're up against a hungry, polite, Excel proficient Indian army.'

Damn I'm jealous. So why should CEOs at FTSE 100 companies have all the fun? His PA even settled arguments in his marriage and took on his stress for him, no joke.

Excuse me dear readers I think I might have to cut this section short and go find myself a new PA. You can read the full article or find out more of Ferris's ideas to make you one of the New Rich on his blog, www.fourhourworkweek.com.

In Praise of Idleness – The Philosophy and the Foolishness of the 9–5

Of course Ferris wasn't the first to propose the end of the formal working week. Bertrand Russell, that intellectual giant of the twentieth century, likened the principle of work for work's sake to the fabricated ethics of 'slave-state' thinking from pre-industrial societies then applied to circumstances totally unlike those in which they arose. Quite simply he explained, 'wage-earners are expected to overwork or starve'.

He argued that in the modern world (this was 1932) we were totally capable of providing for everyone in society and enjoying leisure time for non-passive leisure pursuits. 'Modern technique has made it possible to diminish enormously the amount of labour required to secure the necessaries of life for everyone. This was made obvious during the war [the First World War]. At that time all the men in the armed forces, and all the men and women engaged in the production of munitions, all the men and women engaged in spying, war propaganda, or government offices connected with the war, were withdrawn from productive occupations. In spite of this, the general level of well-being among unskilled wage-earners on the side of the Allies was higher than before or since. The significance of this fact was concealed by finance: borrowing made it appear as if the future was nourishing the present. But that of course would have been impossible; a man cannot eat a loaf of bread that does not yet exist.'

This is a lesson that could so easily have been learned in the recent banking chaos. Russell like Ferris was quite clear on the time needed to supply the basics of a happy life: 'The war showed conclusively that, by the scientific organization of production, it is possible to keep modern populations in fair comfort on a small part of the working capacity of the modern world. If, at the end of the war, the scientific organization, which had been created in order to liberate men for fighting and munitions work, had been preserved, and the hours of the week had been cut down to four, all would have been well. Instead of that the old chaos was restored.'

Notably the production of unwanted goods. 'We keep a large percentage of the working population idle, because we can dispense with their labour by making the others overwork. When all these methods prove inadequate, we have a war.'

If you think that I might be losing the plot here then read up on Ferris's life or check out www.anxietyculture.com, which parodies the excesses of the work ethic. It explains how phoning in sick is good for the economy, questions the rise of meaningless jobs, provides subversive stats that refute common media fallacies and is a welcome addition to online civilisation. It makes for good reading in your cubicle. Your boss might disapprove of the laughter but then most Satan worshippers do.

Russell was also adamant that most of what we call civilisation is contributed by those with time on their hands. Active leisure, he argued, cultivated the arts and discovered the sciences, wrote books, invented philosophies and refined social relations. 'Without the leisure class,' he said, 'mankind would never have emerged from barbarism.'

MAN THINGS

A few things worth knowing

Lost Erections – Where Do They All Go?

My doctor nods his head and smiles. He has a wicked little glint in his eye. 'So you would like some Viagra?'

'Yes please.'

'I have at least one man a day coming through here asking for this. I will give you a double dose. Take half a tablet half an hour before sex or whenever you think you might have a problem, and don't worry it's perfectly normal. According to a study in the *British Medical Journal* every man will have this problem at some point in his life. These should sort things out and take away the fear.'

So what is an overly endowed, high-flying stud muffin like me doing asking a doctor for Viagra? Research obviously and I'm nothing if not thorough, which is why my next stop is Soho's sex shops. Behind the frilly curtains and dark entrances the shops are surprisingly clean, colourful and full of housewives. The shop assistants go out of their way to be helpful, which is lucky for me because if there's one topic liable to make a man turn away in sheer horror and flinch at the imagined fingers pointing in his direction it's this one.

According to the Sexual Dysfunction Association nearly every man will at some point be unable to get or sustain an erection and roughly 10 per cent of all men will have a more severe problem with erectile dysfunction (ED) – the shiny new phrase for impotence. However only 10 per cent of those will ever seek help. That's 1 per cent of all men. I can understand why. I feel tense and defensive just writing about it. It's a far more terrifying subject than jumping from planes, shooting machine guns or learning to power slide, which is why I'm duty bound to put myself out there for your reading pleasure.

The only male shop assistant I can find looks just like Lurch from the Addams Family. When I ask if he has any-thing new in the keeping-it-up stakes he guides me to a glass cabinet filled with wicked-looking chrome devices that would look more at home in the Science Museum. He points out a long 5mm wide metal tube with a black rubber handle. It comes with a black box that has settings for swinger, climax and shooter.

'What exactly is that?'

'A urethra probe, sir. You slide it in and then send an electric current into . . .'

I'm not ready to be quite that adventurous. I settle for some herbal Viagra and an adjustable rubber cock ring instead. An old school gent complete with school tie unashamedly prices up bondage gear in his best colonial voice behind me. Good for him.

So here's what I know about impotence. It strikes fear into the hearts of men because the threat of it means you are somehow less of a man; in dictionary terms you are either

sterile or unable to sustain an erection. Its main meaning . . .
weakness.

The threat of it is probably the cause of more flaccid
penises than any other reason, the fearful question of unman-
liness; no wonder it's such a problem and one that once it
starts can recur again and again.

The crippling effects of the experience haven't changed
much in two thousand years. The Roman satirist Petronius
had this to say in his play *Satyrica*:

> Three times I whip the dreadful weapon out,
> And three times softer than a Brussels sprout,
> I quail, in those dire straits my manhood blunted,
> No longer up to what just now I wanted.

He used humour to show how his hero Encolpius encounters a problem all too familiar to modern ears. But for the
Romans and Greeks the ability to penetrate regardless of
whether it was a woman or a boy was more important than
the ability to conceive.

Sex became focused solely on fertility and conception with
the spread of monotheistic religion and the incitement to go
forth and multiply. After all, growing your own believers is far
simpler than trying to convert them. So successful was that bit
of religious propaganda that by Charles II's time his inability to
sire an heir cost the Hapsburgs Spain while rumours of Louis
XVI's failure to consummate his marriage led in no small part
to the French Revolution. George Washington's ability to
found a dynasty even helped ensure the future of the fledgling
United States. Talk about performance anxiety. Imagine if the
fate of a nation rested on your next nocturnal frolic.

Fiascos in the bedroom have at one time or other been
attributed to witchcraft, masturbation, repressed homosexual

desires, shell shock, sexual excess, sin, bad habits, evil spells, feminism, the Oedipus complex and the unconscious. In the scientific age we've pretty much come full circle again with the main focus on penetration. Happily we may even have sorted the problem out. Thank goodness.

Causes

The most common reasons are stress, tiredness, anxiety and excessive alcohol consumption. Worrying about it can create a more persistent problem due to 'fear of failure'. Until very recently psychological factors were thought to be behind most problems but apparently physical conditions feature in about 75 per cent of sufferers as well. Most men with impotence inevitably have a combination of psychological and physical causes.

Okay so here's the outrageously good news: in nearly all cases there really is nothing to worry about. In fact since the turn of the twenty-first century treatments for erectile dysfunction have improved so much that nearly every sufferer can be assured of a return to successful intercourse.

No wonder my doctor was smiling so much. A treatment that works.

Physical

Your erection works by allowing blood into the spongy tissues of your penis and not letting it back out again. So anything that affects the veins, arteries or nerves in the penis can cause a problem such as:

- Excessive alcohol consumption (brewer's droop).
- Smoking.
- Recreational drugs (e.g. cocaine).

- Being overweight and out of condition.
- Blocked arteries caused by high cholesterol.
- Diabetes.
- Certain medications for blood pressure and depression.
- Even drinking too much coffee.

Lack of testosterone is often cited as a physical cause but clinics charging large piles of cash to cure 'Male Hormone Deficiency' are often taking the gullible for a ride. According to most authorities lack of male hormone is very rare so buyer beware.

Psychological

Do you get an erection in the mornings? Are you still able to get it up for masturbation? Then the likelihood is that when your wee man is 180° shy of heaven it's due to one of the following:

- Anxiety – usually worrying about your performance.
- Guilt – infidelity is the usual cause.
- Relationship issues – such as no longer being attracted to your partner.
- Repressed sexuality – if you're gay and trying to have sex with a woman or if you're straight and trying to have sex with a man.
- Depression.
- Exhaustion.

What's more different stressors are likely to affect you at different ages.

Young men: anxiety about performance, nerves about pregnancy and the age old condom problem.

Middle age: stress and exhaustion are most common here along with post-bereavement problems of either a spouse or close family member. Problems related to diabetes also become more prevalent at this age.

After middle age: seventy per cent of seventy-year-olds are still sexually potent. However the prevalence of ED does increase with age. Deterioration of the blood vessels is the most common cause. Recent studies from 2007 showed that this coincided with deterioration of arteries to the brain and heart. Therefore staying healthy and keeping blood pressure and cholesterol levels down will help to avoid heart attacks, strokes and ED.

So What Works?

Take your time. Spending time just to be with your partner naked or otherwise takes the onus off performance and allows your unconscious to relax. You'll be surprised how effective this is. Touching, feeling, talking, caressing all work to arouse and stimulate and take the focus off standing to attention. For most men this alone will work.

Deal with Underlying Issues

Anxiety, stress, poor diet or too much alcohol all kill your libido. Change whichever element of your life isn't working and gradually sometimes suddenly your libido will return from the dead.

Pills

Viagra works. And even if you don't have problems after the experiments for this chapter I recommend taking one every once in a while just to remind yourself how it was to be a rampant, uncontrollable teen. Although the physical effects last for four hours the positive psychological after-effects last for weeks. Cialis is a newer ED treatment that lasts for up to thirty-six hours. I've not tried it myself but the side effects strictly warn that if your erection lasts for more than four hours you should seek help. Unless you're Cuba Gooding Jr who in a recent US TV commercial was seen to trip people up, knock them out and steer a car with his Cialis filled man thang and then finally get it trapped in a lift door.

Alternatives

Herbals from the sex shop do seem to work although more testing is needed. The ones I tried made me a little on edge and lasted about twelve hours. There are also several alternative treatments out there such as horny goat weed, traditional Chinese medicine and ayurveda; feel free to try any of them and see what works.

Another sex shop toy I did pick up was a cock ring. These work by trapping the blood in your penis after it's erect so they do work in maintaining your erection – seemingly for ever – but they won't necessarily help if you're having problems getting started.

Condom Correction

Ripping, tearing, slipping off and not being able to get them on in the first place are often immediate passion killers and a cause of sexual stress. The condom represents torment for many couples out there. According to the UK Family Planning Association, 35 per cent of men have problems with them slipping or falling off. Why? Simply because a quarter of UK males (and women too one would imagine) don't realise that they come in different sizes. And it's not the length that counts, it's the girth. So if you're using condoms here's how to use them successfully 100 per cent of the time. Measure the girth of your penis when it's erect in centimetres. If it's between 12 and 13 centimetres regular condoms from the chemist or vending machine will fit you just fine. If it's larger than 13 centimetres then opt for anything with 'large' written on it. For 12 centimetres or less go for the 'trim' and 'close fit' varieties. Do this and you'll never ever be scared of a condom again.

Hopefully I've removed some of your fears about this subject. I genuinely hope I have because if you're out there agonising over this there really is no need to. Find a willing partner and try any or all of the suggestions in this chapter and you will find something that suits you both and ensures 'manhood' is never an issue again. However finding the time to fit in all your fun sex play might be. So don't go blaming me if you break each other.

Forever Fit

The good news is we're now living longer than ever but the upshot of this is that if we want to enjoy our lives as we get older we need to look after ourselves or face a long life of illness, pain and inability. But there's really no need to worry: staying healthy and fit doesn't have to involve extortionate gym membership or Lycra. Not unless you want it to. So here are the basics of how to hit your target weight as well as some ideas to keep you bouncing with energy and make sure you're still a troublemaker when you hit the old folks' home. As long as they can keep you there.

What Weight Would You Like to Be?

It's easy to be the size you want to be; there's really no mystery to it. Whether you exercise or not, whether you want to put weight on or take weight off, it all boils down to this: calories in vs calories out.

It's what every fad diet in the world relies on; it's what

every healthy eating regime depends on and what body-builders use to gain and maintain weight and then strip it back down on demand. But don't worry: you don't have to count every last calorie you consume. Here are the basics.

How Much Food You Need

1. Your weight in lbs (1 stone = 14lbs):   _____

2. Multiply (1) by 11:   _____

3. Then complete one of the following.

   If you do no exercise multiply by   _____
   20 per cent (× 0.2):

   Or for light exercise 30 per cent (× 0.3):   _____

   For moderate daily exercise   _____
   40 per cent (× 0.4):

   For intense exercise 3–4 days per week   _____
   50 per cent (× 0.5)

4. Add the results of (2) and (3) together   _____

   The final figure in (4) is how many calories a day you require to maintain your current body weight.

5. To lose 1lb per week subtract 500 from (4)   _____

Say you are a totally sedentary 210lbs (15 stone). To maintain your current weight you will need 2772 calories per day. As 3500 calories is equal to one pound of body weight you can lose 1lb per week simply by cutting 500 calories from your diet each day, either by increasing the amount of exercise you do, decreasing the calories you consume or both. A brisk half-hour walk will burn nearly 180 calories; then skip a chocolate bar, a pint of premium lager or one pre-packaged sandwich and you've covered the rest.

Take It Easy

Lose more than 2lbs per week and your body enters starvation mode and you burn muscle rather than fat. So don't rush it. Even at a rate of 1lb per week that's one stone every fourteen weeks or so. Drop or burn an extra 1000 calories per day and that's a stone in seven weeks.

Gain Muscle

A pound of lean muscle tissue stores 2000 to 2500 calories. To build yourself up as quickly as possible you should eat 300–850 calories a day above what you need. Recalculate the previous figures using your desired body weight as the starting point to find out exactly how much you need. However you must also train regularly for muscular growth, otherwise those extra calories become fat not muscle.

Ensure you eat lean proteins (30–35 per cent), complex carbs (50–60 per cent) and a low-fat (10–15 per cent) diet if you want to bulk up rather than become obese.

Fat Is Your Friend

Often people totally strip out fats in an effort to lose weight but this prevents the body absorbing certain proteins and vitamins. You will always need some fat in your diet. Calculate your fat allowance here:

> You target calorie intake (from (5) above)   _____
>
> Multiply (1) by your desired percentage   _____
> of fat calories, e.g. 0.2 = 20 per cent,
> 0.3 = 30 per cent
>
> Divide by 9 (calories in a fat gram).   _____
> This is your daily fat allowance in grams

Keep It Simple – The Easy Way to Count Calories

Write down a list of all the foods you consume both regularly and irregularly. Calculate the calories for each one and then average it. So if you eat apples give each apple an average calorie value of 85 cals. The same for a medium slice of wholemeal toast. The trick here is to keep it effortlessly simple so that you do it without thinking and don't have to constantly refer to charts and lists.

So even though calories vary for both apples and toast if you know roughly what each food item you eat is worth you will easily be able to track your calorie intake. It doesn't really matter if one apple is 85 calories and the next 95. Over a week you won't notice it but you will have lowered your overall intake.

If you like keep a diary for a fortnight and include everything you consume in it including coffee, alcohol and snacks. You will see a pattern emerge in the foods you eat. By the end of two weeks you will be used to calculating accurately how many calories you've consumed and find it easy to do without it.

For an easy online food diary check out www.fitday.com

Don't Beat Yourself Up

There's going to come a time say Christmas Day when you will eat more than your weight goals will allow. After getting used to calculating your calories on the fly you'll soon be able to tell that the extra servings of stuffing, pudding, chocolates and wine you consumed came to roughly 4000 calories. Now really how long will it take you to lose that? A long walk? Two? Not long at all. So don't stress. Even when you're losing weight you can still eat well, socialise and enjoy your favourite foods.

Forget Calories

If you want to lose weight but don't want to estimate calories then there are three quick strategies you can use that will also help you achieve your goals.

Strategy A

Eat lean meats, fish, eggs, low fat dairy, fruit, vegetables and nuts only. No limit on fruit and veg (chips don't count). Minimal pasta, bread and rice, a maximum 100 grams at any sitting and preferably only one of those a day usually in the evening.

Strategy B

As above but with vegetable proteins and/or low-fat dairy and eggs instead of meat and fish.

Please note: the meat vs vegetarian debate is not even a debate. Morally vegetarians win. *Not killing wins* always. If you're a meat man get over it. I say that as a meat eater myself. Many cultures still rely on meat as their primary source of food and ultimately only you decide what you eat. The quickest way I've ever found to lose weight is to eat vegetarian. There is a nonsense argument that the body doesn't get enough proteins from a meat-free diet; it does if you combine proteins just as you would with ham and eggs, stews or roasts and so on. Don't get bogged down by this whiny non-debate. Do what's right for you.

Strategy C

Blood sugar balancing diet/low GI (glycemic index). Many people including myself react strongly to sugars in food whether it's straight processed sugar or the kind that comes from the carbs in pastas and breads. I know that if I eat even one slice of a farm-house loaf I'll eat the whole thing; same goes for all the other processed carbs. Unfortunately due to my genes I'm primed for diabetes in later life so I have to be careful.

There are many types of low GI eating strategies out there and to one degree or another they all work. If you want a strategy for this that you can implement as soon as you put the book down try three meals a day, no snacking. With each meal eat your own fist size in protein and the same for complex carbs and vegetables e.g. poached eggs on whole-meal toast and an apple for breakfast. Both strategies A and B also work well for low GI types.

None of the above are actually strict diets. In all of them you will eat extremely well and often better than you are eating now while losing weight and increasing your energy levels.

Fun Ways to Be a Real Man Without Being a Gym Bore

For some the gym is everything; for others it's simply a chore. If you're looking to tone up and lose weight then just join a programme at your local gym or try *G-Force* by Gunnar Peterson, 'the man behind the best bodies in Hollywood'. Think Sylvester Stallone or Matthew McConaughey. He provides a good, all-round system for a handsome body that works on diet, anaerobic and aerobic exercise. If it's size you're after I'd recommend Mike Mentzer's High Intensity Training and the excellent www.bodybuilding.com. For all-round fitness try *Chris Ryan's SAS Fitness Book*. For everyone else there's this.

Exercise through doing

The basic principle is this. If you want to lose weight, tone up, become more flexible, more relaxed or be constantly stimulated then pick a pursuit that you can learn and master and go hard at it – high intensity – until you've got it. It doesn't matter whether it's wu-shu stick fighting, the high dive, running a 10k, learning to do the splits, capoeira, horse riding, samba or sword fighting. Better to spend forty minutes maxed out in the gym, the park, on the dance floor or in the back garden than an hour and a half putting the minutes in but not really any effort. Regularly changing your routines and interests also helps you to avoid physical or psychological plateaus.

Jason Statham, the black-market trader turned Hollywood action hero, exemplifies these principles and favours a strategy that involves having the right attitude first. In a recent interview he described building muscle just for the sake of it as pointless. 'Muscle-men grow on trees,' he said. 'They can tense their muscles and look good in a mirror. So what?

I'm more interested in practical strength that's going to help me run, jump, twist, punch.' And so are a lot of other people.

Yoga for Psychopaths

If the thought of deep stretching positions in quiet rooms or out-of-the-way retreats surrounded by lithe alluring women in the prime of their lives doesn't make you reconsider yoga then maybe this will.

Yoga improves your flexibility, strength, balance, joint range, concentration, breathing, pulse rate, mood and eyesight and lowers the levels of just about every toxic substance in your body from cholesterol to blood glucose and salt. Because of this detoxification process it also helps to delay ageing. And just in case you're saying 'Yeah right, yoga's for girls', consider this: Charles Bronson, the most notorious convict in the British prison system, renowned for serial hostage taking and rooftop sieges, has been practising it for more than twenty years. He takes it further than

your average yoga class too – well he would wouldn't he? –
and uses it for everything from pranayama breathing exercises to cleansing his system and nadi-suddhi visualisations
as well as his infamous cow punch – like a rabbit punch but
it'll knock out a much bigger animal. He's covered his fitness
regime in the book *Solitary Fitness* where he describes how
he used his exceptional strength to throw a fridge up a flight
of stairs and punch through bullet proof glass (with wit-
nesses). So if you still think yoga's for girls I suggest you take
it up with Mr B.

Ironman, Ultramarathons

While yoga on the surface at least seems more sedate you
just know that anything with the word 'ironman' in the title
is going to be tough. If you've never heard of it the Ironman
Triathlon is the toughest one-day race in the world and has
the slogan 'Swim 2.4 miles! Bike 112 miles! Run 26.2 miles!
Brag for the rest of your life'.

The race started out in Hawaii in 1978 when a bunch of
Navy Seals argued about who was the fittest athlete.
Commander John Collins suggested that the best way to
decide would be to combine the Waikiki RoughWater Swim,
the Around-Oahu Bike Race and the Honolulu Marathon.
Whoever finished would be a real Ironman. From its humble
beginnings as a twelve-man race the following year just from
word-of-mouth alone it had fifty entrants. It then caught the
attention of a bored golfing journalist who wrote a ten-page
report on it for *Sports Illustrated* and the rest is history. Its
popularity has spread worldwide and you can now run races
from as far afield as Britain, Canada and Malaysia in the
northern hemisphere and New Zealand in the south.

Triathlons became an Olympic sport in 2000 and demand is so high for the race that several non-Ironman-brand races have also been established and Ironman have set up a half-distance triathlon called the Ironman 70.3. If you'd like to have a go the best way to get started is to pick up a running magazine, look through the local event calendar and start training for an adventure race near you.

However if a one-day event just seems too easy you could opt for the Marathon des Sables (Marathon of the Sands) instead. The MDS covers 243 kilometres/151 miles (in sections similar to 25, 34, 38, 82, 42, 22 kilometres) run over six days. That's the equivalent of five and a half regular marathons. If that isn't harsh enough competitors also have to carry everything they will need for the duration (apart from a tent) on their backs in a rucksack (food, clothes, medical kit and sleeping bag). The average speed is between 3kph and 14kph for competitors aged between sixteen and seventy-eight. The message 'Welcome to the world of lunatics and masochists' greets you on www.saharamarathon.co.uk the British entrants' portal, and no wonder: with temperatures as high as 120°F/49°C it's justifiably called the toughest foot race on earth.

And even though some previous competitors have died of dehydration that doesn't stop eight hundred or so new ones enrolling every year. They don't even do it for the prize money as that's virtually nonexistent. They do it to challenge themselves and raise money for charity. The camaraderie and profound bond that develops between people who don't even speak the same language is another reason. Often just as you're thinking of quitting a guardian angel strides out from behind a rock and walks or jogs with you for an hour or so and gives you the support you need to carry on. Then it's your turn to do the same for someone else.

Everyone wants you to finish. As water is also rationed and handed out at each checkpoint you'll need all the help you can get.

Does the thought of the MDS make you feel old? Everything aches I bet. Things aren't what they used to be are they? And kids today they don't know they're born. Well rather than sitting around the house watching *EastEnders* or *Match of the Day* and feeling sorry for yourself you could take to the streets like Fauja Singh. He took up running at eighty-one because he was bored sitting around his son's house. At the age of eighty-nine he ran his first London Marathon and set a world record time when he turned ninety, defying the idea that with age he should get slower. At the age of ninety-two he ran almost an hour quicker than his own personal best to complete the Toronto Marathon in five hours forty minutes. That's the fastest time yet recorded for someone of his age. He even had a copycat, Buster Martin, who claimed to be 101 but turned out to be a mere ninety-four. The oldest man yet to complete a marathon was the ninety-eight-year-old Greek runner Dimitrion Yordanidis in Athens in 1976. He finished in seven hours thirty-three minutes.

I suddenly feel decidedly young and lazy.

Sex Olympics (DIY)

Sorry there isn't actually any official contest where you can compete against other teams to win medals, not that I know of anyway. Still at least you don't have to go all the way to the Moroccan desert to push your limits or burn calories. You could simply stay home and have more sex. The bed may possibly be the single greatest piece of exercise equipment ever invented. Here's why.

Burn Calories
You can burn three hundred calories every hour depending on how and what you are doing. Obviously the more vigorous the activity the higher your heart rate.

Live Longer
According to a ten-year study by the Department of Social Medicine at the University of Bristol in 2002, regular sex of more than twenty minutes more than three times a week, reduces the likelihood of heart attack or stroke. 'Mortality risk was 50% lower in men with high frequency of orgasm than in men with low frequency of orgasm,' the report said.

Relieve Pain
Levels of the hormone oxytocin surge to five times their normal level immediately before orgasm. This also releases endorphins, which alleviate the pain of everything from headache to arthritis and migraine.

Fewer Illnesses
Researchers at Wilkes University in Pennsylvania found that sex once or twice a week increases the antibody Immunoglobulin A by 30 per cent, which strengthens the immune system and helps fight off colds, flu and other illnesses. Sexually active people also take fewer sick days. Perhaps a sex at work programme could be in the offing?

Heightened Sense of Smell
Post-coital hormone surges increase production of the hormone prolactin. This causes stem cells in the brain to

develop new neurons in the olfactory centre, which means your nose might not grow to the size of granddad's after all.

Better Sleep

Sex, including masturbation, helps prevent insomnia. After all the stereotype is men demanding a corned beef and pickle sandwich after sex followed immediately by sleep. Make the most of it.

Defy the Ageing Process

According to some researchers sex may lead to shiny hair, a healthy complexion and bright white eyes. This is because it increases the youth-promoting hormone DHEA (dehydroepiandrostone). In his book *Secrets of the Superyoung* neurophysiologist Dr David Weeks of Scotland's Royal Edinburgh Hospital said, 'An active sex life slows the ageing process.' It's a virtuous circle: you look good and feel more attractive, which then charges up your sex life even more and round we go again.

Greater Self-Esteem, Greater Intimacy

Oxytocin released at orgasm also stimulates feelings of affection, intimacy and closeness between you and your partner. In a loving relationship physical touch and sex can lead to a better quality of life and an even stronger relationship. It's no wonder that healthy, loving intimacy in a positive relationship makes you feel better about yourself, your partner and life in general.

Stress-Buster

According to NHS Direct in one study 'Participants kept a diary of sexual activity, recording penetrative sex, non-penetrative sex and masturbation. In subsequent stress tests including public speaking and doing mental arithmetic out loud, the people who recorded no sex at all had the highest stress levels. Those who had only penetrative sex had the smallest rise in blood pressure, indicating that they coped better with stress.

Plenty of people find that the feel-good factor of intimacy or orgasm without penetration helps them feel relaxed as do exercise or meditation. It doesn't have to be penetrative sex; it's whatever works for you.'

A Healthy Prostate

Some studies show a relationship between *infrequent* ejaculation and prostate cancer. A study recently published by the *British Journal of Urology International* showed that men in their twenties can reduce by a third their chance of getting prostate cancer by ejaculating more than five times a week (flushing the prostate). For Australians another study gave a figure of seven times a week. Who knew cancer prevention could be fun? Just check your palms regularly for extra hair. That's if you can still see them of course.

Time to Get Busy (Hint: Give This to Your Girlfriend)

According to *Women's Health* there are numerous reasons why as soon as you put this book down you should do the nasty, knock boots, bump uglies, shag, boink or boff that handsome man lying next to you. They say sex helps relieve tension and anger, heightens your senses (which makes chocolate taste even better), it's the only way to get pregnant and it gives you an unarguable excuse to go shopping for frilly, sexy, expensive lingerie. Sex also brings you closer together and apparently strengthens your tummy, pelvis and hips even better than Pilates.

If you don't use it you'll lose it too – just like men your

hormone production ceases if it isn't called for. Sex also boosts body image, triggers labour, improves communication and keeps menstruation regular. Not only that, as we've already seen sex provides pain relief which means . . . no more headaches. And lastly do you even need an excuse either of you? I mean come on. Put the book down already.

How to Be a Great Dad

I don't have children. I'd love some but the clock is ticking and circumstances just haven't been right yet. I do know they don't hand out a rule book for dads at the hospital so I've included Leo Babauta's twelve awesome tips for being a great dad. It certainly hit home in terms of what I'd like for my future unborn. Leo is married with six kids and author of the bestselling book *The Power of Less: The Fine Art of Limiting Yourself to the Essentials . . . in Work and in Life* and also runs www.zenhabits.com, one of the top one hundred internet blogs.

You can of course adapt, scrub out or add to this list to suit your needs – you might be a stay-at-home dad or separated from an abusive partner . . . who knows – but even if you haven't had kids yet or you have and just want to compare notes here it is in Leo's own words.

Twelve Awesome Tips

I'm often asked about raising six kids and being productive and achieving goals and changing habits in the midst of raising so many kids. But here's the thing: I do all the other stuff, the productivity stuff, because of my kids. They, and my wife, are my reason for being.

It is my lifelong goal to be the best dad possible, and while there are many ways I can still improve, I think I'm a pretty great dad already, when I sit back and think about it. I know there are some readers who are just starting out in their careers as dads, and this is for you.

How can you be a great dad? In no particular order here are my tips:

Teach Them Self-Esteem

This is one of the most important points. There is nothing you can do that is better than giving them high self-esteem. How do you do this? A million ways, but mainly by showing them (not telling them) that you value them, by spending time with them, by talking and listening to them, by praising things they do, by teaching them (not telling them) how to be competent. Praise and encourage, don't reprimand and discourage.

Put Their Interests First, Always

Do you enjoy drinking or smoking? Guess what – it's not good for them, and you're setting an example with everything you do. I quit smoking about 18 months ago not for my sake, but for my kids. Now, it is still important to take care of yourself (otherwise you can't take care of them), but you should still have them in mind.

Protect Them

As a dad, one of your main roles is protector. There are many ways you need to do this. Safety is one: child-proof your home, teach them good safety habits, set a good example by using your seatbelt. But financial protection is also important: have life insurance, car insurance, an emergency fund, a will and talk to your family or friends about what could happen if the worst were to happen to you. If there's someone suitable elect a godfather or godmother too.

Spend Your Spare Time With Them

When we get home from work, often we're tired and just want to relax. But this is the only time we have with them during the weekdays, often, and you shouldn't waste it. Take this time to find out about their day, lay on the couch with them. On weekends, devote as much time as possible to them. While work may be your passion, it won't be long before they're grown and no longer want to spend time with you. Take advantage of these years. *The thing kids want most from their dads is their time.*

Give Them Hugs

Dads shouldn't be afraid to show affection. Kids need physical contact, and not just from their moms. Snuggle with them, hug them, love them.

Play With Them

Go outside and play sports. Do a treasure hunt. Have a pillow fight. Play Transformers or Pokemon with them. Don't just watch TV. Show them how to have fun.

Do the 'Mom' Stuff

Things that are traditionally considered 'mom' duties are not just for moms anymore [in fact they never were: during the Industrial Revolution separating you from your children gave you less reason to leave the factory and go home to your family] – changing diapers, feeding, bathing, rocking them to sleep in the middle of the night. Dads should help out as much as they can, sharing these types of duties equally if possible. And in fact, if you're a dad of a baby, this is the perfect time to bond with your child. You should leap at the chance to do these things, because that's how you start a life-long close relationship with your child.

Read to Them

This is one of the most important things you can do for your child. First of all, it's so much fun. Kids' books are really cool, and it's great when you can share something this wonderful with your child. Second, you are teaching them one of the most fundamentally important skills (reading) that will pay off dividends for life. And third, you are spending time with them, you're sitting or lying close together, and you are enjoying each other's company.

Stand By Mom

Don't contradict their mother in front of them, don't fight with her in front of them, and most definitely don't ever abuse her. How you treat their mother affects their self-esteem, and the way they will treat themselves and women when they grow up. Be kind and respectful and loving of their mother. And always work as a team – never contradicting statements of the other.

Teach Them About Finances

This is a point often missed in articles about dadhood. You might not need to teach your one-year-old about index funds or portfolio diversity, but from an early age, you can teach them the value of money, how to save money to reach a goal, and later, how to earn money and how to manage money properly. You don't want your child to go into the world knowing as little as you did do you?

Be Good to Yourself

You shouldn't give up your entire life when you become a dad. You need to take care of yourself, give yourself some alone time, and some time with your buddies, in order to be a great dad when you're with your kids. Also take care of your health – eat healthy, exercise – because 1) you can't take care of your kids if you're sickly, 2) you are teaching your kids how to be healthy for life, and 3) you want to enjoy those grandkids someday.

Be Good to the Mom

This isn't the same as 'stand by mom' – if she's at home and you're at work then you should be good to their mom even when they're not looking. Take her to dinner, give her a massage, do chores around the house for her, give her some time alone and baby-sit while she goes out, show affection to her, give her little surprises. Because when mom's happy, the kids are happy. And dad will be happy too! If you're at home and she's at work expect the same treatment.

Thanks Leo. For my part I would also add the following:

Control Your Temper

If you have anger issues you need to learn how to own that anger. Anger is usually your own unexpressed needs and *your kids need you* to have a level head and show them the way. Always control your temper and unless they're about to run in front of a car never, ever scream at them. If you feel you're about to scream or yell go for a walk, a run, find an errand to do in the garden or at the shops and ask yourself,

'What are my unfulfilled, unasked needs?' Once you've figured out your own issues and dealt with your anger in a healthy way i.e. not hitting things, shouting or screaming (that's just practising your anger) then go back.

Let Them Fall

Sometimes you have to look the other way when they are about to fall down. One fall is worth a thousand verbal warnings. The trick of course is to let them fall on something that will hurt without inflicting too much damage such as the last step rather than the whole flight of stairs. Letting them touch something very hot but obviously not scalding and experience the sensation will make 'Careful, that's hot!' that much more effective

Show Them How to Do Things

Help them out around the house. Remember how everything seemed the biggest chore when you were little? When you ask them to tidy their room do it with them, make it fun, quick and easy. As they get older do the same with washing up, fixing bikes, doing the laundry. Praise them for the effort they put in not the task so that the same positive, playful, 'let's get on with it' attitude is applied to all tasks. Think how that translates to exams, relationships or jobs. When you turn up at their first apartment you might even find a clean floor.

Never Use Them to Win an Argument

If you're separated from their mother or even if you're not when you undermine the other parent by feeding the children contradictory information or setting up an argument they will learn to mistrust what you say. It's emotional abuse so don't do it.

Listen to Your Kids and Value their Opinions

Your children have real opinions and real desires. Always listen to them and take them into account. Of course they're not always realistic. Explain why. Never say: 'Because I say so'. Kids can be more rational and understanding than you might think even when they're only three years old.

Help Them Become Who They Truly Are – Not Who You Want Them to Be

Don't project your desires or your failures on to your children. Help them try things out, give them the discipline and encouragement to keep at things when they feel unconfident, uncertain or scared as well as the ability to let go of things they realise are not for them.

Eat Dinner with Them

This could also be called 'turn the TV off'. Quite simply if the TV is on all evening and all through dinner especially then you'll spend more time with fictional families on the tube than your own. Which means your family will also be fictional capiche?

Daughters

Many men have special rules for daughters; usually about sex. My agent told a good story about a high-ranking American military friend who gave the following sage advice to his teenage daughter:

1) Always scream or they won't believe you.
2) If you bite, it will come off.

However I would caution:

Never Teach a Daughter to Exchange Sex for Food

Sounds like a yarn but I once had dinner with two women friends who jokingly said, 'If you weren't a friend you'd be paying for this meal.' They then told me how both their fathers had taught them to 'put out' only when the 'date' had paid for the meal or drinks. Now I do understand that a father wants his daughter to meet a nice guy who'll treat her well but teach them this and you're turning them into 'burgers for blowjobs' prostitutes and your future sons-in-law into their johns. Just don't do it.

Things You Wish Your Dad Told You

You can figure out certain things about childcare by what you lacked. For me many of the subjects in this book are about showing my future children that they can go out there and do whatever they want to do. We often assume as adults that things we take for granted like kicking a ball, speaking to women, looking after yourself are obvious. But remember: childhood can be a confusing time when you really wish someone would tell you all the answers.

I remember my father and uncle showing me how to bowl and bat in cricket and then how to tackle in rugby. That was one afternoon but just those basic skills gave me more confidence in high school than anything else. I would have liked many more of those afternoons.

If I had my childhood over again the one thing I'd want my father to say is 'It's okay to ask about anything, whatever you don't know. Even if I don't know the answer we'll find out together.' What would you wish for?

But most of all if you've got kids always count your blessings and try to get as much sleep as you can.

Being the Strong Man Women Really Want

'What shall we do for dinner tonight?' she said.

'Well we could go here, here or here,' he said pointing to three different restaurants, one a burger joint, the second an Italian and the third the most expensive restaurant in town.

She gave him a look.

'I don't know,' he said. 'What do you want to do?'

'I don't mind.'

'I don't either.'

He's a nice guy. Like most of us he's been brought up to dismiss the patriarchal stereotypes of the past and been told he must evolve and learn how to try and please women at all costs. So that's what he does, try. And most often fails. Why? Well just look at the scenario above: he wants her to be happy so he thinks by offering her a choice she can decide and she will be happy. When the discussion ends up in the inevitable back and forth of 'Well you decide,' 'But I don't mind,' 'Well neither do I,' neither is willing to back down because neither of them wants to make the wrong decision. For him if he picks a place he feels he will be a 'typical' dominant male, a bad man. But if he doesn't he's weak, passive and ineffectual and once again a bad man.

We need to get past this. Instead of trying to be nice guys we need to be good guys. We need to relearn how to be manly and not macho, to be strong, assertive, decisive and confident but not dominating. We are stuck in outmoded concepts of masculinity both in the 'man's man' and the feminised, emasculated male of recent decades.

Take a moment to reread the *OED* definition of manliness from the introduction. Elliot Katz used it in his thought provoking book *Being the Strong Man a Woman Wants*. That is how we need to redefine ourselves; let's give ourselves noble qualities and not the boyish, immature mannerisms so readily touted as masculine today. Let's forget the one-dimensional stereotypes from movies, TV and the street corner and move on. Here's the math.

What Women Want

A man who can make a decision, a man who can be depended on, a man who can look out for the best interests of his loved ones, a man who does the right thing not the easy, popular or expedient thing.

Take Responsibility

Never blame your partner or others. Take full responsibility. A relationship is a mirror of what you put into it as is every area of your life so use each challenge as an opportunity for personal growth. The things that are happening to you, you allowed to happen. Own them. And when things don't go as planned know that you are responsible for the outcome and act to change it.

Learn from Other Men

When you learn to play rugby or learn to sell or act or fight or write or manage other people you regularly observe others that you respect. Emulate their actions then learn what works for you and adapt it to your own life. Do the same with men you respect, the noble ones; avoid the noisy, obnoxious ones and the passive ones.

Let Go of Control

Part of not making decisions about simple things like dinner is the fear of getting it wrong. What if you pick Italian and the pasta is overcooked, the waiter rude or the wine cheap? Well what of it? You cannot make everything perfect. Ever. Sometimes things aren't going to go as planned and as soon as you let go of trying to be perfect it won't be such a big issue and the decisions will come more easily. You may even find it's the best Italian you've ever had.

Accept Challenges for What They Are

When she challenges you sometimes she does it just to see how you'll react. She needs to know what your boundaries are. Don't react just to humour her or please her; do the right thing. Especially when it's hard and not the easy answer. If she constantly pushes your buttons even when you set your boundaries then there's something else going on – manipulation, control, neuroses – and you need to evaluate whether she's for you. If she isn't and you stay with her whose fault is that? Yours of course.

Don't Be Passive

Most passive aggression is just aggression dressed up to look nice. If you have unfulfilled needs and aren't stating directly what they are you are being a passive aggressive little puss, blaming the other person and not taking responsibility.

Passive aggressive: 'Yeah but *you* never choose where we eat. *You* always leave it to me.'

Assertive: 'I always love your choices. But unless you have any objections . . . tonight let's go here. If it's awful we can always have bulimia for dessert.'

Be Decisive

When you need to make an on the spot decision let go of control and decide something. Toss a coin if you have to. You may even decide that none of the options are what you want and do something completely different instead. Or be pleasantly surprised by the decision you eventually do make.

Be Independent

Don't do everything together. You need time to be yourself, to experience other things whether that's time with friends, a good book, family, travel, some grease and oil or whatever your passion is. Those of us who do this always bring new experiences into a relationship and strengthen it. Do the opposite and you become dependent on each other for self worth. Always maintain your independence to keep things fresh.

Know What's Going On

Let them know you care. Pay attention to your significant other. Take the time to really talk to them. Knowing what's going on in their lives will mean that when things aren't working for them or they need a little extra help you can step in and lend a hand. When the crisis or need has finished then step back and let them regain their independence. It will also mean that when your guidance is offered not imposed it is more likely to be accepted as genuine rather than controlling.

Don't Buy Her Happiness
Q: Who is rich?
A: He who is happy with his share.

Don't break the bank to keep her happy. If you are trying to please her by buying things neither you nor she can afford then ultimately the only person who's going to take the blame when you go broke is you. As Katz says, 'Does it make you feel needed? Being strong means knowing when and how to say no.'

Never Lose Your Temper
If someone is trying to goad you and you let them they've won. If they aren't and you do lose your temper then you've lost again. Think of a time when you're fuming about something, spitting and frothing at the mouth almost. If your boss suddenly calls or a customer you always switch the anger off and you're suddenly personable, strong and in control again. Do the same whatever the circumstance. Put your angry child tantrums in a box. Control yourself not your partner.

Know When to Ask for Help
Being strong is also about admitting that you can't handle everything. In the same way that you are strong for your partner they sometimes need to be strong for you. But

asking for help is the first step and then allowing them to help you the next. Let me give you a painful example. When my father died I couldn't handle it. Did I admit it? Did I hell. Which made me weak. If I'd been a strong man I could have asked for help – there's no such thing as losing face in these circumstances.

Don't Infantilise Your Partner

While you may be strong, if you're the controlling type your partner will feel weak. Encourage them to be independent, to make decisions for themselves, to take responsibility and know what's going on. Never bully or cajole.

Remember being a strong man isn't about controlling or dominating. It's about being who you really are and being an equal partner in a relationship rather than a dependent, needy man child. Forget about being the nice guy who tries to do everything perfectly to please their partner and concentrate on being a good guy who does the right thing.

Don't believe me? Perhaps you think all this is just macho posturing? Well here's some advice to 'Nice Guys' or women who think that's what we should be from the straight-talking *femmes fatales* at Heartless Bitches International:

I get letters from self-professed Nice Guys, complaining that women must WANT to be treated like shit, because THEY, the 'Nice Guy' have failed repeatedly in relationships. This is akin to the false logic that 'Whales are mammals. Whales live in the sea. Therefore, all mammals live in the sea.' If you have one bad relationship after another the only common denominator is *YOU*. Think about it.

What's wrong with Nice Guys? The biggest problem is that most Nice Guys™ are hideously insecure. They are so anxious to be liked and loved that they do things for other people to gain acceptance and attention, rather than for the simple pleasure of giving. You never know if a Nice Guy really likes you for who you are, or if he has glommed onto you out of desperation because you actually paid some kind of attention to him.

Nice Guys exude insecurity – a big red target for the predators of the world. There are women out there who are 'users' – just looking for a sucker to take advantage of. Users home in on 'Nice Guys', stroke their egos, take them for a ride, add a notch to their belts, and move on. It's no wonder so many Nice Guys complain about women being horrible, when so often the kind of woman that gets attracted to them is the lowest form of life . . .

Harsh but fair words, I think so anyway. You can read the full article at www.heartlessbitches.com. But I'd hate to give you justification to feel like a victim here. The piece concludes by saying:

Get this Guys: Insecurity isn't sexy. It's a turnoff.

You don't have to be an ego-inflated, arrogant jerk. You just have to LIKE yourself. You have to know what you want out of life, and go after it. Only then will you be attractive to the kind of woman with whom a long-term relationship is possible.

So remember it's never about being dominating or controlling on your part. And you should never permit that kind of behaviour from your partner either. Bottom line: neither sex ever should.

Being pro-man is never about being anti-woman in the

same way that being pro-woman is never about being anti-man. Be pro-everyone fool.

Nice guys finish last.

Bad guys wind up dead or in jail.

Good guys don't even have to compete.

LUST AND LOVE

All we think about is sex

The Best Sex She's Never Had – Keep Her Coming Back

Sex isn't just about technique. You also have to know how to keep things fresh, to tailor your skills to suit your lover, to be able to talk openly about what you both want and to listen. You must always be respectful but always playful. As a modern gentleman simply imagine you're a little trickster devil with very good table manners.

First you need to master some essential techniques then forget them. A bit like learning to drive a car: when you're learning you have to think about how to turn the wheel using technique then by the time you've mastered it and you're giving it everything you've got you're not worried how you turn the wheel, you just want to make the tyres squeal.

The Most Important Erogenous Zone

Okay there are endless areas of delight on a woman's body – inner arms, inner thighs, nape of the neck, shoulders, behind the ears, those little dimples at the base of the spine. Each woman is different: for some their toes are it, for others it's a gentle nibble of their cheek just above the bone. I recommend becoming familiar with all of them. Especially the biggest and most neglected of them all. The mind. Now you're probably thinking, 'What? I can't nibble her brain.' Of course you can't but as you know yourself just the thought of sex can make you aroused. You don't need to be touched, see anything or even be in the same room for that to happen.

The same is true of her. So use all the social skills you have to make her want you and to feel sexy, desirable and wanted herself. This could be creating a tailor-made place or time for carefree seduction and sex. For example does she prefer the early morning wake-up call, long, languorous afternoons or passionate evenings? Ask her.

Or try building anticipation through flirting and eroticism. If she's gone out for the day slowly tease her with short, simple text messages, emails or phone calls. Make them erotic not pornographic. When you're out with friends flirt with her even if you've been together for years. Whisper in her ear and tell how amazing she looks and all the ways you're going to make her melt when you get her home. An intimate touch as she passes your seat or a pressing embrace against a wall on the way back will only serve to heighten the anticipation.

The Kiss

Often overlooked the kiss is one of the most erotic actions in the sexual repertoire. It's often seen as a precursor to the main event or as something fleeting to do in a club. You know grab the back of her head, stick your tongue in and wiggle it about and that's the extent of it. Dear god!

The lips are actually one of the most sensitive areas of the human body and when kissed the stimulation causes nerve endings to fire rapid signals straight to your brain that release a surge of pleasurable neurotransmitters and endorphins like dopamine and phenylethylamine, which are responsible for feelings of euphoria, pleasure and motivation as well as enhancing focus, mood and attention. So when you kiss properly your body floods with feelgood chemicals. No wonder good kissing is so much fun. Try varying your rhythm, pressure and technique. Kiss both lips separately and together, run your tongue along the inside of her lips, nibble gently on her top lip then her bottom, brush her lips with yours, open her mouth wide with your lips and engage her tongue with yours. Play, add pressure, make it fleeting and barely touching, lose yourself in each other. Feel your way.

The Breasts

Did you know that you can give a woman an orgasm through her breasts alone? Many woman love having their breasts, nipples and areolae touched, flicked, nibbled, bitten, breathed on, tickled or squeezed. Often a man's touches are simply too fleeting or of the squish-and-move-on or turn-the-dial-on-the-radio variety. Spend a good laid-back half-hour on her magnificent mammaries some time in much the same way you would with her lips. Ask her to close her eyes and fantasise as you gently tease those nerve endings until they vibrate with pleasure. Ask her to tell you what she wants as you're doing it. If there's something she likes you can repeat the action or change it. For some women soft touch is what they want; for others nothing but a good biting and nipple clamps will do. Again every one of your lovers will be different. Also be aware that breast play works better at different times of the month. At certain points during the menstrual cycle the nipples and breasts can be quite painful to the touch. Take your time and enjoy yourselves.

The Vagina and the Clitoris

Most men of my generation were beaten around the head and told that because previous generations didn't know where this magic little button was we were all evil, women-hating chauvinists. However when I came to explore women's bodies as a younger man I was often surprised to find that many young women didn't know where the clitoris was either. So if you are a younger man you may have to assist your partner as she gets to know her body (I'm sure you won't need asking twice) and learns what she likes and doesn't like and work through any of that hand-me-down, repressed sexual shame and nervousness.

The fact that the vagina and its various parts have been celebrated, cherished and turned on in many cultures from the ancient Celts through to the 'divine passage' or yoni in Hindu culture, makes the point. It's only since Victorian times that as a culture we've forgotten what these bits were for. Until then a woman's pleasure was often seen as an essential part of procreation.

A good lover will help you understand their body and help you find out about yours. So take some time to explore your partner and get to know her. If you part her legs you'll first see the kissable outer labia with the same colour skin as the rest of the body. Part the lips and you'll see the equally kissable inner labia, the inner lips, which surround the vaginal opening; they are certainly lip-like in colouring and texture although they do come in all sorts of colours, shapes and sizes. Every single woman is different: they can be slim and narrow, fluted or flared. They can protrude past the outer lips or be hidden within. The texture ranges from crinkled or smooth to deeply textured or even glassy. There isn't a wrong shape or size.

If you follow the line of the inner lips up towards the pubic bone where the two top corners of the lips meet in an A-frame you'll find the protruding tip of the clitoris. It's the powerhouse of your woman's orgasm and is densely packed with over eight thousand sensual nerve endings, more than any other part of the body either male or female. Twice that of the penis and in a much more compact package. Lucky her.

So intense is the pleasure from the clitoris that some women don't even like direct stimulation. Luckily it is surrounded by the clitoral hood and vulva, which can be used as a sensation buffer. So let's get down to it.

Cunning Linguists

Women reach orgasm through intercourse roughly 25 per cent of the time but through oral 82 per cent of the time and unless you've turned them into a total orgasmic mess they're nearly always ready for more. So for high percentage sexual techniques this is it.

Cunnilingus usually happens in four stages.

1. You set the tone with thoughtfully placed starting licks, nibbles and kisses. Unless your lover tells you to get straight to it in which case obey.

2. You build pleasure with tongue techniques, long and short, in and out, flicking, fluttering or flattened. At this point the clitoris can be extremely sensitive. If you feel an 'electric shock' run through her body it's a sign that you need to ease off or change to another technique. There's no hurry so take your time.

3. Taking cues from your lover you focus on one technique that she most responds to. You establish and maintain a rhythm on her sweet spot that builds sensation until it triggers orgasm. It's important to sustain the rhythm at this point as this is what will lead to climax. She may buck or move without even realising it and you may have to chase her with your mouth. Alternatively pin her thighs to the bed or hold her buttocks in both hands and bring her to you. If she's moving away ease off; if she's pushing forward then add pressure, as the clitoris withdraws just before climax. If she grabs the back of your head and pulls you in try and grab a deep breath.

4. Women orgasm in all kinds of ways; some are quiet and barely make a sound while others are like a volcano. It can be as short as a few seconds or last up to three minutes. Afterwards she'll be extremely sensitive and touching her down there may be too much. If she's multi-orgasmic and wants to go again she'll let you know or just hang out a while and you may find that you'll lead her down that multi-orgasmic path.

You can use your fingers in much the same way as your tongue and sex toys can also add a new and enjoyable dimension to your lovemaking. Violet Blue in her sexcellent book *The Ultimate Guide to Cunnilingus* offers the following advice to heighten pleasure still further.

- Lick lazy circles round her clit.
- Lick side to side or up or down, nipping with your lips between directions.
- Use short, rapid upward strokes, alternated with dipping into her vagina.
- Lick in circles combined with open-mouthed embraces.
- Alternate between circles and side-to-side licks
- Run your tongue back and forth across her inner lips then use gentle suction on the lips.
- Use the same technique on the clitoris.
- Alternate small, focused circles on either side of the hood.
- With your tongue tip, lick in the furrows from top to bottom, pressing in gradually with each stroke.
- Lick, plunge in; lick, plunge in.
- Start with 'ice cream' licks up and down followed with down strokes with your fingertips or flattened thumbs.
- Swirl your tongue in the space between hood and mons and rub the outer labia with flattened fingers.
- Lick the ABCs on her vulva. Start with A and go from there – capitals, lower case, cursive, secret messages. This method is an old standby.

Remember: don't be overwhelmed by this it's just technique. Pick a couple and have fun with them. Then try a couple more. If you pick up a copy of Blue's book make sure to get her companion book on fellatio as well. Oral pleasure works both ways and your partner will usually give as good as she gets.

If you're wondering why I've spent a long time on this section it's simply this: usually what makes a woman come hardest and longest is a man who can use his tongue well. To quote author and sex columnist Anka Radakovich in her essay *Lip Service: On Being a Cunning Linguist* and why knowing how to use your tongue is a very good thing: 'I became tongue whipped (the female equivalent of pussy whipped) and even offered to do his laundry if he would come over and satisfy me. After two months I put a framed photo of his tongue on my desk.'

It's good to have a sense of humour about these things so confession time: I picked up the technique of grabbing the clit between my lips and flicking across it with my tongue from a lover in my early twenties. I used this for years thinking it was a surefire thing with every women I met until a female friend told me over drinks that it would be incredibly painful for her. She explained the wonders of using the hood as buffer, always experimenting and keeping the lines of communication open. Do the same. Now how does one get a good photo of a tongue?

Spotty Logic – the G, the A, the U

Okay here's a bit of uncommon knowledge about the clitoris. It's not just that little nubbin. In fact it's a huge network of nerve endings that goes back away inside the woman. Both the G-spot and the U-spot are part of this network and not separate to it.

The U-spot is easy to find: it's the urethral opening just above the vaginal opening and below the clitoris.

It's easier to find the G-spot when she's already slightly aroused. Insert your finger into the vagina and bend it towards you. When you feel an uneven area of skin a little like the surface of a golf ball you're there. Apply pressure in a massaging, come-hither motion. If it's her first time she may feel like she needs to pee. This is the part of the anatomy responsible for female ejaculation usually anything from a teaspoon to a cupful. Combine it with oral for extreme pleasure. Or try having sex with her on top and facing away from you or doggy style as she holds on to a chair, bed or stairs to stimulate it directly with your penis.

There is also the A-spot. Desmond Morris, author of *The Naked Woman: A Study of the Female Body*, had this to say: 'Its existence was reported by a Malaysian physician in Kuala Lumpur as recently as the 1990s. There has been some mis-reporting about it, and its precise position has been incorrectly described by several writers. Its true location is just above the cervix, at the innermost point of the vagina. The cervix of the uterus is the narrow part that protrudes slightly into the vagina, leaving a circular recess around itself. The front part of this recess is called the anterior fornix. Pressure on it produces rapid lubrication of the vagina even in women who are not normally sexually responsive. It is now possible to buy a special AFE vibrator – long, thin and upward curved at its end, to probe this zone.'

Try rotating stimulation to each area in turn to really blow her mind.

Less Mouth, More Trousers

The techniques for penetrative sex are far too numerous to cover here. Entire books have been written about them tackling every kind of variation: legs open, legs closed, one leg or two bent and pushed up for deeper penetration, her on top for greater orgasm control – for both him and her – standing, kneeling, straddling, multiple entry, anal, forwards, backwards, in public, her in control, him in control, bondage, S&M, role-play, massage; all the animals: tiger crouching, the bear, the snake, the lion hunting, eagles in flight, the birds, the Viennese oyster; the cowgirl, the drill ... I could go on. Basically if all you're ever doing is the missionary and the occasional doggy style try banning those positions for a month and seeing what playful variations you can come up with. Try www.sexinfo101.com for inspiration.

Vary your thrusting technique as well. Mix deep thrusts with shallow, forwards and backwards movement with side-to-side and figure-of-eight rotations; learn to use your hips, pull all the way out and dive back in. No holds are barred in this full-contact sport.

Desmond Morris also said, 'It has been claimed that two out of every three women fail to reach regular orgasms from simple penetrative sex. . . . most of them find that only digital or oral stimulation of the clitoris can be guaranteed to bring them to climax. This must mean that, for them, the two "hot spots" inside the vagina are not living up to their name. The reason for this, it seems, is monotony in sexual positioning. A group of 27 couples were asked to vary their sexual positions experimentally, employing postures that would allow greater stimulation of the two vaginal hot spots, and it was found that three-quarters of the females involved were then able to achieve regular vaginal orgasms.'

I've already pointed out the G-doggy variation earlier. Try the CAT (coital alignment technique). From a standard missionary, position yourself slightly higher up her body so that your shoulders are above hers. Use a shallow penetration and use the base of your penis to stimulate her clitoris. This combination can provide an intense clitoral climax for her and an intense climax for you.

Or try the inverted jockey. From the missionary put her legs together with you inside her and yours on the outside of hers. Lean forward and thrust shallow or deep as you can manage. But as usual do what's right for both of you. Some women don't get anything from these, for others it's the answer to all their orgasmic prayers. The tightness of her also makes for concentrated pleasure for you.

Multiple Orgasms – Yours Not Hers

It's time for a male sexual revolution. Did you know men can fake orgasm? Did you know men can have multiple orgasms? Did you know that ejaculation and orgasm are not the same thing? Did you know that you can have an all-body orgasm?

If you're happy with what you've got now then I'm happy for you; you don't have to read on or believe me. But if you do . . .

Most men learn to ejaculate during masturbation as a teenager. This is usually a rushed, tense period with little time for finding out what happens if you do anything other than race to get it over and done with.

Let's try something different.

Homework assignment #1

Multiple orgasms – non-ejaculatory

- Masturbate until the point of no return. This is the point where if the house was burning down you wouldn't be able to stop. If that's too much to begin with try 50, then 70, then 90 per cent. Stop, breathe and feel the sensations flying around your body. Wait until the sensations have subsided and then go again.

- Make time for this; having to rush to work or put the fire out won't give you the time you need to get to know how your body responds.

- Relax. Don't rush, take it slow. Pay attention to your body; maybe you get pleasurable sensations other than just in your penis. Touch any part of you that turns you on.

- Breathe. Breathing deeply during build-up and especially once you hit the point of no return will help you control what is happening.

- Discover your PC (pubococcygeus) muscle. Tense as if you were trying to stop the flow of urine when you pee. That's your PC muscle. Doing Kegel exercises will help strengthen this muscle which helps you control your ejaculation and orgasm.

- Visualise and breathe. When you are near the point of orgasm imagine the energy normally released through orgasm flowing to other areas of your body and away from your genitals. Notice the build-up of heat and breathe deep, steady breaths to control the pace.

- Let go. Allow yourself to have an orgasm while using your breath, body awareness and by squeezing your PC muscle. As you orgasm keep squeezing your PC muscle and redirect the flow of energy around your body. It may not work the first time so you'll just have to practise again – poor you! Remember this is fun; it's not about keeping score.

- If it works you will find that you get to the point where you're about to explode, pass it and experience a tingling orgasm without ejaculation. It will feel different from a normal ejaculatory orgasm and as you learn to control it more you can build and heighten the sensation. Keep redirecting the flow of energy and breathing and eventually it will turn into an all over body orgasm. Which will really make you go blind, at least for a few seconds.

Troubleshooting (excuse the pun): if you have problems stemming the flow try one of the following just before peaking:

- Place two fingers on the underside of the penis and one on top either at the base or just below the head and squeeze.
- Press the million dollar spot and squeeze the PC muscle. This spot is just in front of the anus and before your testes. You'll feel an indentation at the correct spot. Push your finger in until the first joint.
- Scrotal tugging. Pull your testicles gently away from the body just before orgasm as they have to draw into the body to supply the necessary goods.
- Breathe. This is the best technique combined with the redirection of energy as ultimately all the above are difficult to perform while lovemaking. If you have a few ejaculatory orgasms while you practise don't worry about it, seriously.

There have been several studies conducted on men who experience multiple orgasms in this way. The most famous involved thirty-three men and their partners in a clinical setting conducted by William Hartman and Marilyn Fithian.

During a variety of tests the men experienced between two and sixteen orgasms with an average of four. They monitored pelvic contractions and heart rate and found that the arousal charts for these men were identical to multi-orgasmic women.

When you practise the above exercise don't use porn. It places your focus elsewhere and your attention away from what is happening to you.

When you transfer the above exercise to a partner take your time, explain to her what you're doing and what you'd like to try. If you've ever had to use the withdrawal method of contraception you may have found yourself already using these techniques without realising it. Initially you might want to take control by withdrawing in a similar manner but always remember to focus on your breathing and redirecting as well.

Women discovered that they could do this and men in other cultures have known how to do this for thousands of years so why shouldn't you? You should also expect similar attention and treatment from your lover with kissing, touching and oral too. Remind her that you're more than just a branch she has to shake occasionally. It's not a question of fingerpointing any more it's simply this: if you don't ask you don't get.

Homework assignment #2
    Multiple orgasms – ejaculatory
Now there is a subset of men not widely reported I must add who say they can achieve multiple ejaculations as well as orgasms. I have one friend who can do this and it has happened to me on three occasions, each time with a partner but personally I suffer from what is known as *le petit mort* after too many ejaculations and feel totally drained of

energy. So it's not for me although it is certainly enjoyable to practice.

Basically you masturbate in pretty much the same way as for assignment #1 but then instead of holding back you come a little and then apply the PC control, breathe, relax and wait for the orgasm to subside then restart. It might take a while to train yourself to do this but again I'm sure you'll have fun trying.

There is some mild argument over which technique constitutes a proper orgasm. Personally if there are positive results from both, do either one or both together as and when it suits you. To find out more about #1 check out *The Multi-Orgasmic Man* by Mantak Chia.

Many men apparently have the natural ability for #2 from an early age. According to www.multiorgasmic.com one study subject 'experienced six natural and fully ejaculatory orgasms within a 36-minute time span with no decrease in erection or ability to continue'. Most report an escalation of intensity similar to the non-ejaculatory orgasms.

The point of highlighting these techniques is not to make you feel that you must do them all the time every time or have a mind-blowing, full-body orgasm every time you have sex. That's just unnecessary social pressure. Sometimes no orgasm is what you want. Other times a regular ejaculatory orgasm is equally as good. Who doesn't like a delicious quickie before work or while swimming in remote rock pools? It's all about context, time, space and what you're in the mood for. Most of all sex isn't just about orgasms it's about being open and learning to explore, communicate and enjoy yourselves. And if you apply even half of what you learned in these chapters you will definitely do that.

THE DIVINE COMEDY

For those rainy days

Laughing and Crying

You my friend are going to die. I hate to break it to you like this. I know we've only just met. But there it is and the end is always going to come sooner than you'd like, that much you can be sure of.

Yes I know your Great-Aunt Ermintrude lived to be a feisty 102 and your Uncle Stan smoked thirty Woodbine, drank every day and only stopped working when a steamroller squished him flatter than a 45rpm picture disc – remember them?

But if you're anything like me there comes a point when realisation dawns. My dad died at fifty-five and my gran at fifty-six and who doesn't have friends in the prime of their life with fat bank accounts and even fatter kids who drop dead in their thirties or early forties?

As I'm already in my late thirties that means if I'm anything like my dad I'm already at the end of my middle years and due a midlife crisis. How about you? Yeah I'm still holding out for those life-extension pills too. Like Woody Allen says, 'I don't want to achieve immortality through my work. I want to achieve it through not dying.' Hopefully one day a little pill or a genetic tweak will keep us ticking over until we're all celebrating five hundred. That is if we manage not to scorch away our atmosphere, enslave ourselves to debt, TV or vacuous celebrities in the meantime. But even then we're liable to slip in the shower and break our necks.

Buddhists have the right idea. No please bear with me. They regularly meditate on their mortality because it gives them a greater appreciation of life. That's a pretty sensible, logical and healthy approach to things.

However in Western cultures most of us don't have the dubious luxury of wearing sheets all the time – it's too bloody cold for one thing – and we barely have the moral fortitude to go without streaky bacon for more than a day. No what we have are accidents, bankruptcy, the quarterlife and midlife crisis and the occasional crisis of conscience. Oh my god the world is about to come to an end or is it?

Crisis: it's definitely not glamorous or men's-mag glossy but what are you going to do? Run? Hide? From yourself? There's no need. If you listen to what your inner moppet is trying to tell you life is going to be more fun than it's ever been. I mean take the midlife crisis. When was the last time you saw a guy in an orange sheet driving a Ferrari with a twentysomething blonde on his arm?

Exactly and what's more that's just the small stuff so don't sweat it. The really good things happen when you work out what the hell it was you were put here to do. You'll find a passion in your heart and a fire in your eyes that you haven't felt since the first time you saw your team win, fell in love or reached for the lasers.

A crisis can either be a new beginning or the beginning of the end. Seize the opportunity now and your remaining years whether you're eight or eighty will be the best years of your life. So take a deep breath and smile. Life's about to get a whole lot better.

So What's in a Crisis?

Well apparently they're inevitable and if you read most of the media they're bad bad bad. But actually what they are and what they have always been is a time to re-evaluate. They usually fall into the following categories.

- Financial.
- Spiritual.
- Midlife.
- Quarterlife.

Let's take them one by one.

Financial

You're about to lose everything. You've ballsed up your figures, the economy has gone to the wall. So what? I know you feel stressed right now but as you're going through this process you're probably learning more about how money and markets work in the real world than all those courses, financial guru guides and MBAs combined. Worst case scenario? You lose everything you own. What think you can't handle it? Of course you can. Far worse things happen every day. People get raped, trapped in war zones, tortured or lose a child. Accept it for the challenge it is. You can handle it.

It doesn't matter what other people think about you. Concentrate on doing everything you need to do for you.

Learn everything about your situation. If your financial problem is debt based what are *all* your options? From minimum payments to lower-rate 'full and final' settlements to individual voluntary arrangements to bankruptcy or working it off: there is always an option that is going to be the best one for you.

Take Donald Trump. He or the companies he runs have famously either gone bankrupt or been close to bankruptcy on four separate occasions. In 1991 he was forced to declare business insolvency as he had $3.5 billion in outstanding loans and with a $900 million personal debt he was almost forced to declare personal ruin as well. As I write this one of the casinos he is on the board of filed for Chapter 11 once again.

Think he won't bounce back? Of course he will. What do I know about this? I've lost everything and bounced back myself. I'll do it again if I have to. I also learned more about myself through the hard times than I ever did during the easy times.

Try the Citizens Advice Bureau as a starting point or the excellent forums at www.debthelpuk.co.uk. It is one of the longest running forums with sound advice from people who've all been there and done that.

Spiritual

Personally I think this is harder than financial loss. If you feel like you've lost your path, you're losing your faith, the things that you have learned to value suddenly seem worthless or as I did have a profound realisation about your own mortality then the effects of this are likely to be far more wide ranging. It's usually that your experience of reality has jarred with the mental map you have of the world around you. So typically the go-getting financial high-flyer suddenly finds his trophy wife, cars and kids empty and valueless. Perhaps the strict religious template you had for the world is rocked by scandal within your community or you find ancient teachings have little bearing on current times.

Whatever it is this type of crisis requires you to explore and find answers for yourself. Don't just rely on other people to tell you. Examine and research everything in front of you and then rewrite the template. Try www.spiritualcrisisnetwork.org.uk for inspiration and people going through similar experiences.

Midlife

Are you holding in your stomach right now? Have you gone in over your head for a new Aston Martin? Or are you working up the courage to tell your wife about your strange new feelings for the au pair? If so you could be having a midlife crisis. But it needn't all be clichéd and dreadful. You can have your cake, car, curvy cutie and eat whichever one you want.

The midlife crisis is so steeped in cliché it's often hard to take it seriously. But midlife crises do happen. Most often they are triggered by events that commonly happen during that age such as the death of a loved one, close friend, sibling or parent. Stagnation at work or business failure are also key triggers as are more everyday situations like the kids leaving home. Questions of your own mortality become more relevant as often you have a health scare or serious illness. This often leads to a re-evaluation of life's priorities.

For an excellent source of inspiration and people going through similar things try www.lifetwo.com.

Quarterlife

This is a relatively new category but equally painful if you're experiencing it. It comes on in the late teens, kicks in with a vengeance in your twenties and can linger on indefinitely if not resolved. The 'symptoms' of a quarterlife crisis derive primarily from a working environment where job insecurity and high turnover are the norm and self-worth is determined through advertising standards rather than moral, community or family frameworks. These include:

- Feeling 'not good enough' because you can't find a job that is at your academic/intellectual level.
- Frustration with relationships, the working world and finding a suitable job or career.
- Confusion of identity.
- Insecurity regarding the near future, long-term plans, life goals.
- Insecurity regarding present accomplishments.
- Re-evaluation of close interpersonal relationships.
- Disappointment with your job.
- Nostalgia for university, college, high school or elementary school life.
- Exhibiting a tendency to hold stronger opinions.
- Boredom with social interactions.
- Loss of closeness to high-school and college friends.
- Financially based stress (overwhelming college loans, high cost of living etc.).

- Loneliness.
- Unfulfilled desire to have children.
- A sense that everyone is somehow doing better than you. Try Alexandra Robbins' or Damien Barr's books on quarterlife crises for detailed advice.

Notice a theme developing here in all of these crises? When reality does not meet expectations cognitive dissonance and crisis occur.

They all boil down to one basic question: 'What you are currently doing with your life and where do you want it to go from here?' Go back to the section entitled Never Get Ripped Off Again and try the LIM technique on yourself.

What They Are, What They Aren't

Since the midlife-crisis concept made its way into popular culture the idea of specific triggers has crowded out more detailed analysis of the causes of all types of crisis so remember that any label given to your situation is just shorthand and you may have to explore several avenues to find the right answers for you. One size does not fit all.

Hitting the Wall – What to do/What not to do

Whether or not a crisis becomes a long dark night of the soul often depends on how we choose to perceive it. If you only take the negative then that's all you'll have. Try focusing on the positive aspects of what's in front of you and see where it takes you. It's hardly likely to be any worse is it?

Do:
- Take stock of your situation and then take responsibility for it.
- Talk to those around you. You don't have to agree with their replies or opinions but simply voicing your thoughts

can help. Find a professional third party if you want con-
fidential help, say a professional insolvency firm if you
want clear cut advice on business issues or a therapist for
personal issues.
- Take time for yourself, be good to yourself.

Don't:
- Force a decision for immediate change.
- Ignore your problems.
- Get carried away with the first idea that comes into your
  head.
- Drink or take drugs to avoid dealing with the problems.
- Make fun of your problems.
- Be afraid to ask for help.

How Long Will It Last?

Adversity makes us stronger so the saying goes. But it can
also make us live longer, have more fun, do things we never
thought possible become the person we truly want to be.
However just like any other form of ailment the symptoms
normally get worse before they get better.

Depending on whose data you believe studies suggest that
anything from 26 to 80 per cent of adults between the ages
of forty and sixty experience some form of midlife crisis. For
some this is the 'classic' crisis brought on by the ageing
process, for others it's those troubling life events that often
leave each generation feeling directionless and as if time is
quickly running out.

Currently this traditional 'turbulent' crisis is believed to
last from around two months to two years. However a
recent study from Britain's Warwick University and America's

Dartmouth College demonstrated that the unhappiest years of life are forty-four for men in the UK and fifty for men in the US. This however appears to be perfectly normal behaviour for the mid to late forties and according to LifeTwo, 'The good news, and this was true across almost all 80 countries in the study, is that if you make it to aged 70 and are still physically fit, you are on average as "happy and mentally healthy as a 20-year old".'

As for all the other crises it usually takes a trigger event to make us change our current dysfunctional path and adapt for the better. How quickly you can make these changes and find suitable adaptations whether they are financial, professional, spiritual or otherwise will determine how long it lasts.

The Excuse
Bad times can be the easiest of means to justify dodgy ends. So if you do really want to run away with the au pair pick a crisis and go for it. I'm sure that's not the usual advice you'll hear but how often do you get the chance to really take risks and throw caution to the wind? However do make sure you've thought it all through properly and that you're not going to regret it when you come back or else you'll be right back where you started.

Near-Death Experience
On the other hand life is for the living. If you have postponed your happiness on the never-never plan – you know work until sixty-five, retire, wonder what the hell to do with your life, muddle along for a few years and drink every day so that you don't have to face what's coming – then you might want to take a good look at those itches you've been meaning to scratch all these years.

There is no shame in experiencing a crisis no matter how other people might try to make you feel. To prove my point here's an alternative personal biography with all my own crises included:

Frank Coles had his first classic midlife crisis at the age of eight when he realised that one day he really was going to die. In his twenties he worked on developing TV formats with the author of *The Quartersomething Crisis* (the midlife crisis for those under the age of forty) and then had a career crisis about TV. He trained to Master's level in Science and Computing before realising it wasn't for him. He quickly lost everything he'd worked for up to that point then began writing and travelling under his own name. At thirty-three his father died suddenly, causing the most painful crisis yet. Since then he has written two books, edited two more and been published by lots of household names. He's travelled the world, trekked through jungles, skied to the North Pole and got to know his family again. He firmly believes we could all do with a little more crisis in our lives.

I'm sure I'll have a few more crises before the towel I'm supposed to throw in is ripped from my hands. I hope you will too.

Smile at the Devil and Spit in His Face – Depression and How to Deal with It

There is an elephant in the room. It's sitting in front of the TV, blocking the view and generally making a nuisance of itself. Nobody wants to mention it.

It's you.

Initially you thought it was just a prolonged period of sadness but then one sunny day when you were with people you loved and everyone was happy you just couldn't be. I know you tried, I mean you really tried but it just wouldn't happen. It wasn't out of choice; no matter what you did you just couldn't physically be happy.

The problem was that nobody else could see that little devil sitting on your shoulder. Whenever your lips began to curl upwards he pressed down on them with all the weight of the world; whenever you opened your mouth to laugh he clamped it shut.

You've barely admitted it to yourself. You went to the

doctor for colds, tiredness, aches, pains and never told him. When he couldn't help you started to self medicate with drink and drugs. When you took them you felt fine and the little devil disappeared for a few hours but the next day he had grown in stature and took up more of your time, more of your energy and whispered in your ear about how truly bad you were. How you deserved everything you got.

He told you that he would eventually have in his power one in six of the population and that at any one time one in ten would be under his spell. He told you that three out of four people suffering never even asked for help. What chance did you have?

Then one day worn down by the constant battle against the demon you decided enough was enough. You contemplated severing those tusks and calling it a day. But somewhere deep inside you found a tough inner core and decided to fight. You knew it wouldn't be easy but you knew from the many who had gone before you that it could be done, that you could prevail and walk out the other side smiling and victorious. So here's how.

But first if you are feeling suicidal right now whether you're browsing in a bookshop or reading this at home please know that your situation is not irreversible. You need to put this book down right now and contact either the police, your doctor or the Samaritans. The Mental Health Foundation estimates that 70 per cent of recorded suicides are by people experiencing undiagnosed depression. Don't be another statistic; be a demon killer instead.

Know Your Symptoms

According to MIND, the mental health charity, if you tick off five or more of the following symptoms it's likely you're depressed:

- Being restless and agitated.
- Waking up early, having difficulty sleeping or sleeping more than usual.
- Feeling tired and lacking energy; doing less and less.
- Using more tobacco, alcohol or other drugs than usual.
- Not eating properly and losing or putting on weight.
- Crying a lot.
- Having difficulty remembering things.
- Having physical aches and pains with no physical cause.
- Feeling low-spirited for much of the time, every day.
- Being unusually irritable or impatient.
- Getting no pleasure out of life or what you usually enjoy.
- Losing interest in your sex life.
- Finding it hard to concentrate or make decisions.
- Constantly blaming yourself and feeling guilty.
- Lacking self-confidence and self-esteem.
- Being preoccupied with negative thoughts.
- Feeling numb, empty and despairing.
- Feeling helpless.
- Distancing yourself from others; not asking for support.
- Taking a bleak, pessimistic view of the future.
- Experiencing a sense of unreality.
- Self-harming (by cutting yourself for example).
- Thinking about suicide.

Know Your Type of Depression

Major Depression

This is the most common form and is through the use of wildly mixed metaphor described in the opening paragraph. The sufferer appears to walk around with the weight of the world on their shoulders. You probably know several people who have this. They usually seem disinterested in everyday or enjoyable activities and are convinced that they are in a hopeless condition. Loss of sex drive, appetite and weight are also common in this form of depression.

Atypical Depression

This is quite common and subtly different to major depression. The sufferer can feel moments of happiness and elation. Symptoms include fatigue, oversleeping, overeating and weight gain. People who suffer from atypical depression believe that outside events such as success, attention and praise control their mood. Episodes of atypical depression can last for months or a sufferer may live with it for many years.

Bipolar Disorder (Manic Depression)

People who suffer from manic depression have alternating mood swings where deep depressions swing to manic highs and back again. When manic they are often highly excitable and enthusiastic and may plan and try to execute grandiose schemes and ideas.

Seasonal Affective Disorder (SAD)

SAD is one of the most common forms of depression. It usually occurs in colder latitudes where the days grow short and exposure to daylight is reduced. It's known as the 'winter blues' but also with the increased use of air conditioning and tinted windows in hot climates or where sunlight is artificially restricted as the 'droopy dims'. It's easily treated with a SAD lamp and by being outside every day.

Psychotic Depression

Those with severe depression lose touch with reality and may hallucinate, experiencing frightening sounds, voices and images. Eventually they are unable to distinguish between what is really happening and what in their imagination they believe is happening.

Dysthymia

This is a mild but persistent type of depression that often occurs for two or more years in adults or one year in children. Many suffers are not aware of it and just live with it, considering it simply part of the daily grind. They often feel unimportant, dissatisfied, frightened or simply don't enjoy their lives. Although the symptoms are not as severe as other types of depression the length of time they persist can have a particularly distressing impact on everyday life.

Spit at the Devil

Don't get weighed down any further by these definitions. Depression is usually not incurable. It feeds on itself and the more you think or believe it is hopeless the more you'll prove your point. Instead revel in the knowledge that you are now doing something about it and are soon going to run that scrawny little devil's arse into touch and slam him to the floor.

There are several options for treatment that will suit the severity of your illness from medication to changes in diet and psychological treatment. The point is to educate yourself so that *you* feel in control of it. I guarantee that if you try any of the following you will begin to feel better in one to three weeks.

Medication

This is usually the first form of treatment for all levels of depression if you visit a GP. If you're 'stuck' in a negative place or scared that you are only getting worse then it is a positive first step. The most popular drug is Prozac, the brand name for Fluoxetine. There are several brand variations of this on the market and they all fall into the family of drugs known as selective serotonin reuptake inhibitors (SSRIs). Their basic job is to regulate serotonin in the brain, one of the chemicals responsible for mood. For more severe forms like manic depression a combined high and low mood management approach is used e.g. Fluoxetine to manage the lows and Lithium to manage the highs.

However speaking from my own experiences of the medical profession and these types of illnesses, medication alone simply isn't enough. Many SSRIs are poorly regulated and some with short half lives have withdrawal symptoms which have been described as worse than those from heroin. So do your own research first. One or more of the following needs to happen as well as and in many cases replace medication.

Therapy

According to MIND your doctor will typically be able to refer you to or offer one of the following traditional therapies:

- Five or six sessions of problem-solving therapy to help break down your problems into manageable portions and provide strategies for coping with them.
- Cognitive behavioural therapy (CBT), which helps identify and change negative thoughts and feelings affecting your behaviour. Computerised CBT is also available for those with social anxiety problems. You can get started by trying out the exercises in the Mind Control section.
- Guided self-help over six to eight weeks under the guidance of a healthcare professional.
- Interpersonal psychotherapy (IPT) focusing on relationships for up to six to twelve months.
- Counselling. Either short or long term. This is simply talking with someone trained to listen with empathy and acceptance. This allows you to express your feelings and find your own solutions to your problems.

Non-Medical One: FOOD

You are what you eat

The food we eat affects our mood. Eat too much sugar what happens? Drink too much Red Bull what happens? Drink alcohol, a plant extract, what happens? Eat to the point where you are bloated and overfull what happens? The same chemical triggers are at work in your everyday foods but at less noticeable levels and all go some way to affecting your mood.

Blood sugar

If your energy or mood levels fluctuate wildly eat a low glycemic index (GI) diet. To do this simply cut out white processed food such as pastas, breads, cakes, biscuits, pastries and anything containing sugar. One of the earliest studies on this was written up as *Potatoes Not Prozac* in which Kathleen DesMaisons Ph.D. researched the link between diet and mood for recovering alcoholics. She proposed a simple seven-step programme focused on eating three protein-rich meals a day that shifts you from high-sugar, simple-carb foods to balance your serotonin levels and increase beta-endorphin production. Additionally you have to cut back on alcohol and coffee both of which also affect mood. The only side effect of this programme is that you lose weight and eat more interesting food. There are many resources for low GI foods out there; simply Google or Amazon to find out more.

5-HTP

According to the charity Food for the Brain, 'Serotonin is made in the body and brain from an amino acid 5-Hydroxy Tryptophan (5-HTP), which in turn is made from another amino acid called tryptophan. Both can be found in the diet; tryptophan in many protein rich foods such as meat, fish, beans and eggs.'

People who don't eat enough tryptophan rapidly become depressed within hours. Both tryptophan-rich foods and 5-HTP have been shown to be useful antidepressants in clinical trials and in comparison studies between 5-HTP and SSRI antidepressants 5-HTP often came out slightly better.

You can buy it in health food stores or online. Reported side effects such as bad guts and sleepiness normally pass after a few days.

Omega 3

In clinical trials this fat commonly found in fish oils has repeatedly been shown to have beneficial effects on mood usually within a three-week period. Food for the Brain reports that 'the average improvement in depression was approximately double that shown by anti-depressant drugs, and without the side effects. This may be because Omega 3s help to build your brain's neuronal connections as well as the receptor sites for neurotransmitters; therefore the more Omega 3s in your blood the more serotonin you are likely to make and the more responsive you become to its effects.' Omega 3 EPA and DHA is the more concentrated form and has also been shown to have statistically significant effects on brain function making you smarter too.

B-Vitamins

A recent study from Kuopio University in Finland published in the journal *BMC Psychiatry* found that high levels of B vitamins complemented other treatments and in *The Rotterdam Study* they found that 'vitamin B12 may be causally related to depression'. So combining B vitamins with Omega 3 may be even more effective. Supplementing with B vitamins has also been shown to lower homocysteine levels as high levels of this toxic protein in the blood increase the likelihood of depression.

Chromium

If you suffer from atypical depression then upping your chromium intake helps regulate your blood-sugar levels because insulin can't work to clear the excess glucose without it. Food for the Brain reports that in a small double-blind study when ten patients suffering atypical depression were given chromium supplements of 600mcg a day and five others a placebo for eight weeks, 'The results were dramatic. Seven out of ten taking the supplements showed a big improvement, versus none on the placebo. Their Hamilton Rating Score for depression dropped by an unheard of 83%; from 29 – major depression – to 5 – not depressed. A larger trial at Cornell University with 113 patients has confirmed the finding. After eight weeks 65% of those on chromium had had a major improvement, compared to 33% on placebos.' Try supplementing 600mcg per day with 400 in the morning and 200 at lunch.

Non-Medical Two: Exercise

Twenty to thirty minutes a day of regular exercise from walking to running has been proven to be effective treatment for depression within a three-week period and to have continuing positive effects on mood, health, energy levels and self-esteem throughout your life. Studies have shown that aerobic exercise alone is almost twice as effective as standard drug treatments.

So if you do nothing else, for the next three weeks or more run, walk, swim, hit the gym, ramble, jump up and down on the floor or dance like you mean it every day. Whatever it takes, whatever you're comfortable with, whatever you can face try it. Start today. What have you got to lose? For quick inspiration reread Hal Higdon's 30/30 running plan in the Forever Fit section.

Change Your Life Today

Self-Medication

If you drink or smoke find a way to reduce or stop either one or both of these drugs. With smoking you'll be amazed at the positive difference on your mood when you don't have to suffer nicotine withdrawal every half an hour.

Forget Lifestyle

If all you have is a lifestyle you've got nothing. Get a *life* instead. You wouldn't settle for a certain style of child would you? You'd take the time to find the right person and then work hard to create something wonderful. Why is your life any different? So perhaps it's your job, perhaps it's your relationship or even the area where you live. If you've tried all the above treatment options and have neither learned to manage your depression or remove it then it's very likely that what you needed all along was to begin to live life more passionately. Try some of the NLP exercises in the next section to get started.

Through my own experiences of depression in my early twenties I found that changing my diet and beginning to exercise again was more effective than any drug treatment. I then found that changing an unhappy job situation improved it even more and then found stopping smoking was a revelation. When I started doing some of the things I'd always been passionate about everything changed for the better again. So pay attention to what your mind and body are telling you; if you've always been 'searching' for something in life there's probably a good reason.

Professor Irving Kirsch from the Psychology Department at the University of Hull and lead researcher on a recent paper on SSRIs and clinical trials said, 'The difference in improvement between patients taking placebos and patients taking antidepressants is not very great. *This means that depressed people can improve without chemical treatment* [my emphasis]. Given these results, there seems little reason to prescribe antidepressant medication to any but the most severely depressed patients, unless alternative treatments have failed to provide a benefit.'

What's certain is this: exercise, sunlight, reducing your stress levels, eating healthily and well and limiting excessive use of alcohol, nicotine and drugs all help to increase or stabilise your natural levels of serotonin and beta-endorphins – the things that keep your mood level buoyant.

A positive mental attitude to this sometimes unwieldy depression thing also makes all the difference. So act like you mean it. Throw out all those depressing CDs, books, movies and decor that you've become addicted to and that only serve to deepen your depressive mood. Stop wearing black and restock your life with funny movies, satirical novels, vibrant colours and silliness instead.

P. G. Wodehouse said it best: 'I'm all for rational enjoyment, and so forth, but I think a fellow makes himself conspicuous when he throws soft-boiled eggs at the electric fan.'

So make yourself conspicuous and next time that little devil turns up at your side smile at him, spit in his face if you want to, but more than anything feel sorry for him. He's dependent on you feeling blue and believing you have no way out to keep him alive. It's a relationship that will soon be over. Give it three weeks using any of the above and it's almost certain he will shrink in size. You'll see he's not so tough after all. Then a few weeks or months down the line when you find yourself in a good place again surrounded by good people you'll barely remember he was ever there.

MIND CONTROL

Use it or lose it

Mind Mastery – Be Happy, Handle Anything: Some Cognitive Tools

In the last thirty years two psychological toolsets have been developed that promise to help us transform what we think and feel about ourselves by changing *how* we think.

Neuro-Linguistic Programming (NLP)

NLP is in the strictest terms a pseudoscience as its claims are not based on the scientific method. The *Oxford English Dictionary* defines it as a system of alternative therapy 'which seeks to educate people in self-awareness and effective communication, and to change their patterns of mental and emotional behaviour'.

According to Wikipedia 'NLP was originally promoted by its founders, Bandler and Grinder, in the 1970s as an extraordinarily effective and rapid form of psychological therapy, capable of addressing the full range of problems which psychologists are likely to encounter, such as phobias, depression, habit disorder, psychosomatic illnesses, learning disorders. It also espoused the potential for self-determination through overcoming learned limitations and emphasized well-being and healthy functioning. Later it was promoted as a "science of excellence", derived from the study or "modelling" of how successful or outstanding people in different fields obtain their results. It was claimed that these skills can be learned by anyone to improve their effectiveness both personally and professionally.'

It takes less than a week to become a certified practitioner. You can then go out and teach corporations how to build efficient teams and streamline economies through recession as well as change their own internal neuro-linguistic associations by calling a recession a 'credit crunch'.

Still once you get past the hype of NLP and its pre-ordained ability to turn you into a post-modern superman it does have its uses. I'm all for hacks and shortcuts that circumvent the pre-programmed noise in our heads and get us doing what we want to do. I was going to present you with a few techniques that I'd found useful over the years and that I use once in a while when I need to get past something and then found that that talented swine Derren Brown had done a similar thing in his book *Tricks of the Mind*. As he eloquently put it, 'If we remove from the NLP equation the grinning, flaccid course-junkies, delusional flower fairies and ridiculous tactile businessmen, and some of the taken-as-read wild claims made by NLPers at all levels, there are some sensible enough tools and techniques from that world which are worth knowing about, as long as you don't become a True Believer.'

Quite so and without further ado here's my pick of the bunch.

The Fast Phobia Technique

1. Think of a fearful situation that you have to face in the next few hours or days. Nothing potentially traumatic just something like a public speech, a job interview or a first date. Think about it until you get that feeling of fear. You've probably imagined a small sequence of events just like a short film or movie.

2. Imagine you're watching that movie in a darkened cinema with your movie paused just before you are about to enter the fearful situation. Now imagine yourself at the back of the cinema in the expensive seats on the balcony, the ones that provide you with endless popcorn and nachos and limitless barrels of cola. You can now barely see the picture, its colours are so muted that it's almost black and white. And you can see yourself watching the movie in the stalls below. Now watch the film from beginning to end and pause it at the end. From this small third person perspective you'll be surprised at how little emotional effect it has on you.

3. Now step into the picture, make it as big as you can, an IMAX screen, larger than your field of vision, louder and more vibrantly colourful than is necessary.

4. Now run the film quickly in reverse and add a comedy soundtrack.

5. Now step back out of the screen and sit in the front row. Then white-out the screen in front of you.

6. Repeat as necessary until the desired effect is achieved.

One worthy NLP observation is that how we portray a situation to ourselves influences its effect on us. Ever noticed how when you're worrying late at night it is usually a movie repeating endlessly in your head? If you have a fear or phobia it's often the same; the image becomes loud and almost unbearable and like a scab we keep picking at it and making it worse.

By using the above technique and repeating it until it sticks you can minimise the effects of unwanted behaviours on your conscious mind. Derren adds a useful addition to this technique: 'If something is bothering you, shrink it down, desaturate the colour, move it away and shift it to that third person perspective; if you want to feel more excitement, make the picture big and buzzy and colourful, bring it in close and make sure you see the thing through your own eyes.'

I've personally never tried this for an outright phobia but with hindsight maybe it would have been a more sensible first stop than actually jumping out of a plane.

Develop a Grand Vision

Richard Buckminster Fuller aka 'Bucky' was a visionary designer, architect, author and inventor. Born in 1895 his most famous creation was the geodesic dome. He was also one of the modern thinkers who popularised the idea of sustainability here on 'spaceship earth' well before the current zeitgeist. This came about because although he considered himself an average individual without special monetary means or academic qualification he chose to devote his life to this question: 'Does humanity have a chance to survive lastingly and successfully on planet Earth and if so how?' He tried to identify what he as an individual could do to improve humanity's condition in ways which large organisations, governments and private enterprises inherently could not.

So as you might have noticed a big part of this book is about letting go of your 'can't do' and embracing your 'can do'. If you've ever felt there was more for you out there or you just plain well want it right now take some inspiration from Bucky Fuller and try this.

Examine your core values and principles

1. Picture your passions, interests and desires. Look into the future and see how they might be realised. Pick the most important ones to you and see your goals being achieved. This is your potential future.

2. Discover your values and principles. Take a few minutes to explore each goal. What value or principle is most important to you about it? If it's travel is it the excitement and the fun to be had or the learning and challenge of new cultures. Usually this provokes answers like 'making the world a better place', 'freedom' or 'money'.

3. For each goal ask yourself: What do I most value about this goal? Make a list.

4. Find the underlying principles. When you have your list ask yourself: What is important about all these values? What are the common denominators?

5. Record these core values and principles for future reference.

Develop your vision

1. Picture your interests, values and abilities. Take the time to imagine yourself using them. Play with them. Create images of what is most important to you. This will give you an idea of what direction you would like to take.

2. Picture your heroes. See yourself doing things that give you the same feelings you get when you imagine them. Let any other images disappear.

3. Direct a movie; you're the star. Go wild here. Now take those images and put them together into a movie of the things you'd like to become and achieve. Make it as loud,

vibrant, colourful, dramatic and emotionally engaging as you can until you feel tingles down your spine.

4. Recall your core values and let them inspire the images you see.

5. Get out of your own way. Ask for your inner wisdom to guide this vision and then relax. Know it is the right thing and it will come. It's a process of discovery so take your time and play with it. When you feel you've found the edges of this grand vision write it down.

Own your mission

1. Stand up or lie down for this. Picture your vision in front of you as a movie.

2. Add special effects and sound

3. Add a voiceover, a sentence or two that summarises your vision.

4. Add feeling, pride, confidence, power, nobility, whatever you associate most strongly with your vision.

5. Now picture the star of your movie from behind, your future self standing directly in front of you in three dimensions. It is the you that you will eventually become.

6. Now move forward into your future self. Feel what it truly feels like to be that future you; let the emotions and confidence fill you from the tips of your fingers to the tips of your toes. Feel the energy of potential vibrate inside you. Feel what it's like to know where you are going in life and what you want to achieve. That image is now a part of you.

7. Repeat as necessary to reinforce the feeling or when waiting for an appointment, stepping out of a lift or sitting on a train.

If you want to find out more about NLP then there are hundreds of resources online that will teach you everything you need to know from swish patterns for self-empowerment to rapport building, reframing and the anchoring technique of tying emotional states to specific physical cues. *NLP: The New Technology of Achievement* by Andreas and Faulkner is also a very good workbook for your collection.

Cognitive Behavioural Therapy (CBT)

Unlike NLP, CBT is rigorously tested and applied in clinical situations. In layman's terms the basic premise of CBT is that you take a thought based on faulty reasoning like those for people with low self-esteem such as 'I'm worthless' and replace it with something more realistic like 'Hey check me out, I'm really rather groovy, look at me go.'

It's been found to be incredibly useful and widely applicable to a range of areas from the prison system and schools to everyday clinical issues like addiction, post-traumatic stress disorder, clinical depression, OCD and bulimia. In the UK it is the treatment of choice for the National Institute for Health and Clinical Excellence for a wide range of mental health difficulties

In self-help terms it has been shown to be effective for problems like excessive worry, anxiety, procrastination, insomnia and depression. It has come under some criticism as it has become a catch-all treatment for governments especially with a recent move by Gordon Brown to have a six to sixteen week programme that aims to make the depressed undepressed and get them out to work. All fine and dandy but it kind of missed the obvious no-jobs/no-money scenario that usually comes with a massive recession. And that if the jobs are unfulfilling and low paid CBT is unlikely to help. For that you would need some serious brainwashing.

Still that said I personally have found CBT one of the most useful psychological techniques around. Because when situations call for an immediate change of perspective re-examining the minutiae of your childhood one hour a week for the next six months can seem a little ineffective but changing your internal monologue in a few short minutes quite the opposite. Here are the basics to get you started.

You Feel the Way You Think

Cognitive distortions affect the way we see the world. The most common distortions are as follows:

- All or nothing thinking.
- Overgeneralising.
- Mental filter – focusing on one negative against all else.
- Disqualifying the positive.
- Jumping to conclusions.
- Magnification (or catastrophising).
- Emotional reasoning.
- 'Should' statements.
- Labelling.
- Personalisation.

So say for example you've just handed over a report to your boss that you've been working on all week as well as late nights and early mornings. He barely looks at it, grunts and tells you he's got an important meeting to go to.

The following thoughts rampage through your internal monologue: 'I work like a slave and this is the thanks I get from that pillock? I'm completely unimportant. I can't take it any more. I'm a failure. I never do anything right. What's wrong with me?'

Now can you spot the cognitive distortions there? 'I'm completely unimportant' is all or nothing thinking. You were significant enough to be given the assignment in the

first place. 'I'm a failure' is overgeneralisation and jumping
to conclusions, and really you've never done anything that
wasn't a failure? Whatever? You managed to leave the
house with your clothes on this morning didn't you? 'I
can't take it any more' is magnification of your pain; you
are blowing it out of proportion because you are taking it.
Maybe you don't want to but you are. Also you are not a
slave; that is labelling as is calling your boss a pillock.
Okay he may be exhibiting insensitive and ungracious
behaviour but pillocks don't really exist, at least not like
that.

While it might be unrealistic to think that you will walk
away from that interaction not thinking your boss is a
complete tool, he may genuinely have an important meeting
that he is sweating about and isn't even aware of his behaviour. He may genuinely be a pig of course. But we have all
had those situations where we've jumped to conclusions
only to have someone come back to us at the end of the day,
humble, grateful and very human. But either way it would
be unwise to walk away feeling that you are a failure, a slave,
a victim, unimportant and that there is something wrong with
you. That will lower your self-esteem, make you angry and
possibly inspire self loathing.

Emotional Accounting

At its most basic CBT will help you restructure your
thoughts so that they are more realistic. It is a form of talking back to your internal critic and learning to counteract
your self defeating inner voice.

Examine this effortless triple-column technique that helps
you do this. It can be used to restructure the way you think
about yourself when things have gone wrong. The aim is to
substitute more rational thoughts for the illogical, harsh

self-criticisms that automatically flood your mind when a
negative event occurs.

Automatic thought	Cognitive distortion	Rational response
I'm completely unimportant	All or nothing thinking	Nonsense. I'm important to myself, my family and my boss who gave me the assignment in the first place
I'm a failure	Overgeneralisation, jumping to conclusions	I'm not sure I have failed my boss yet. Let alone anyone else. And if I did so what? It's not the end of the world is it? And yes look I am wearing clothes today
I can't take any more	Magnification	I can't take finishing a report? Now it's finished I can relax. Is that really a problem?
I am a slave	Labelling	Oh yeah? Can I write a resignation letter? Can a slave?
etc		

Based on source: *Feeling Good*, by David D. Burns, MD.

CBT techniques will become part of your normal cognitive processes as you start to use them but when beginning you must always write them out. It is a process of active learning or ritual that helps reinforce the new thought processes in your brain and it forces you to be much more objective as opposed to being subjective in your analysis.

If you use this simple three column technique for a fortnight or the more detailed Daily Record of Dysfunctional Thoughts also found in *Feeling Good* it will almost certainly transform your thinking and help you identify the part of your psyche that reacts negatively when it doesn't need to. If you want to take it further there are many good books on this subject that will help you work on all areas of your life from job interviews to dealing with anger or procrastination. Apart from David Burns's book I also recommend *Mind Over Mood* by Greenberger and Padesky.

Assertiveness – The Art of Saying No or . . . How to Grow a Pair

Assertiveness isn't about aggression or control; it's simply about being able to say what needs to be said in a way that resists the pressure of overly dominant people. Gandhi's use of non-violent assertiveness against the British to find freedom for India is an inspiring example.

Passive communicators: do not protect or value their personal boundaries which allows aggressives to dominate and influence them.

Aggressive communicators: do not respect others' personal boundaries and are liable to cause harm while trying to influence others.

Assertive communicators: are not afraid to speak their minds or influence others but do so in a way that respects other people's personal boundaries.

Like good steel it's a skill that needs to be tempered. A healthy balance of assertiveness is important in making relationships and friendships work well. Get it wrong and you're either a walkover or an emotional bully. But get it right and you will come across as confident, people will feel comfortable approaching you and there will be nothing vague about dealing with you.

David Straker, author of *Changing Minds*, and myself have put together the following assertiveness primer just for you.

Assertive Beliefs

Much of what we do, say or feel is based on our beliefs. Problems occur when we hold contradictory beliefs about ourselves and about other people. If you have assertive beliefs then assertive behaviour will follow.

Beliefs that drive assertive behaviour include:

- I am equal to others with the same fundamental rights.
- I am free to think, choose and make decisions for myself.
- I am able to try things, make mistakes, learn and improve.
- I am responsible for my own actions and my responses to other people.
- I do not need permission to take action.
- It is okay to disagree with others. Agreement is not always necessary or possible.

Non-Assertive Beliefs

Non-assertive beliefs assume we are not equal to other people and hence drive passive or aggressive behaviour.

Beliefs that drive passive behaviour include:

- Others are more important, more intelligent or better than me.

- Other people do not like me because I do not deserve to be liked.
- My opinion is not of value and will not be valued.
- I must be perfect in everything I do otherwise I am a complete failure.
- It is better to be safe and say nothing rather than say what I think.

Beliefs that drive aggressive behaviour include:
- I am cleverer and more powerful than other people.
- Other people cannot be trusted to do as they are told.
- It's a dog-eat-dog world. I must get other people before they get me.
- The only way to get things done is to tell people. Asking is a sign of weakness.
- People who do not fight hard for what they want get what they deserve.

Developing Assertive Beliefs

There are several things you can do to develop and stabilise beliefs that will make you more assertive:
- Notice how your current beliefs drive your decisions and actions. Identify the beliefs that you want to change (CBT is an effective tool for this).
- Consider how the beliefs of others drive their decisions and actions.
- Choose the beliefs you want to adopt. Write them down. Pin them on the wall. Carry them with you in your wallet or pocket.
- Start by acting assertive. You may not feel it but you can always act it.

- Start small: be assertive in relatively simple contexts such as asking for things in shops and restaurants where it is not a 'life or death' situation.
- Reflect on your successes. Realise how new beliefs are making a difference.

Assertiveness Techniques

Saying No

When you are asked to do something you do not want to do you can just say no.

- When you say 'no' keep your refusal short but not so abrupt that it upsets the other person. Make sure what you are saying is crystal clear with no scope for the other person to think that you might yet be persuaded.
- Make the message clear by starting your response with 'no'.
- You do not need to qualify or explain your response. The fact that you have made a decision is enough. It may be helpful sometimes to explain a decision but do not offer this as something for them to challenge.
- Don't apologise for your refusal and don't be apologetic in your tone. 'I'm sorry but . . .' often appears weak and leads to challenges and further argument. Be firm: neither weak nor aggressive.
- Don't make excuses. If you give a reason be honest even if it is uncomfortable. Be careful about giving explanations on which they might try objection-handling. Defending an excuse can be very hard to sustain.
- Disregard pleading, whining and wheedling. Only listen to rational argument and make rational decisions based on what you hear. Only change your mind if it makes real sense.

- It helps to acknowledge the other person, by using their name for example.
- Show that it's you making the decision rather than hiding behind other people or impersonal rules. Say 'I' rather than 'we' or 'they'.
- If the other person persists repeat your reasons (do not look for new reasons to decline). Use the broken record method if necessary.

Example

'I can't take on any extra work. My calendar is completely full for the next month.'

'Sorry Kylie. You're a nice girl but I do not want to go out with you.'

'No I do not want double glazing. I am happy with my house as it is thank you.'

Many people have problems saying no. It is much easier to say yes. By saying no we risk the wrath of the other person or the other people they might tell. Ultimately refusal may seem to risk hurting a relationship, being ostracised from the group, being fired from the company or otherwise being severely punished for your lack of cooperation. When you refuse it may seem as if you are also giving up your right to ask something of the other person.

All this is of course untrue. You have a basic right to refuse. The good news is that reality is nowhere near as bad as imagination. When you say no assertively and clearly you are more likely to gain respect than lose it.

The Broken Record

Method

When the other person repeats their request to you simply repeat the same words of refusal. *But* you may have to do this a number of times *but* eventually they will get the message. You can add other words of acknowledgement *but* . . .

Example

'Yes I know it's important but I don't want to go . . . Sorry but I don't want to go . . . I realise what it means to you but I don't want to go.'

'It's too expensive . . . I know it's good value but it's too expensive . . . I know about finance deals but it's too expensive.'

If someone is trying hard to persuade they often do not really hear your refusal. At best they may just see it as an objection that can be overcome.

When you repeat the same words the pattern-recognition ability of the brain eventually notices that something is being repeated here and the other person starts to take notice of what you are saying. When they realise they are bashing their head against a brick wall they will eventually give up (with most people this will be quite quickly).

Praise – Giving and Receiving

You can use assertion both in giving praise and receiving it.

Giving Praise

- In giving praise assertively be specific about how the other person has done well. Mention the value that the other person has created and how you feel about it.
- Make the praise heartfelt. Do not say anything that you do not really mean.
- You can praise superiors as well as peers and subordinates. Many managers receive very little recognition from their charges and a little appreciation can go a long way. Be careful and succinct with this – it is easy to appear as if you are sucking up to them. A simple way of doing this is to thank them when they have helped you in some way.

Accepting Praise

- When other people praise you accept it with a slightly surprised thanks.
- Do not be arrogant or show that you expected the praise. Avoid saying, 'Yes it was rather good I thought.' Nor be excessively diffident, effectively refusing to accept the praise or downplaying your part in it as, 'Oh it was nothing really.'

Example

'Jed you did a great job of getting the project completed to schedule. I have had several very complimentary comments from our customers about it.'

'Michelle I really liked the way you handled Steve yesterday. That was a tricky situation and could easily have got out of hand.'

'Thank you. That's very kind of you to say that [accepting praise].'

Praise is a powerful motivator. If offered in the right way it affirms the other person's sense of identity, increasing their sense of worth. It also tells them what they are doing well. Generally people will do more of the things for which they are praised but only as long as they believe that they deserve the praise and that it was genuinely offered and without ulterior motive.

Weak praise can sound like empty flattery seeking to appease the other person rather than offering genuine appreciation. When you give praise that is not really deserved then you make worthless any praise that is deserved. As a result the other person will never really feel praised (and will dislike you for 'assassinating praise').

Aggressive praise can sound like cynicism or sarcasm that seeks to keep the other person in an inferior position. It happens when someone realises that the other person has done a good job but rather than truly admiring the other person they feel threatened and that their own limitations have been shown up (perhaps deliberately).

These techniques are great starting points. If you want to find out more head over to www.changingminds.org or take a class. Hands on practice with assertiveness techniques that deal with inquiry, criticism and handling arguments is one of the most valuable things you can do with your time and will help you in your work, your family life and yourself.

More than Mnemonics

Our brains are hard-wired to use the full range of sensory input: smell, touch, taste, sight, structure, space, position, rhythm, emotion and language. However most of the things we have to remember come verbally in conversation or on the printed page. By simply using all of our senses we can increase our recall whether it's for a simple shopping list when we don't have a pen to hand, birthdays, blueprints of Dr X's secret base, exam revision or a big presentation without notes.

There are simple ways to make difficult information easy to remember. We've all used mnemonics: think of the 'thirty days hath September' rhyme, or Every Good Boy Deserves Fudge (EGBDF) for musical notation. Adding humour and playfulness really helps. 'Me Very Excited, Me Just Sat Upon New Paint' is a good way to remember the order of the planets in our solar system – Mercury, Venus, Earth, Mars, Jupiter, Saturn, Uranus, Neptune and Pluto. The trick is to make it big, make it colourful, use positive images (as your brain blocks out unpleasant ones), exaggerate for effect and use all the senses. Adding in everyday totems like traffic lights or a thumbs-up is also highly effective as is making them rude. Find a rude word beginning with F to make an alternative rhyme out of 'Every good boy deserves . . .' Picture it in your mind, give that good boy a gold star on his shirt, make it you, bring it up close, give yourself a silly hat, a stupid grin, make a lot of noise, add humour. Got a clear image in your mind? Good: now run it through a couple of times until it's easy to see. If I ask you a year from now what the notes in a scale are do you think you'll be able to remember? Now try making the planet mnemonic both rude and colourful.

The Loci Palace

This is one of my favourite memory tools. It's simple and powerful as well as being quick and adaptable. I use it regularly when I am travelling and need to remember things without notes.

In ancient times loci were physical locations usually a large, familiar public building like a market or a temple. The idea is that you walk through your chosen building several times and view distinct places within it in the same order each time.

After several repetitions when you can reliably remember and visualise all the various nooks, cubbyholes and rooms in order you break up whatever you want to remember into pieces and choose vividly imagined objects or symbols to replace the key points.

In your imagination you then place each of these images into the different loci. They can then be recalled in the correct order simply by imagining you are walking through the building again, visiting each loci in order and viewing each of the images placed there.

Let's try it now. Pick a list of something you have to remember either real or imaginary. Today's to-do list for example.

Pick up dry cleaning	Pay water bill
Shop for goldfish	Cash cheque
Call Mum	Reply to emails
Buy this book for everyone I know	Take dog for a walk

Pick a place you are very familiar with, perhaps a park, your mother's house or a favourite gallery. I usually use my apartment. Now sit back and imagine you are at the entrance. Walk into the hallway: what's the first thing you see? In mine there's a chest on the right-hand side, two closets on the left and several pictures on the wall.

So whatever you have in your hallway, stop at each location and picture it in your mind's eye. Imagine that it is brightly lit even if in reality it's not. Once you have it firmly fixed move on to the next memory location until you've worked your way through. Now enter a second room, say your living room. What do you immediately notice? Is there a TV, a settee, a table and chairs, pictures on the wall, a door leading to the garden?

Whatever immediately springs to mind is your loci. Once you have the route and the locations fixed in mind you will have an always available blueprint that you can reuse any time simply by retracing your steps in your imagination.

Now walk through it again populating each location with

the items on your list. As it is imaginary you can make your palace as big or as small as you like. If your list is a short one like the one above then a hallway and a living room are more than enough.

Fix each memory subject in place as you work your way round. So for the dry cleaning imagine your suit on its hanger. Sex it up. Let's have that boring old suit waving, maybe even doing a little can-can. Add music. Now hang it or lay it in the first stop in your loci palace. Make sure there is plenty of light. For me it hangs on a picture frame above the chest.

Now move on to the second item on your list: shop for goldfish. Mine is another picture frame this time with a goldfish looking directly at me. It's in a little movie; I can hear the blooping noise and see the bubbles. Then it gets scooped up by a hand and placed in a plastic bag and then the movie resets.

In the living room I add item three. There is a phone permanently moored to the wall and it's ringing but instead of a bell I hear my mother's voice saying 'Call me.'

Repeat this simple procedure until you have filled up all the loci. Then walk through your route again stopping at each location. The images you've created should now present themselves.

If they are a bit hazy or fuzzy re-imagine them. Make them as bright and colourful as you can and if you like make them rude. Go wild, obscene even: as long as the image is memorable and clear there's no need to hold back.

The great thing about the loci palace is that it's totally adaptable. You can add more locations at any time and even add imaginary rooms to make your humble flat a true palace of the mind. There is no reason why the wardrobe in your bedroom can't lead to the V&A or Wembley Stadium.

If you find that one of the loci is just not presenting itself you can move on to the next one and carry on from there. Unlike learning by rote as we do in school the loci technique is also extremely flexible. You can start at any arbitrary point and recall the list in any order even in reverse.

This technique has been in use for more than two millennia and all top memorisers use it to this day. It's even in everyday language even though we don't realise it in phrases like 'in the first place' and 'in the second place'. And whereas it usually takes an average man up to an hour to memorise the sequence of a deck of cards, with this powerful technique it takes Ben Pridmore, the current world memory champion, just 26.28 seconds. Could be a useful skill if you've just read the gambling chapter and are now contemplating card counting as a hobby.

Control Your Thoughts – Never Fall for Advertising, Politicians, Religious Authorities or Con Men: What They Never Taught You at School or on the Job

Take enough small steps, and a respectable middle-class citizen can be turned into a cold-blooded murderer.

Kathleen Taylor

Brainwashing is an art form that has been formalised for such a long time that it has become a part of our everyday lives so much so that we are barely even aware of it. It is delivered to us through family, the media, workplace ideology, government, religion, schools and any other social force. Some forms of coercion such as elections are socially acceptable while others such as religious cults or state torture are anything but.

According to Kathleen Taylor, a research scientist at the Department of Physiology, Anatomy and Genetics at the University of Oxford and author of *Brainwashing: The*

Science of Thought Control, it usually happens either by force or stealth. It is she says, 'part of a wider array of influence techniques, from television to terrorism'. She argues that influence attempts 'may change the inner world in many ways, from the lightest persuasion – a wind brushing the grass – to the catastrophic coercion of forceful brainwashing'.

As somebody who has worked in several fields that involved techniques of persuasion I'd like to share with you some thoughts and experiences.

But first you need to know how the brain functions. It's quick and easy so just dive straight in.

A neuron is the fundamental building block of the brain and nervous system.

Each neuron can communicate with each other neuron via electrical signals (stimulated by external events or internal processes like temperature change or memories). These signals travel along axons (pathways) floating between each neuron. There is a gap at the end of each axon called a synapse.

When the signal reaches the synapse chemical neurotransmitters are fired into the neuron and have the effect of switching genes on and off, increasing the production of various responsive proteins and enzymes within the neuron itself. With more frequent or intense signals new receptors are opened and the stronger the connection becomes.

Each neuron learns to represent features of the real world such as colour, sight, sound, physical feel, movement. This is why repetition is key to so many learning techniques whether it is language, sky diving and combat drills or advertising and brainwashing tactics.

Through repetition neurons then learn to fire together and build cognitive webs, cogwebs for short. They fire together when a memory or sensation is triggered. This could be anything from a stranger's smile, the sound of an old song, to the collection of neurons that remember how to drive. In a well-formed brain there are many neural maps of your interactions with the outside world.

Simple stuff right?

This is how we all work and we need these cogwebs in order to function – if we need to turn a corner as we walk the cogweb for that action takes care of it rather than your conscious, processing mind.

But is there an inherent design flaw? Is there a hack? You bet.

The clever persuader knows how this works, sometimes intuitively, sometimes consciously, and exploits the inherent vulnerability in the system. Specifically that because you aren't aware of how your own mind functions most of the time it can be changed without you even realising.

This is why companies spend fortunes on advertising, governments on public broadcasting, public relations and state events and churches on distributing free materials, missionary work and encouraging current members to 'spread the word'.

We used to call it propaganda but then Edward Bernays, the self proclaimed 'Father of PR', and nephew of Sigmund Freud, reworked the term as 'public relations' because he said Hitler and Stalin had given it such evil connotations.

The first time I personally became aware that words changed minds was back when I worked as a TV researcher. I had an argument with a friend in a pub about some hot topic of the day and was happy to banter with him until he gave me a piece of information using exactly the same words I'd written for a documentary broadcast the previous week. I let him win that one. I'd have been arguing with myself otherwise. Somehow I'd managed to make him think something he hadn't previously thought. It was a thrill.

But it was also an argument that I'd thrown in to the mix at the last minute to fill a narrative gap in the programme. It wasn't coherent, well reasoned or well thought out.

That is one of the dangers of believing third-party sources. Even half-hearted, time-pressed persuaders will attempt to change your beliefs.

So what exactly is a belief?

Imagine that the route a neuron takes to reach the next synapse is like a path through a forest. The path is formed by regular use and becomes easier to walk down the more you use it. Over time this path becomes so well trodden and familiar that you wouldn't really consider using any other even if you knew there were easier or better paths out there.

There's nothing wrong with this, this is normal people, this is you, this is me. But here's the thing: if all you ever do is walk the same path you will find it hard to navigate in a storm. If suddenly there's a heavy downpour of unfamiliar thoughts, feelings and emotions that then flood your normal route where do you go? What options do you have? Trudge along the same old path now flooded and hard to get out of?

This slippery-sided path is where brand loyalty, a point of principle or a firmly held belief begins and personal choice ends. If you stick to the path too closely your options for navigation become limited.

Metacognition – Thinking about Thinking

Have you ever faced an unexpected challenge mid-argument and found that you quickly develop new and sometimes conflicting arguments to protect your position and rout the enemy? If you have then you'll enjoy what follows.

If we want to stay in control of our thoughts or grow as human beings then it is essential to develop new pathways for us to survive attempts at influencing our thoughts. Any experience or input out of the ordinary will do. Travel for example literally broadens the mind. Walk a different way to work every day, always vary your sexual routine, your eating habits, your choice of music. Observe how quickly and easily your mind maps the new territory that you were previously scared of. The trick is to regularly do things outside your comfort zone.

But what if there are people like me waiting for you when you're accidentally knocked off your normal path? For example your car breaks down for the last time; it's a write-off. But now that you cannot do what you normally do suddenly the noise of all those advertisements, the arguments of marketers, can make you consider my client's latest model, brand sexy, as your next new purchase.

If they've done their job right you'll only need a small push to take a step on to this new pathway that will lead you to – getting to work, dropping the kids off, driving fast, looking cool – and with enough repetition of the message and a few walks along these pre-prepared neurological pathways you'll be convincing yourself that their brand is exactly the one you will buy. Of course you reached that decision all on your own didn't you?

We had to do this when I worked as a development producer for a UK broadcaster. It was my job to encourage small independent companies, the 'film varnishers' as the marketing department used to call them, to make low-cost, long running repetitive series, think fifty-plus episodes as opposed to one-off documentaries. It was important to the broadcasters. The digital switchover that is happening now was originally going to take place at the turn of the century but in non-digital households the five main broadcasters had crappy audience share. They needed time to create branded channels and get the audience used to coming to them for long running series and emotionally familiar branded content.

It worked: we'll all be switching over soon and TV on demand is now here. We just needed to tailor the market first to meet our revenue needs. A bit like a paedophile grooming their prey.

Sometimes it happens slowly like the above or quickly like after 9/11. When everyone was still stunned the propaganda machine, sorry PR machine, kicked in and before you knew it a whole new language had appeared with the 'War on Terror' including such thought-terminating clichés paraphrased from the Bible as 'You're either with us or against us.'

The reason was simple, Taylor says: 'Human brains tend to associate two stimuli perceived at the same time, and a skilled speaker will make use of this, trying for instance to associate a perceived or real injustice with an ethereal idea'. Think x number of towers falling and you think why? Just fill the hole and repeat the message until the new connections are fixed in place – until it sticks.

At the same time emotions like fear, anger or arousal flood the synapses with neurotransmitters such as dopamine, noradrenalin and serotonin and are useful tools for influence technicians to anchor word phrases or ideas with emotions.

Trust me: we know what we're doing and making you believe that advertising doesn't affect you, that you are somehow immune, was our best trick so far.

There is a thing called the placebo effect where a larger

than expected percentage of people recover from an illness because they believe the pill they're taking is real simply because it is given to them by a man in a white coat (who told them a white coat made a difference?).

Link that with a bit of crowd psychology: convince roughly 45 per cent of people that your argument is right and the remainder will usually go along with you. There you have the mechanism we use to convince people to go to war or to win an election.

What's Wrong with This Picture?

Before you get too worried there is a way to protect yourself. Simply give yourself neural options, educate yourself through physical, experiential or academic means, or as Taylor recommends, 'Stop and think.' This sounds easy; you probably think you do this already. Don't kid yourself; it isn't and you don't.

Demagogues, cult leaders, advertisers and brainwashers know how this works. Human brains are designed to minimise the amount of work they do. Simple information gets processed faster which is why their messages are usually short and simple so that they are interpreted by your brain as 'true' before you've had time to consciously stop and think i.e. the neural pathway has already been created and it's easier for them to make the neuron fire again when they repeat the same message.

Learn to Recognise Cognitive Dissonance

This is the feeling of uncomfortable tension which comes from holding two conflicting thoughts in the mind at the same time. Take the 'you're either with us or against us' statement earlier. Break it down and it is simply two polar opposites presented as an either/or option.

In reality there is no option; it's designed to immobilise but we are so used to thinking of messages on TV from politicians as being authoritative that we don't question it. It's no different to the school bully, teacher or parent who says, 'Answer the question' and then when you do says, 'Don't answer back.'

Try this as a counter: 'We're neither with you nor against you.' Left unchallenged these conflicts between what is real, 'the territory' and the 'map' you overlay on it can lead to schizophrenia.

The easiest way to spot this feeling of cognitive dissonance is simply to ask yourself, 'What's wrong with this picture?' It's a line from cop show *The Wire* where two drug squad officers watching some dealers know that something is up but can't quite put their finger on it. Trust your instincts.

Zealots for the Brand

I tried an experiment when I was a teen to believe in as many widely disparate systems of belief as I could wholeheartedly and with as much conviction as I could muster. For this end I chose belief systems that I wasn't necessarily comfortable with such as esoteric religions and hard line political doctrines. Only for a week at a time. And without going into the nitty gritty here's the conclusion I came to after I'd overlaid a few of these maps on the world around me. It's possible to believe anything you want to; some belief structures are complex networks of cogwebs, some are simply one or two well-worn neural paths or thoughtless maladaptive dogmas.

The more you believe one thing or walk a set path the harder it is to consider other possibilities. But belief can also provide a great short cut to get past blocks in your way.

Consider the mother who needs to lift the car off her child and from somewhere finds the strength to do so. Or any number of other emergency situations where your self belief changes from the culturally ingrained can't do to can do.

So What Can You Do?

Ever wanted a more positive self-image? One method to get yourself believing is to imagine that whatever you want to be true is already true.

Now you may have some dissonance here because how can believing what isn't true make it true? Stop and think: quite simply it's not possible. As much as you believe that your skin is the colour blue, unless you've just fallen in a vat of paint or are reading this naked at the South Pole it isn't and isn't likely to be any time soon.

However for most things that are inside your head – you know confidence, public speaking, being good with people or world champion MasterChef – they are already potentially true. You simply need to give yourself permission for this to be the case. Then pretend it is already true. The next time you try a bit of public speaking for real you will have already established the necessary neural connection and the existing belief will channel a positive response where you want it to go with quite dramatic effects in the real world.

Put It All Together

An example of how powerful all these techniques are hit me when I switched on *News at One* just a few months ago, a politician was being interviewed and they were debating Heathrow's position as an international and transatlantic hub in the face of overseas competition principally China and the Middle East. I'd thrown this fear hook out there in the marketing materials I wrote for the launch of Dubai

World Central – destined one day to be the largest airport in the world. I'd love to take credit for this politician using this idea and for spin doctors like Alastair Campbell using the reverse fear hook in his own work on Heathrow's third runway but that would be arrogant and naive on my part. It does however highlight the inherent problem with propaganda, PR, or whatever you want to call it. Some of the persuasive arguments used actually do mean something and do have relevance. It's worth not being too paranoid about all this.

That said it does influence millions of minds and is used to shape virtually every area of modern life from shopping centres and celebrity crises through to international conflicts and the environment. It's learning to recognise when you're being played that is important and strengthening your own mind so that your decisions are your own.

So remember as you develop the cognitive webs that define your world always challenge, always add new experiences and learning and never assume there's only one path.

As it is estimated that 20 to 80 per cent of all news is either a direct copy of, sourced from or influenced by public relations, you also need to learn that when you are the horse being led to water you don't always have to drink. That goes for TV programmes, magazines, movies and special interest groups too.

Or to put it in Bernays's words from his book *Propaganda*, 'So vast are the numbers of minds which can be regimented, and so tenacious are they when regimented, that a group at times offers an irresistible pressure before which legislators, editors and teachers are helpless. Making of those powerful beings [. . .], the leaders of public opinion, mere bits of driftwood in the surf.' He wrote that at a time when he was busily persuading Western industrial leaders to replace political and religious morality with commercialism. They wanted everyone to find the meaning of their lives at the shop counter. Think it worked? That change happened before most us were born.

Understanding that brains can be changed is the first step in resisting change imposed by others.

Essential Survival Skills for Your Mind

Stop and Think
Whenever you read a headline, hear an advertising slogan or listen to a soundbite on the news notice how it affects you emotionally or if you have any dissonance. Then stop and think about it. You don't have to do this 24/7 just enough to give you an edge.

Break Thought-Terminating Clichés
The stingy Scot, the thieving Scouse, the fighting Irish, the arrogant French, the obnoxious English, the loud American, the sheep-shagging Welshman or Kiwi, the lazy foreigner/they're stealing our jobs (how about that for a contradictory either/or), the dumb blonde, the terrorist suspect (notice how the phrase is structured, desired role first and oh by the way he's only a suspect as an afterthought), football hooligan . . . and so on. If you hear one of these or anything like it again watch your emotional reaction.

Ignore Absolutes
Be wary of any statement that something is absolutely true or a moral imperative. For example 'all [insert ethnic group] are xxxxx'. Politicians use this all the time. Focused as they

are on short-term political goals they also use words like 'should', 'must' and 'ought' to make you feel obliged and as if what they'd personally like to happen is a moral certainty.

External Sources
Politicians also use external sources to convince people that there's something they don't know about. As the whole WMD fiasco demonstrated by simply quoting a student report Gulf War II was sanctioned. It's a powerful technique. I use quotes in my writing for the same reason. As do religious leaders. Also if you ever hear a politician invoke science, god or their own beliefs as their absolute 'proof' of something that is only their opinion you have my permission to put their head on a spike at the city gates.

Them and Us
There is actually no them and us. We are all one. If someone tells you that there is smile knowingly and ignore them. Of course certain social forces impact social groupings more than others either men or women, rich or poor, black or white, Muslim or Christian, left or right, you and me, but even then we are still all one. Never forget that. Many magazines or books with either women or men as their demographic (such as this one) use this technique via the 'All men are bastards' argument or the 'All women are bitches' ruse. You'll notice I've tried not to do that in this book. These arguments are used to simply sell more products. So be wary of demonising others or anyone trying to.

The Map Is Not the Territory
Always ask yourself 'How am I interpreting this?' If you're stressed about your finances and get into a discussion about money do you think that will affect the tone of the debate?

However you see the world, your office, your family, your pets, your life, how you think about it is just one possible map of the territory. Don't become trapped in the map it's only an approximation. In fact it has been shown that the most high-performing people in whatever field economics, music, chess or sport, use multiple maps of their specific field to effortlessly outperform others. Do the same. One size really does not fit all. Reality is complex.

So now that you have the basics pay attention to the world because it is paying attention to you.

Religion and Spirituality

What can you say about gods that their followers haven't already said about them? Well how about this? Most gods' pitches are the equivalent of a hard sell online sales letter that says something like: Learn the Secrets of Holy Unarmed Combat: What the Other Religions are Too Scared to Tell You. Amazing Special Offer, Save $$$$, Kick Ass the Way God Meant You To. Limited Time Offer. You're Either With Us or Against Us. Do You Have the Dim Mak Death Touch? Get it Now OR Go To Hell. Call 0800 GOD GOD GOD.

Anyone with an internet connection can look up the gods. There are a lot of them. There are literally thousands of deities from a staggering range of pantheons from the ancient Incas and Celts to the modern Japanese and the Middle East.

From ancient Greece there's the ever popular Zeus, the big cheese of the ancient Greek gods and ruler of the earth. With a roving eye and a string of illegitimate deity children there's so much going on in his household that you'll never need to watch *EastEnders* again. But that's only to be expected with Aphrodite, the goddess of love, bedding down in your house

Gods get everywhere, their legacies linger in our minds and our language. From goodbye – god be with you – to the days of the week. Thursday for example, a day named after Thor, the hairy Norse god of thunder – it's a bit like Friday but without the beer and onion rings. Like Zeus's, Thor's romantic flings were legendary although he may have regretted waking up one Saturday morning after a Thank Me It's Friday evening to find he'd had a fling with the giant Jarnsaxa because this naughty little god was already married to Sif and had a daughter called, well . . . Thrud. No seriously that's not the sound she made when she fell from heaven and hit the floor, that's actually her name. Clearly both he and Sif were on the sauce when they came up with that one.

There are also certain bodily functions that as humans we normally do behind closed doors or at the very least with the lights out. Unfortunately the same rules don't apply to gods. Abeguwo, a Melanesian god, is known as the god of rain. Which sounds nice at first: crops need rain, rivers need to flow, where's the harm hey? Well let's see. That rain has to come from somewhere and according to www.godchecker.com, 'The world is her lavatory, [she] lives in the sky, and whenever she needs to relieve herself she has no inhibitions about letting loose all over the planet.' That explains that whole great flood obsession then, when you've got to go . . . I won't even tell you about the gods with a preference for spreading 'seed' around.

Gods are also lazy swines. They never turn up in person; they're a bit like the CEO who's always on the golf course leaving the PA to manage the schedule. Throw in a few minions, sorry disciples, and a new shop front or two, sorry place of worship, and they're good to go. Of course every organisation needs its mission statement, oops there I go again, sorry commandments or holy book. Clearly they'll have to be cc'd to all members of the board of disciples who will then add the first thoughts that come to mind or something their two-year-old said on the potty at breakfast. They will of course insist on complete revisions throughout the entire document. That's all fine and dandy; they are the head honchos after all. Then three minutes before deadline they'll say something along the lines of, 'Hmm no, I don't like it can we change it back?'

'What all twenty-five thousand copies?'

'Yes and can we take out the bit about sleeping with virgins? My wife might read it.'

Cerrunos, Buddha, Yahweh, Monkey, the Eight Immortals, the Jade Emperor, Bochica, Huitzilopochtli, Thoth, Ra, Set and Osiriris, Venus, Mars, Cupid and Bacchus and, and, and . . . I could go on but I won't: there's thousands of the little blighters. Many of them promote love, virtue, honour but a lot of them, well let's just say they're still at the toilet humour stage of existence. Until very recently human sacrifice was demanded by many religions, as many as eighty thousand in one ceremony for the bloodthirsty Aztec Huitzilopochtli – COO of the war department – although some scholars think twenty thousand sacrifices a year for this god is a more plausible figure. Think about that for a moment. Jeepers.

The thinking behind these rituals makes about as much sense as a scribbled memo after a long Friday lunch translated through an overworked PA's frazzled mind. 'Pick up the dry cleaning' becomes 'Execute weeping boys in spring to prevent end of world,' at least for the Aztec deity Tlaloc.

Human sacrifices still happen today with modern Tantriks

in India (not to be confused with Tantric Buddhism) and the traditional religious act of eating human hearts before battle in Liberia. Personally before battle I'd opt for peace talks but hey what could I a mere human possibly know compared to these wonderful magical beings.

That's what happens when you let an overworked PA with a god complex run the company. Suddenly we're all expected to confess our sins or follow what some dude in a dress says because the CEO has now gone AWOL – apparently in important development talks in the Bahamas.

This explains why from our modern religions the ones with the dresses and the pointy hats had to build a box for confessionals, sorry performance reviews, to prevent the middle managers having sex with those under review while the ones with the beards and the dresses unquestioningly propagated the teachings of a known paedophile. Oh boy where do I sign up?

Once upon a time polytheism was all the rage, the market was diverse and there was lots of competition, and let's face it it was a hell of lot more fun. According to Godchecker 'Dionysus made two exciting discoveries. 1) How to make wine. 2) How to make orgasms which could drive you to the brink of madness.' That explains nymphs and orgies then.

Sadly the monotheists then got in on the act and spoiled everyone's fun, the gods' included. Now apparently there is only one true god. Only problem is that while all members of the world's main religions now agree that there is only one supreme being they can't agree on anything else. That's the problem with monopolies. Clearly the organ grinding CEOs have gotten a little carried away and left the monkeys in charge – simple brains need simple answers after all. Can you count to one?

It's also quite apparent that the holy mission statements

that everyone hands around as proof of existence are cobbled together by humans. I've done it too many times for too many CEOs not to spot the signs of mixed messages, contradictions, exceptions and generally just sounding like you were written by committee. So let's face facts: any omnipotent universe-creating being worth his bunions could figure out the 'send to many' feature on his mobile phone and avoid misinterpretation. He hardly deserves to be worshipped if he can't.

And why would he need to be worshipped anyway? Do you know what a narcissist is? If you met one in the street would you prostrate yourself in front of one?

By this point you might be thinking I'm one of those atheist types. Actually you'd be completely and utterly wrong. I believe in all gods, I know they exist, at least in people's minds. But a god that needs to be worshipped is no god at all; it's simply a human with a good sales patter trying to lure you into their god shop. Nobody needs to go to one of those to get their spiritual fix.

Nope simply find a suitable field and pick a few mushrooms. At least that's according to a recent study by researchers at Johns Hopkins University in Baltimore, Maryland. Using unusually rigorous scientific conditions and measures Johns Hopkins researchers have shown that the active agent in 'sacred mushrooms' can induce mystical/spiritual experiences descriptively identical to spontaneous ones people have reported for millennia.

They were very clear on one point: 'We're just measuring what can be observed. We're not entering into "Does god exist or not exist. This work can't and won't go there."'

In the study more than 60 per cent of subjects described the effects of psilocybin in ways that met criteria for a 'full mystical experience' as measured by established psychological scales. 'One third said the experience was the single most spiritually significant of their lifetimes; and more than two-thirds rated it among their five most meaningful and spiritually significant. Subjects likened it to the importance of the birth of their first child or the death of a parent.

'Two months later, 79% of subjects reported moderately or greatly increased well-being or life satisfaction compared with those given a placebo at the same test session. A majority said their mood, attitudes and behaviours had changed for the better. Structured interviews with family members, friends and co-workers generally confirmed the subjects' remarks. Results of a year-long follow up are being readied for publication.'

Well Johns Hopkins can't go there but I will. Gods and religions are human creations and they can be extremely powerful; they can create consensus and provide moral guidance and structure. I'm all for avoiding usury for example (charging extortionate interest rates); however when I lived in the Middle East they advertised Mecca credit cards with wait for it *profit* rates instead of interest rates and 'Steps to Mecca' air miles. Not to be outdone the Catholics also have their own World Missions Visa card that supports evangelism. I'm also against murdering people and definitely for being good to one another but I don't need a religion to tell me that. I actually don't mind if they do as long as there's a forum in which open discussion is permitted.

That's not always the case however so next time a sales storm trooper on my doorstep working on the never-never afterlife commission insists that their brand of one-size-fits-all deity has the monopoly on morality or spirituality then I might just invite them in for a chat over dinner. Mushroom Surprise perhaps.

You see spirituality is something that everyone can experience not just prophets and sages, while a consensus morality is something that as adults we should all work hard to have not just expect to have handed to us by some self-proclaimed authority figure. No god-botherer gets away with trying to get me addicted to their repackaged version of reality.

The insight of oneness that mystical experience gives us (specifically no us and them, definitely no denominations) either by formal religious experience or through a simple food gives those of us who've forgotten what it's like to be a non-judgemental child a healthy reminder.

But you also need the constant reminder that you are not part of a flock being tended to by a shepherd. Ultimately here's the thing about any moral system worth a damn: you need active questioning and heretical human input for it to have any long lasting value. You need to be willing to test it to find out what's good and what's bad.

Otherwise we may as well go back to passive worship and unchanging acceptance and wait for the human sacrifices to begin again.

Screw that. Personally I'd rather take a walk in the country or gaze at a clear night sky if I need a bit of one on one time with my god.

My view is that one size does not fit all and if you don't like what I've written, well here's the thing . . . the gods *made* me do it.

The Meaning of Life

It's a question that has bothered mankind for eons it seems or at least that's the perceived wisdom of people whose interests this question serves. The idea is that somewhere out there someone omnipotent or otherwise has written a rule book. In that rule book there's a secret and once you have trodden the dutiful path all will be revealed to you. Wisdom and the greater glory will be yours. Or at least the silly hat, the ceremonies and the long flowing robes will be.

But by the time you reach the point of initiation all that hopping around on one leg under a full moon in the sign of the rabid cat will probably have played havoc with your tendons and you'll be too nervous to care. When you arrive in that learned chamber full of the pious and the wise you will ask your humble question, 'What is the meaning of life?'

The venerable sage who knows everything, the bearded one who has been handed all the wisdom of the ages, will lean forward and say, 'You mean you don't know? Damn! Another one. We were hoping you would. You see our people have been waiting all these generations for someone who does. Every Tuesday every month for forty years in my case dear lord . . . just think what I could have been doing . . . I could have learned to rumba.'

So like the bloody-minded individualist I am here is the answer or at least an answer. It is simply this: 'Ask better questions!'

Try this: 'What is the meaning of *my* life?'

The meaning of life is yours to own. Not anyone else's. If somebody tells you what *the* meaning of life is, a singular point anchored in time for all eternity, well then that is just their opinion isn't it? What good does it do you or anyone else?

You need to find your meaning. It's not hard. It takes time sure, a little thought too. You might take a few wrong turns even get lost for a while but eventually the thing that you were looking for all along will be right where you left it and you'll say, 'Oh how silly of me. Of course.'

Finding the meaning of your life is one of the most rewarding things you will ever do. Whatever it is will probably boil down to one word or one sentence and if you live by it you will never take a wrong step because it is the meaning of *your* life. It may be humble or grandiose, it certainly won't mean you'll never make an idiot of yourself or say the wrong thing or never make a mistake. But when the Grim Reaper lowers his cowl, gives you a fleshless bony grin and runs a finger along the sharp edge of his scythe you won't be left wondering. You'll know . . . you'll smile back.

Afterword

Men: we do drink beer, own remote controls, play football and even apply moisturiser (or Swarfega). Although that's not all we do but all too often they are the only ideals we ever see. And they're the smallest aspects of what it means to be a man. So let's demand more, much more, especially from ourselves. Seek out every opportunity to find your heart's desires, make mistakes, fail (i.e. find out what doesn't work) and to succeed beyond your wildest dreams.

By playing small and shrinking so that other people won't feel insecure you neither serve the world nor yourself.

To do that you need new ideals – defined by you, more daring goals, self-awareness and fundamentally a set of balls. So buckle your swash, pick a horse you want to ride and as a modern gentleman with a healthy dose of badass pick a path ahead that makes you feel truly alive.

> If you want to conquer fear, do not sit home
> and think about it. Go out and get busy.
> *Dale Carnegie*

Acknowledgements

Books don't happen in a vacuum. People go out and make them happen. First off thank you to my agent Ian Drury of Sheil Land Associates and Jo Fletcher for inspiration, insight and feedback. Then to all the hard working people at my publisher Little, Brown Book Group especially Tim Whiting for 'getting it' and then commissioning it; along with Iain Hunt, Zoë Hood, Bobby Nayyar, Darren Turpin as well as legal eagles Siobhan Hughes, Maddie Mogford, photographer Charlie Hopkinson, illustrator Jamie Keenan and Stephen Guise for catching the calculation gaffe.

Thank you also to all my family and friends especially those who have helped and supported me along the way: Claire Haswell for getting me started, Jo Summers and Jean Coles for a place to work, Peter Vidler, Emma Nugent and Emma-Kate Dobbin for their input and to Professor David Wilson for the fatherhood gibe. As well as Caithlin Tracey, Peter Taylor and my niece Amber. Also Andrew (Billy) Thomas and Faye Keegan – thanks for the necessary nudge in the right direction all those years ago.

Extra special thanks must go to contributors Leo Babauta, Paddy Smith, Mike Phipps, Colin Gautrey, David Straker, Olivier Bonnefoy and Violet Blue, you've made this a much richer book and prove that it never hurts to ask.

To all the companies and individuals that helped me out and that feature throughout the book: you taught me new and often scary skills and in the process changed my life. I thank you more than I can say.

Dynamic Drivers, Tank School, Core Combatives, Edelweiss Tactical, Target Skysports, Skydive Spain, Action Park, Inghams Travel, Woodsmoke, P1 and all the teams, Thundercat Racing UK, BSM Rider Training Silverstone, Access Yachts, Tesla, as well as the Kakslauttanen Hotel & Igloo Village and Holiday Club Hotel Saariselka. Although I can't thank everyone at these companies individually – there's just so many of you – I'd particularly like to thank JC, Mick Coup, Angharad Gibbs, Lynsey Devon, Fiona Pascoe, Alastair Scott, Janne Ylimys, Glenn Chidzoy, Shelley Jory, Andy Lovemore, Alf Batchelor, Duarte Masmo, the BSM boys: Andrew Freeman, Ray Earle, Will Charters; not forgetting Steven Hanton, Matt Upson, Ben McNutt, Don Cochrane and Sanna Korteklainen. To find out more about each of these companies visit: www.howtodriveatank.com. To anyone I've omitted, forgotten or edited out please accept my humblest apologies.

To all the great people I met along the way – James Clarke, Cem Behar, Carl Zahra, Mark Maddison, Richard Ratcliffe, Karri Gibson, Sophie Denman, Jane Brant, Jason Woolley, Stefan, Mark Taylor, Minty Clinch and all those who cannot be named in Switzerland (stay safe) – you made it all worthwhile.

And to you dear reader thank you. Without you we writers and publishers are nothing.